WILEY
CPA EXAM REVIEW
UPDATE 2011

What You Need to Know for the New Exam Format

Roger Philipp, CPA

WILEY

JOHN WILEY & SONS, INC.

The following items, Copyright © by the American Institute of Certified Public Accountants, Inc., are reprinted with permission:

1. Material from Uniform CPA Examination Questions and Answers, 1978 through 2000.

2. Example audit reports from Statements on Auditing Standards and Statements on Standards for Accounting and Review Services.

3. Information for Uniform CPA Examination Candidates, Board of Examiners, 2000.

4. Material from AU 319 (SAS 55 and SAS 78) and an AICPA Audit Guide, both titled Consideration of Internal Control in a Financial Statement Audit.

5. Material from AICPA Auditing Procedures Studies: Consideration of the Internal Control Structure in a Computer Environment: A Case Study; Auditing with Computers; Auditing in Common Computer Environments; Audit Implications of EDI.

6. Material from the Certified Internal Auditor Examination, Copyright © 1994 through 1997 by the Institute of Internal Auditors, Inc., is reprinted and/or adapted with permission.

7. Material from the Certified Management Accountant Examinations, Copyright © 1993 through 1997 by the Institute of Certified Management Accountants, is reprinted and/or adapted with permission.

Material adapted, with permission, from *Writing for Accountants*, Aletha Hendrickson, South-Western Publishing Co., 1993.

This book is printed on acid-free paper. ⊗

ISBN 9781118011485 (book); ISBN 9781118016374 (ebk);
ISBN 9781118016381 (ebk); ISBN 9781118016398 (ebk)

Printed in the United States of America.

10 9 8 7 6 5 4 3 2 1

CONTENTS

1 INTRODUCTION

USING THIS INFORMATION

This booklet is by no means a comprehensive stand-alone study guide but instead is meant as a supplement to review lectures and practice questions. This information will familiarize candidates with the exam and all CBT-e changes including content, scoring weights, and the new exam formats. This information can accompany any 2010 CPA exam review materials purchased from any vendor but should not be used alone to prepare for the 2011 CPA exam.

Each of the four topics is broken down between the newly created material and any material that was previously tested but is shifted or moved from one topic to another in the CPA exam after January 1, 2011. All current CSOs/SSOs may be found on the AICPA's Web site at www.aicpa.org; candidates are encouraged to stay current on exam changes in the event they are using older or outdated review materials. This booklet provides CSOs to be tested in 2011, but this information is subject to change by the AICPA Board of Examiners.

This material provides new and updated information when used in conjunction with other CPA Review material. If a candidate has not prepared for the CPA exam previously, it is recommended that he or she purchase new study material for the new 2011 CPA exam. This booklet on its own will not provide enough information to prepare for the exam but will familiarize candidates with the new format and outline topics tested in 2011.

THE CPA EXAM

Purpose

The Uniform CPA Examination is designed to test the entry-level knowledge and skills necessary to protect the public interest. These skills and required knowledge base were identified through a Practice Analysis performed in 2000, which served as a basis for the development of the content specifications for the new exam. The skills identified as necessary for the protection of the public interest include:

- *Knowledge and Understanding.* Expertise and skills developed through learning processes, recall, and reading comprehension. Knowledge is acquired through experience or education and is the theoretical or practical understanding of a subject; knowledge is also represented through awareness or familiarity with information gained by experience of a fact or situation. Understanding represents a higher level than simple knowledge and is the process of using concepts to deal adequately with given situations, facts, or circumstances. Understanding is the ability to recognize and comprehend the meaning of a particular concept.

- *Application of the Body of Knowledge, including Analysis, Judgment, Synthesis, Evaluation, and Research.* Higher-level cognitive skills that require individuals to act or transform knowledge in some fashion.
- *Written Communication.* The various skills involved in preparing written communication including basic writing mechanics, such as grammar, spelling, word usage, punctuation, and sentence structure.

The CPA Examination is one of many screening devices to ensure the competence of those licensed to perform the attest function and to render professional accounting services. Other screening devices include educational requirements, ethics examinations, and work experience.

The examination appears to test the material covered in accounting programs of the better business schools. It also appears to be based on the body of knowledge essential for the practice of public accounting and the audit of a medium-size client. Since the examination is primarily a textbook or academic examination, candidates should plan on taking it as soon as possible after completing their accounting education.

In 2008, the AICPA and NASBA announced the latest evolution of computerized testing, called CBT-e or Computer-Based Testing *evolution*. The new exam format uses the same psychometric testing criteria as CBT but features shorter, task-based simulation problems and assigns an increased weight to research problems.

These implemented changes will increase the efficiency of scoring, security levels of the exam, and continue ensuring that the testing of entry-level knowledge and skills that are important to the protection of the public interest is consistent across examination administrations.

The following are just some of the many changes that will be implemented on **January 1, 2011,** when CBT-e is launched:

- New Uniform CPA Examination Content and Skill Specification Outlines (CSOs/SSOs), including International Financial Reporting Standards (IFRS), will go into effect. (See pages 21–22 for new CSOs)
- A new release of authoritative literature, with codified FASB Accounting Standards, and a new research task format will be introduced on the CPA Examination.
- The components of CPA Examination sections will be reorganized, with all written communication tasks to be concentrated in one section—Business Environment and Concepts (BEC); section time allocations will be adjusted.
- Short Task-Based Simulations (TBS) will replace simulations in the current (long) format in Auditing and Attestation (AUD), Financial Accounting and Reporting (FAR), and Regulation (REG).

A tutorial that reviews the revised examination's format and navigation functions is now available at www.aicpa.org. Choose the "Become a CPA" tab and then pick "CPA Exam" from the options on the left. From there, candidates can find the tutorial and practice questions. All exam candidates are encouraged to review it prior to sitting for the examination. The tutorial is intended to familiarize candidates with the functionality and types of questions and responses used in the new examination format. The tutorial does not focus on examination content and is not intended as a replacement for study materials.

Structure

The Uniform CPA Examination spans 14 hours and consists of four separate sections:

Computer-Based Uniform CPA Exam
1. Auditing and Attestation (4 hours)
2. Financial Accounting and Reporting (4 hours)
3. Regulation (3 hours)
4. Business Environment and Concepts (3 hours)

Examination Specifications

Below are the main content areas for each section of the Uniform CPA Examination. For more detailed information about examination content specifications, visit www.aicpa.org and choose the "Become a CPA" tab.

AICPA released final weights as follows:

	Financial Audit and Regulation	**Business Environment and Concepts**
M/C	60%	85%
Task-Based Simulations	40%	–
Written Communication	–	15%

Types of Questions

A candidate's score on each section of the exam is determined by the sum of points assigned to individual questions and simulation parts. Thus candidates must attempt to maximize their points on each individual item. Candidates should review the examination tutorial at www.aicpa.org prior to attempting the first exam part to familiarize themselves with the computerized exam format. A test that contains a few sample multiple-choice questions and a sample simulation for each applicable section is currently available. Neither the tutorial nor the sample test will be available at the test center; therefore, familiarization with the format is encouraged prior to exam day.

Objective Formats (Multiple Choice)

A format is considered objective when it can be graded without subjectivity. Grading objective examinations is a mechanical process that requires little judgment. Any format that can be graded by machine is generally considered objective. Objective formats result in very consistent scores because the acceptability of particular responses is determined before grading begins. The most widely used objective format is multiple choice (i.e., four-option questions) because it has a restricted set of alternatives from which the correct answer must be selected. Objective questions make up 60% of FAR, AUD, and REG and 85% of BEC.

The multiple-choice questions within each section are organized into three groups, which are referred to as testlets. Each exam section will have three testlets of objective questions (24–30 questions per testlet) worth up to 85 points per exam. The multiple-choice testlets vary in overall difficulty. A testlet is labeled either "medium difficult" or "difficult" based on its makeup. A "difficult" testlet has a higher percentage of hard questions than a "medium difficult" testlet; however, more difficult questions carry a higher point percentage rate, and therefore fewer must be answered correctly to pass. Every candidate's first multiple-choice testlet in each section will be a "medium difficult" testlet. If a candidate scores well on the first testlet, he or she will receive a "difficult" second testlet. Candidates who do not perform well on the first testlet receive a second "medium difficult" testlet. Because the scoring procedure takes the difficulty of the testlet into account, candidates take equivalent but different exams and are scored fairly regardless of the type of testlets they receive.

Each multiple-choice testlet contains "operational" and "pretest" questions. The operational questions are the only ones that are used to determine the candidate's score. Pretest questions are not scored; they are being tested for future use as operational questions. Candidates have no way of knowing which questions are operational and which questions are pretested so they must approach each question as if it will be used to determine their grade. Pretest questions make up about 14% to 16% of total multiple-choice questions.

Task-Based Simulations (TBSs)

Task-based simulations (TBSs) will make up 40% of the FAR, AUDIT, and REG exams. Each TBS is worth approximately 6 points. The Business Environment and Concepts section does not contain simulation problems but instead consists of three written communication problems. The points assigned to each requirement will vary according to its difficulty. Each TBS should be allotted about 15 minutes to complete. Candidates will be required to demonstrate their ability to apply certain skills (knowledge, understanding, and application of the body of knowledge) in each section of the CPA exam using task-based case studies. These skills will be tested in a variety of methods, such as simulation or relational case studies, which test candidates' knowledge and skills using work-related situations. Simulations require candidates to have basic computer skills, knowledge of common spreadsheet and word processing functions, the ability to use a financial calculator or a spreadsheet to perform standard financial calculations, and the ability to use electronic tools such as databases for research. Therefore, candidates need to become proficient in the use of these tools to maximize their scores on the task-based simulation component of each applicable exam section.

Each TBS contains three distinct tabs: the work tab, the information tab, and the help tab. The work tab (identified by a pencil icon) is the part of the question that will be graded and contains directions for completion of the task. The information tab(s) may contain authoritative literature or other relevant information to assist in completing the task presented in the work tab. Some task-based simulations may contain more than one information tab while others may not have any information tabs at all. The help tab provides assistance with the exam software, such as instructions on using the provided word processor for written communication problems. While the exam environment closely mirrors common software programs that candidates have used previously, it is recommended that candidates view the help tab for specific instructions on using the exam's provided software as it can differ from commercially available software programs.

Much like the multiple choice testlets, candidates can go back and forth between different task-based simulation questions but cannot go back to previous multiple-choice testlets or review their simulations once they have submitted their exam as complete.

Authoritative Literature   While completing the task-based simulations, candidates will use financial accounting, auditing, or taxation databases. The financial accounting database will include certain portions of the FASB's Original Pronouncements and Current Text. The auditing database will include certain portions of the AICPA's Statements on Auditing Standards. The taxation database will include certain portions of the federal tax code. The databases include all the excerpts that are necessary for completion of the case study simulations. As they relate to the simulations, the databases will be updated annually. In a rare situation, a recent FASB or AICPA pronouncement or a change in the code may impact the simulation. In those situations, a candidate should answer the simulation using the database provided.

CPA Exam Candidates: Free Online Access to Professional Literature Package   CPA exam candidates can get a free six-month subscription to professional literature used in the computerized CPA Examination. This online package includes AICPA Professional Standards, FASB Current Text, and FASB Original Pronouncements. Only candidates who have applied to take the CPA exam and have been deemed eligible by their state board of accountancy will receive access to this package of professional literature. NASBA will verify that a candidate has a valid NTS (Notice to Schedule). A candidate must possess a valid NTS prior to receiving authorization to the professional literature.

To subscribe, visit: www.nasba.org/NASBAWeb.nsf/ENCD.

Effective Date of Pronouncements   Accounting and auditing pronouncements are eligible to be tested on the Uniform CPA Examination in the window beginning **six months** after a pronouncement's *effective date*, unless early application is permitted. When early application is permitted, the new pronouncement is eligible to be tested in the window beginning six months after the *issuance* date. In this case, both old and new pronouncements may be tested until the old pronouncement is superseded. For the federal taxation area, the Internal Revenue Code and federal tax regulations in effect six months before the beginning of the current window may be tested on the Uniform CPA Examination. For all other materials covered in the Regulation and Business Environment and Concepts sections, material eligible to be tested includes federal laws in the window beginning six months after their *effective* date and uniform acts in the window beginning one year after their adoption by a simple majority of the jurisdictions.

Auditing and Attestation—4 Hours
1. Planning the engagement
2. Internal controls
3. Obtain and document information
4. Review engagement and evaluate information
5. Prepare communications

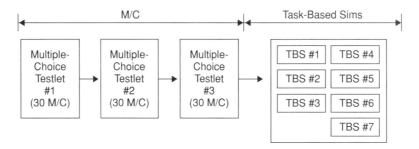

Things to consider:
- Use 1.5 minutes per multiple-choice question as a benchmark (50 minutes per testlet).
- Allocate 15 minutes per task-based simulation.

Financial Accounting and Reporting—4 Hours
1. Concepts and standards for financial statements
2. Typical items in financial statements
3. Specific types of transactions and events
4. Accounting and reporting for governmental entities
5. Accounting and reporting for nongovernmental and not-for-profit organizations

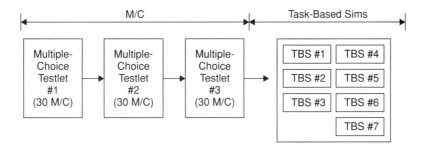

Things to consider:
- FAR includes calculations.
- Allocate 1.5 minutes per multiple-choice question as a benchmark (45 minutes per testlet).
- Allocate 15 minutes per task-based simulation.

Regulation—3 Hours
1. Ethics and professional responsibility
2. Business law
3. Federal tax procedures and accounting issues
4. Federal taxation of property transactions
5. Federal taxation—individuals
6. Federal taxation—entities

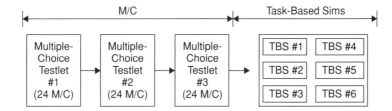

*Regulation has *24* multiple-choice questions per testlet!

Things to consider:
- Allocate 1.25 minutes per multiple-choice question as a benchmark (30 minutes per testlet).
- Allocate 15 minutes per simulation.

Business Environment and Concepts—3 Hours
1. Business structure
2. Economic concepts
3. Financial management
4. Information technology
5. Planning and measurement

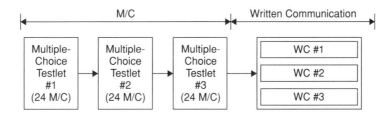

Things to consider:
- Allocate 1.5–2 minutes per multiple-choice question as a benchmark (approximately 45 minutes per testlet).
- Allocate 10–15 minutes for each written communication.

NEW RESEARCH TASK FORMAT (2010)

Starting January 1, 2011, research will no longer be tested as a tab within a simulation but as its own independent task-based simulation problem. Each section with simulation problems (FAR, AUD, REG) will contain one research problem. These problems will carry an equal point-percentage weight to other TBS problems.

Candidates will be asked to search through the database to find an appropriate reference that addresses the issue presented in the research problem. A scenario is presented in which candidates must find their answer in the authoritative literature using a predetermined list of codes (such as Professional Standards or federal taxation code). The candidates will choose the appropriate code title from the drop-down list and then enter a specific reference number applicable to the given scenario.

Authoritative literature for each section appears in the drop-down menus as follows:

FAR: Candidates will search the FASB ASC (Accounting Standards Codification) for their response; this section does not have a drop-down menu to select from.

REG: IRC –Internal Revenue Code
           TS – Tax Services
AUD: AU – U.S. Auditing Standards
           PCAOB – PCAOB Auditing Standards (i.e., AS1–AS5)
           AT – Attestation Services
           AR – Statements on Standards for Accounting and Review Services
           ET – Code of Professional Conduct
           BL – Bylaws
           VS – Statements on Standards for Valuation Services
           CS – Statement on Standards for Consulting Services

For example, a candidate may be asked the following question:

A company appropriates retained earnings for a loss contingency. How should this be disclosed in the financial statements?

Using the Authoritative Literature tab, the candidate will search for keywords associated with the question; in this case, a search for "appropriation of retained earnings" would likely bring up FAS5, paragraph 15, which reads:

> Some enterprises have classified a portion of retained earnings as "appropriated" for loss contingencies. In some cases, the appropriation has been shown outside the stockholders' equity section of the balance sheet. Appropriation of retained earnings is not prohibited by this Statement provided that it is shown within the stockholders' equity section of the balance sheet and is clearly identified as an appropriation of retained earnings. Costs or losses shall not be charged to an appropriation of retained earnings, and no part of the appropriation shall be transferred to income.

Using the provided drop-down menu, the candidates would then select the appropriate literature reference from the list (in this case, FASB codification) and enter the pronouncement and paragraph numbers in the two blank boxes.

Research questions will also alert candidates whether they have formatted their answer correctly by displaying "Your response is correctly formatted" in a box below the response if the candidates have entered reference numbers correctly. For example, single-digit reference numbers (such as "paragraph 3") may be formatted as a two-digit response (such as "paragraph "03").

SKILL SPECIFICATION OUTLINES (SSOs)

The Skill Specification Outlines (SSOs) identify the skills to be tested on the Uniform CPA Examination. There are three categories of skills, and the weightings will be implemented through the use of different question formats in the exam. For each of the question formats, a different set of tools will be available as resources to the candidates, who must use those tools to demonstrate proficiency in the applicable skills categories.

The percentage range assigned to each skill category will be used to determine the quantity of each type of question, as described below.

Weights

The percentage range assigned to each skill category represents the approximate percentage to which that category of skills will be used in the different sections of the CPA Examination to assess proficiency. The ranges are designed to provide flexibility in building the examination, and the midpoints of the ranges for each section total 100%. No percentages are given for the bulleted descriptions included in these definitions. The presence of several groups within an area or several topics within a group does not imply that equal importance or weight will be given to these bullets on an examination.

Skills Category	Weights (FAR, REG, AUD)	Weights (BEC)
Knowledge and Understanding	50%–60%	80%–90%
Application of the Body of Knowledge	40%–50%	–
Written Communication	–	10%–20%

For the computer-based CPA Examination, these skill weightings will be applied in conjunction with the content percentage ranges described in the Content Specification Outline.

Knowledge and Understanding

Multiple-choice questions will be used as the proxy for assessing knowledge and understanding and will be based on the content topics as outlined in the CSOs. Candidates will not have access to the authoritative literature, spreadsheets, or database tools while answering these questions. A calculator will be accessible for candidates to use in performing calculations to demonstrate their understanding of the principles or subject matter.

Application of the Body of Knowledge

Task-based simulations will be used as the proxy for assessing application of the body of knowledge and will be based on the content topics as outlined in the CSOs. Candidates will have access to the authoritative literature, a calculator, spreadsheets, and other resources and tools, which they will use to demonstrate proficiency in applying the body of knowledge.

Written Communication

Written communication will be assessed through the use of responses to essay questions, which will be based on the content topics as outlined in the CSOs. Candidates will have access to a word processor, which includes a spell check feature.

An example of candidate instructions:

Reminder: Your response will be graded for writing skill in the context of specific subject matter. This response is to be written as a business letter. Do not convey any information in the form of a table, bullet point list, or other abbreviated presentation. Your response should include the conventions of a business letter, such as *date, greeting*, and *closing*.

Outlines

The following outlines provide additional descriptions of the skills that are represented in each category.

- Knowledge and Understanding

    Expertise and skills developed through learning processes, recall, and reading comprehension. Knowledge is acquired through experience or education and is the theoretical or practical understanding of a subject; knowledge is also represented through awareness or familiarity with information gained by experience of a fact or situation. Understanding represents a higher level than simple knowledge and is the process of using concepts to deal adequately with given situations, facts, or circumstances. Understanding is the ability to recognize and comprehend the meaning of a particular concept.
- Application of the Body of Knowledge, including Analysis, Judgment, Synthesis, Evaluation, and Research

    Higher-level cognitive skills that require individuals to act or transform knowledge in some fashion. These skills are inextricably intertwined and thus are grouped into this single skill area.
- Assess the Business Environment
    - Business Process Evaluation: Assessing and integrating information regarding a business's operational structure, functions, processes, and procedures to develop a broad operational perspective; identify the need for new systems or changes to existing systems and/or processes.
    - Contextual Evaluation: Assessing and integrating information regarding client's type of business or industry.
    - Strategic Analysis—Understanding the Business: Obtaining, assessing and integrating information on the entity's strategic objectives, strategic management process, business environment, the nature

of and value to customers, its products and services, extent of competition within its market space, etc.
- Business Risk Assessment: Obtaining, assessing, and integrating information on conditions and events that could impede the entity's ability to achieve strategic objectives.
- Visualize abstract descriptions: Organize and process symbols, pictures, graphs, objects, and other information.
- Research
  - Identify the appropriate research question.
  - Identify key search terms for use in performing electronic searches through large volumes of data.
  - Search through large volumes of electronic data to find required information.
  - Organize information or data from multiple sources.
  - Integrate diverse sources of information to reach conclusions or make decisions.
  - Identify the appropriate authoritative guidance in applicable financial reporting frameworks and auditing standards for the accounting issue being evaluated.
- Application of Technology
  - Using electronic spreadsheets to perform calculations, financial analysis, or other functions to analyze data.
  - Integration of technological applications and resources into work processes.
  - Using a variety of computer software and hardware systems to structure, utilize, and manage data.
- Analysis
  - Review information to determine compliance with specified standards or criteria.
  - Use expectations, empirical data, and analytical methods to determine trends and variances.
  - Perform appropriate calculations on financial and nonfinancial data.
  - Recognize patterns of activity when reviewing large amounts of data or recognize breaks in patterns.
  - Interpretation of financial statement data for a given evaluation purpose.
  - Forecasting future financial statement data from historical financial statement data and other information.
  - Integrating primary financial statements: Using data from all primary financial statements to uncover financial transactions, inconsistencies, or other information.
- Complex Problem Solving and Judgment
  - Develop and understand goals, objectives, and strategies for dealing with potential issues, obstacles, or opportunities.
  - Analyze patterns of information and contextual factors to identify potential problems and their implications.
  - Devise and implement a plan of action appropriate for a given problem.
  - Apply professional skepticism, which is an attitude that includes a questioning mind and a critical assessment of information or evidence obtained.
  - Adapt strategies or planned actions in response to changing circumstances.
  - Identify and solve unstructured problems.
  - Develop reasonable hypotheses to answer a question or resolve a problem.
  - Formulate and examine alternative solutions in terms of their relative strengths and weaknesses, level of risk, and appropriateness for a given situation.
  - Develop creative ways of thinking about situations, problems, and opportunities to create insightful and sound solutions.
  - Develop logical conclusions through the use of inductive and deductive reasoning.
  - Apply knowledge of professional standards and laws as well as legal, ethical, and regulatory issues.
  - Assess the need for consultations with other professionals when gray areas, or areas requiring specialized knowledge, are encountered.
- Decision Making
  - Specify goals and constraints.
  - Generate alternatives.
  - Consider risks.
  - Evaluate and select the best alternative.
- Organization, Efficiency, and Effectiveness
  - Use time effectively and efficiently.
  - Develop detailed work plans, schedule tasks and meetings, and delegate assignments and tasks.

- Set priorities by determining the relevant urgency or importance of tasks and deciding the order in which they should be performed.
- File and store information so that it can be found easily and used effectively.
- Written Communication—The various skills involved in preparing written communication, including:
  - Basic writing mechanics, such as grammar, spelling, word usage, punctuation, and sentence structure.
  - Effective business writing principles, including organization, clarity, and conciseness.
  - Exchange technical information and ideas with coworkers and other professionals to meet goals of job assignment.
- Documentation
  - Prepare documents and presentations that are concise, accurate, and supportive of the subject matter.
  - Document and cross-reference work performed and conclusions reached in a complete and accurate manner.
- Assist client to recognize and understand implications of critical business issues by providing recommendations and informed opinions.
- Persuade others to take recommended courses of action.
- Follow directions.

A Few Interesting Facts about the Computerized Exam

- Candidates may take one part at a time.
- Score results will take approximately six to eight weeks and are released twice per exam window.
- Candidates must pass all four sections of the Uniform CPA Examination within a "rolling" eighteen-month period, which begins on the date that the first section(s) passed is taken.
- Any credit for any section(s) passed outside the eighteen-month period will expire and that section(s) must be retaken.
- Candidates will not be allowed to retake a failed section(s) within the same quarter (examination window).
- Candidates will take different, equivalent exams.

Content Specification Outlines
Valid as of 1/1/2011

AUDITING AND ATTESTATION (AUD)

The Auditing and Attestation section covers knowledge of auditing standards generally accepted in the United States of America (GAAS) for public and private companies, governmental entities, not-for-profit entities, and employee benefit plans, standards related to attestation and assurance engagements, and standards for performing accounting and review services and the skills needed to apply that knowledge in auditing and other attestation engagements.

Candidates are expected to demonstrate an awareness of:

1. The International Auditing and Assurance Standards Board (IAASB) and its role in establishing International Standards on Auditing (ISAs).
2. The differences between ISAs and U.S. auditing standards.
3. The audit requirements under U.S. auditing standards that apply when they perform audit procedures on a U.S. company that supports an audit report based on the auditing standards of another country, or the ISAs.

This section also tests knowledge of professional responsibilities of certified public accountants, including ethics and independence.

Auditing and Attestation Content Specification Outline

I. Auditing and Attestation: Engagement Acceptance and Understanding the Assignment (12%–16%)
- A. Determine nature and scope of engagement.
- B. Consider the firm's system of quality control for policies and procedures pertaining to client acceptance and continuance, including:
  1. The CPA firm's ability to perform the engagement within reporting deadlines.
  2. Experience and availability of firm personnel to meet staffing and supervision requirements.
  3. Whether independence can be maintained.
  4. Integrity of client management.
  5. Appropriateness of the engagement's scope to meet the client's needs.

    C. Communicate with the predecessor auditor.

    D. Establish an understanding with the client and document the understanding through an engagement letter or other written communication with the client.

    E. Consider other planning matters.
1. Consider using the work of other independent auditors.
2. Determine the extent of the involvement of professionals possessing specialized skills.
3. Consider the independence, objectivity, and competency of the internal audit function.

    F. Identify matters and prepare documentation for communications with those charged with governance.

II. Auditing and Attestation: Understanding the Entity and Its Environment (including Internal Control) (16%–20%)

    A. Determine and document materiality levels for financial statements taken as a whole.

    B. Conduct and document risk assessment discussions among the audit team, concurrently with discussion on susceptibility of the entity's financial statement to material misstatement due to fraud.

    C. Consideration of fraud:
1. Identify characteristics of fraud.
2. Document required discussions regarding risk of fraud.
3. Document inquiries of management about fraud.
4. Identify and assess risks that may result in material misstatements due to fraud.

    D. Perform and document risk assessment procedures.
1. Identify, conduct, and document appropriate inquiries of management and others within the entity.
2. Perform appropriate analytical procedures to understand the entity and identify areas of risk.
3. Obtain information to support inquiries through observation and inspection (including reading corporate minutes, etc.).

    E. Consider additional aspects of the entity and its environment, including: industry, regulatory and other external factors; strategies and business risks; financial performance.

    F. Consider internal control.
1. Perform procedures to assess the control environment, including consideration of the COSO framework and identifying entity-level controls.
2. Obtain and document an understanding of business processes and information flows.
3. Perform and document walkthroughs of transactions from inception through recording in the general ledger and presentation in financial statements.
4. Determine the effect of information technology on the effectiveness of an entity's internal control.
5. Perform risk assessment procedures to evaluate the design and implementation of internal controls relevant to an audit of financial statements.
6. Identify key risks associated with general controls in a financial information technology environment, including change management, backup/recovery, and network access (e.g., administrative rights).
7. Identify key risks associated with application functionality that supports financial transaction cycles, including:
   • Application access control (e.g. administrative access rights).
   • Controls over interfaces, integrations, and e-commerce.
   • Significant algorithms, reports, validation, edit checks, error handling, etc.
8. Assess whether the entity has designed controls to mitigate key risks associated with general controls or application functionality.
9. Identify controls relevant to reliable financial reporting and the period-end financial reporting process.
10. Consider limitations of internal control.
11. Consider the effects of service organizations on internal control.
12. Consider the risk of management override of internal controls.

    G. Document an understanding of the entity and its environment, including each component of the entity's internal control, in order to assess risks.

    H. Assess and document the risk of material misstatements.
1. Identify and document financial statement assertions and formulate audit objectives including significant financial statement balances, classes of transactions, disclosures, and accounting estimates.

      2. Relate the identified risks to relevant assertions and consider whether the risks could result in a material misstatement to the financial statements.

      3. Assess and document the risk of material misstatement that relates to both financial statement level and specific assertions.

      4. Identify and document conditions and events that may indicate risks of material misstatement.

  I. Identify and document significant risks that require special audit consideration:

      1. Risk of fraud.

      2. Significant recent economic, accounting, or other developments.

      3. Related parties and related party transactions.

      4. Improper revenue recognition.

      5. Nonroutine or complex transactions.

      6. Significant management estimates.

      7. Illegal acts.

III. Auditing and Attestation: Performing Audit Procedures and Evaluating Evidence (16%–20%)

  A. Develop overall responses to risks.

      1. Develop overall responses to risks identified and use the risks of material misstatement to drive the nature, timing, and extent of further audit procedures.

      2. Document significant risks identified, related controls evaluated, and overall responses to address assessed risks.

      3. Determine and document level(s) of tolerable misstatement.

  B. Perform audit procedures responsive to risks of material misstatement; obtain and document evidence to form a basis for conclusions.

      1. Design and perform audit procedures whose nature, timing, and extent are responsive to the assessed risk of material misstatement.

      2. Integrating audits: In an integrated audit of internal control over financial reporting and the financial statements, design and perform testing of controls to accomplish the objectives of both audits simultaneously.

      3. Design, perform, and document tests of controls to evaluate design effectiveness.

      4. Design, perform, and document tests of controls to evaluate operating effectiveness.

      5. Perform substantive procedures.

      6. Perform audit sampling.

      7. Perform analytical procedures.

      8. Confirm balances and/or transactions with third parties.

      9. Examine inventories and other assets.

    10. Perform other tests of details, balances, and journal entries.

    11. Perform computer-assisted audit techniques (CAATs), including data query, extraction, and analysis.

    12. Perform audit procedures on significant management estimates.

    13. Auditing fair value measurements and disclosures, including the use of specialists in evaluating estimates.

    14. Perform tests on unusual year-end transactions.

    15. Audits performed in accordance with International Standards on Auditing (ISAs) or auditing standards of another country: Determine if differences exist and whether additional audit procedures are required.

    16. Evaluate contingencies.

    17. Obtain and evaluate lawyers' letters.

    18. Review subsequent events.

    19. Obtaining and placing reliance on representations from management.

    20. Identify material weaknesses, significant deficiencies, and other control deficiencies.

    21. Identify matters for communication with those charged with governance.

IV. Auditing and Attestation: Evaluating Audit Findings, Communications, and Reporting (16%–20%)

  A. Perform analytical procedures.

  B. Evaluate the sufficiency and appropriateness of audit evidence and document engagement conclusions.

  C. Evaluate whether audit documentation is in accordance with professional standards.

D. Review the work performed by others to provide reasonable assurance that objectives are achieved.

E. Document the summary of uncorrected misstatements and related conclusions.

F. Evaluate whether financial statements are free of material misstatements.

G. Consider the entity's ability to continue as a going concern.

H. Consider other information in documents containing audited financial statements (e.g., supplemental information and management's discussion and analysis).

I. Retain audit documentation as required by standards and regulations.

J. Prepare communications.
   1. Reports on audited financial statements.
   2. Reports required by government auditing standards.
   3. Reports on compliance with laws and regulations.
   4. Reports on internal control.
   5. Reports on the processing of transactions by service organizations.
   6. Reports on agreed-on procedures.
   7. Reports on financial forecasts and projections.
   8. Reports on pro forma financial information.
   9. Special reports.
   10. Reissue reports.
   11. Communicate internal control related matters identified in the audit.
   12. Communications with those charged with governance.
   13. Subsequent discovery of facts existing at the date of the auditor's report.
   14. Consideration after the report date of omitted procedures.

V. Accounting and Review Services Engagements (12%–16%)
   A. Plan the engagement.
      1. Determine nature and scope of engagement.
      2. Decide whether to accept or continue the client and engagement including determining the appropriateness of the engagement to meet the client's needs and consideration of independence standards.
      3. Establish an understanding with the client and document the understanding through an engagement letter or other written communication with the client.
      4. Consider change in engagement.
      5. Determine if reports are to be used by third parties.
   B. Obtain and document evidence to form a basis for conclusions.
      1. Obtain an understanding of the client's operations, business, and industry.
      2. Obtain knowledge of accounting principles and practices in the industry and the client.
      3. Obtain knowledge of stated qualifications of accounting personnel.
      4. Perform analytical procedures for review services.
      5. Obtain representations from management for review services.
      6. Perform other engagement procedures.
      7. Consider departures from generally accepted accounting principles (GAAP) or other comprehensive basis of accounting (OCBOA).
      8. Prepare documentation from evidence gathered.
      9. Retain documentation as required by standards.
      10. Review the work performed to provide reasonable assurance that objectives are achieved.
   C. Prepare communications:
      1. Reports on compiled financial statements.
      2. Reports on reviewed financial statements.
      3. Restricted use of reports.
      4. Communicating to management and others.
      5. Subsequent discovery of facts existing at the date of the report.
      6. Consider degree of responsibility for supplementary information.

VI. Professional Responsibilities (16%–20%)
   A. Ethics and independence
      1. Code of Professional Conduct (AICPA)
      2. Public Company Accounting Oversight Board (PCAOB)

       3. U.S. Securities and Exchange Commission (SEC)
       4. Government Accountability Office (GAO)
       5. Department of Labor (DOL)
       6. Sarbanes-Oxley Act of 2002, Title II
       7. Sarbanes-Oxley Act of 2002, Title III, Section 303
       8. Code of Ethics for Professional Accountants (IFAC)
   B. Other Professional Responsibilities
       1. Sarbanes-Oxley Act of 2002, Title IV
       2. Sarbanes-Oxley Act of 2002, Title I

References—Auditing and Attestation

    • AICPA Statements on Auditing Standards and Interpretations • AICPA Codification of Statements on Auditing Standards, AU Appendix B, *Analysis of International Standards on Auditing* • Public Company Accounting Oversight Board (PCAOB) Standards (SEC-Approved) and Related Rules, PCAOB Staff Questions and Answers, and PCAOB Staff Audit Practice Alerts • U.S. Government Accountability Office Government Auditing Standards • Single Audit Act, as amended • Office of Management and Budget (OMB) Circular A-133 • AICPA Statements on Quality Control Standards • AICPA Statements on Standards for Accounting and Review Services and Interpretations • AICPA Statements on Standards for Attestation Engagements and Interpretations • AICPA Audit and Accounting Guides • AICPA Auditing Practice Releases • AICPA Code of Professional Conduct • IFAC Code of Ethics for Professional Accountants • Sarbanes-Oxley Act of 2002 • Department of Labor Guidelines and Interpretive Bulletins re: Auditor Independence • SEC Independence Rules • Employee Retirement Income Security Act of 1974 • The Committee of Sponsoring Organizations of the Treadway Commission (COSO): Internal Control—Integrated Framework • Current textbooks on auditing, attestation services, ethics, and independence

FINANCIAL ACCOUNTING AND REPORTING (FAR)

    The Financial Accounting and Reporting section tests knowledge and understanding of the financial reporting framework used by business enterprises, not-for-profit organizations, and governmental entities. The financial reporting frameworks that are included in this section are those issued by the standard-setters identified in the references to these CSOs, which include standards issued by the Financial Accounting Standards Board, the International Accounting Standards Board, the U.S. Securities and Exchange Commission, and the Governmental Accounting Standards Board. In addition to demonstrating knowledge and understanding of accounting principles, candidates are required to demonstrate the skills required to apply that knowledge in performing financial reporting and other tasks as certified public accountants.

Financial Accounting and Reporting Content Specification Outline

I. Conceptual Framework, Standards, Standard Setting, and Presentation of Financial Statements (17%–23%)
   A. Process by which accounting standards are set and roles of accounting standard-setting bodies
       1. U.S. Securities and Exchange Commission (SEC)
       2. Financial Accounting Standards Board (FASB)
       3. International Accounting Standards Board (IASB)
       4. Governmental Accounting Standards Board (GASB)
   B. Conceptual framework
       1. Financial reporting by business entities
       2. Financial reporting by not-for-profit (nongovernmental) entities
       3. Financial reporting by state and local governmental entities
   C. Financial reporting, presentation and disclosures in general-purpose financial statements
       1. Balance sheet
       2. Income statement
       3. Statement of comprehensive income
       4. Statement of changes in equity
       5. Statement of cash flows
       6. Notes to financial statements
       7. Consolidated and combined financial statements
       8. First-time adoption of IFRS
   D. SEC reporting requirements (e.g. Form 10-Q, 10-K)

E. Other financial statement presentations, including other comprehensive bases of accounting (OCBOA):
    1. Cash basis
    2. Modified cash basis
    3. Income tax basis
    4. Personal financial statements
    5. Financial statements of employee benefit plans/trusts

II. Financial Statement Accounts: Recognition, Measurement, Valuation, Calculation, Presentation, and Disclosures (27%–33%)
    A. Cash and cash equivalents
    B. Receivables
    C. Inventory
    D. Property, plant, and equipment
    E. Investments
        1. Financial assets at fair value through profit or loss
        2. Available for sale financial assets
        3. Held-to-maturity investments
        4. Joint ventures
        5. Equity method investments (investments in associates)
        6. Investment property
    F. Intangible assets—goodwill and other
    G. Payables and accrued liabilities
    H. Deferred revenue
    I. Long-term debt (financial liabilities)
        1. Notes payable
        2. Bonds payable
        3. Debt with conversion features and other options
        4. Modifications and extinguishments
        5. Troubled debt restructurings by debtors
        6. Debt covenant compliance
    J. Equity
    K. Revenue recognition
    L. Costs and expenses
    M. Compensation and benefits
        1. Compensated absences
        2. Deferred compensation arrangements
        3. Nonretirement postemployment benefits
        4. Retirement benefits
        5. Stock compensation (share-based payments)
    N. Income taxes

III. Specific Transactions, Events, and Disclosures: Recognition, Measurement, Valuation, Calculation, Presentation, and Disclosures (27%–33%)
    A. Accounting changes and error corrections
    B. Asset retirement and environmental obligations
    C. Business combinations
    D. Consolidation (including off-balance sheet transactions, variable-interest entities, and noncontrolling interests)
    E. Contingencies, commitments, and guarantees (provisions)
    F. Earnings per share
    G. Exit or disposal activities and discontinued operations
    H. Extraordinary and unusual items
    I. Fair value measurements, disclosures, and reporting
    J. Derivatives and hedge accounting
    K. Foreign currency transactions and translation
    L. Impairment

M. Interim financial reporting
N. Leases
O. Distinguishing liabilities from equity
P. Nonmonetary transactions (barter transactions)
Q. Related parties and related party transactions
R. Research and development costs
S. Risks and uncertainties
T. Segment reporting
U. Software costs
V. Subsequent events
W. Transfers and servicing of financial assets and derecognition

IV. Governmental Accounting and Reporting (8%–12%)
  A. Governmental accounting concepts
    1. Measurement focus and basis of accounting
    2. Fund accounting concepts and applications
    3. Budgetary accounting
  B. Format and content of comprehensive annual financial report (CAFR)
    1. Government-wide financial statements
    2. Governmental funds financial statements
    3. Proprietary funds financial statements
    4. Fiduciary funds financial statements
    5. Notes to financial statements
    6. Management's discussion and analysis
    7. Required supplementary information (RSI) other than management's discussion and analysis
    8. Combining statements and individual fund statements and schedules
    9. Deriving government-wide financial statements and reconciliation requirements
  C. Financial reporting entity, including blended and discrete component units
  D. Typical items and specific types of transactions and events: recognition, measurement, valuation, calculation, and presentation in governmental entity financial statements
    1. Net assets and components thereof
    2. Fund balances and components thereof
    3. Capital assets and infrastructure assets
    4. General long-term liabilities
    5. Interfund activity, including transfers
    6. Nonexchange revenue transactions
    7. Expenditures
    8. Special items
    9. Encumbrances
  E. Accounting and reporting for governmental not-for-profit organizations

V. Not-for-Profit (Nongovernmental) Accounting and Reporting (8%–12%)
  A. Financial statements
    1. Statement of financial position
    2. Statement of activities
    3. Statement of cash flows
    4. Statement of functional expenses
  B. Typical items and specific types of transactions and events: Recognition, measurement, valuation, calculation, and presentation in financial statements of not-for-profit organizations
    1. Support, revenues, and contributions
    2. Types of restrictions on resources
    3. Types of net assets
    4. Expenses, including depreciation and functional expenses
    5. Investments

References—Financial Accounting and Reporting

• Financial Accounting Standards Board (FASB) Accounting Standards Codification • Governmental Accounting Standards Board (GASB) Codification of Governmental Accounting and Financial Reporting Standards • Standards Issued by the U. S. Securities and Exchange Commission (SEC): Regulation S-X of the Code of Federal Regulations (17 CFR Part 210), Financial Reporting Releases (FRR)/Accounting Series Releases (ASR), Interpretive Releases (IR), SEC Staff Guidance in Staff Accounting Bulletins (SAB), SEC Staff Guidance in EITF Topic D and SEC Staff Observer Comments • International Accounting Standards Board (IASB) International Financial Reporting Standards (IFRS), International Accounting Standards (IAS), and Interpretations • AICPA Auditing and Accounting Guides • Current textbooks on accounting for business enterprises, not-for-profit organizations, and governmental entities

REGULATION (REG)

The Regulation section tests knowledge and understanding of ethics, professional and legal responsibilities, business law, and federal taxation.

Ethics, Professional and Legal Responsibilities, and Business Law: These topics test knowledge and understanding of professional and legal responsibilities of certified public accountants. Professional ethics questions relate to tax practice issues and are based on the AICPA Code of Professional Conduct, Treasury Department Circular 230, and rules and regulations for tax return preparers. Business law topics test knowledge and understanding of the legal implications of business transactions, particularly as they relate to accounting, auditing, and financial reporting. This section deals with federal and widely adopted uniform state laws or references identified in this CSO.

Federal Taxation: These topics test knowledge and understanding of concepts and laws relating to federal taxation (income, gift, and estate). The areas of testing include federal tax process, procedures, accounting, and planning as well as federal taxation of property transactions, individuals, and entities (which include sole proprietorships, partnerships, limited liability entities, C corporations, S corporations, joint ventures, trusts, estates, and tax-exempt organizations). In addition to demonstrating knowledge and understanding of these topics, candidates are required to demonstrate the skills required to apply that knowledge in providing tax preparation and advisory services and performing other responsibilities as certified public accountants.

Regulation Content Specification Outline

I. *Ethics, Professional, and Legal Responsibilities (15%–19%)*
   A. Ethics and responsibilities in tax practice
      1. Treasury Department Circular 230
      2. AICPA Statements on Standards for Tax Services
      3. Internal Revenue Code of 1986, as amended, and Regulations related to tax return preparers
   B. Licensing and disciplinary systems
      1. Role of state boards of accountancy
      2. Requirements of regulatory agencies
   C. Legal duties and responsibilities
      1. Common law duties and liability to clients and third parties
      2. Federal statutory liability
      3. Privileged communications, confidentiality, and privacy acts

II. *Business Law (17%–21%)*
   A. Agency
      1. Formation and termination
      2. Authority of agents and principals
      3. Duties and liabilities of agents and principals
   B. Contracts
      1. Formation
      2. Performance
      3. Third-party assignments
      4. Discharge, breach, and remedies
   C. Uniform Commercial Code
      1. Sales contracts
      2. Negotiable instruments

      3.   Secured transactions

      4.   Documents of title and title transfer

  D. Debtor-creditor relationships

      1.   Rights, duties, and liabilities of debtors, creditors, and guarantors

      2.   Bankruptcy and insolvency

  E. Government regulation of business

      1.   Federal securities regulation

      2.   Other federal laws and regulations (antitrust, copyright, patents, money-laundering, labor, employment, and ERISA)

  F. Business structure (selection of a business entity)

      1.   Advantages, disadvantages, implications, and constraints

      2.   Formation, operation, and termination

      3.   Financial structure, capitalization, profit and loss allocation, and distributions

      4.   Rights, duties, legal obligations, and authority of owners and management

III. Federal Tax Process, Procedures, Accounting, and Planning (11%–15%)

  A. Federal tax legislative process

  B. Federal tax procedures

      1.   Due dates and related extensions of time

      2.   Internal Revenue Service (IRS) audit and appeals process

      3.   Judicial process

      4.   Required disclosure of tax return positions

      5.   Substantiation requirements

      6.   Penalties

      7.   Statute of limitations

  C. Accounting periods

  D. Accounting methods

      1.   Recognition of revenues and expenses under cash, accrual, or other permitted methods

      2.   Inventory valuation methods, including uniform capitalization rules

      3.   Accounting for long-term contracts

      4.   Installment sales

  E. Tax return elections, including federal status elections, alternative treatment elections, or other types of elections applicable to an individual or entity's tax return

  F. Tax planning

      1.   Alternative treatments

      2.   Projections of tax consequences

      3.   Implications of different business entities

      4.   Impact of proposed tax audit adjustments

      5.   Impact of estimated tax payment rules on planning

      6.   Role of taxes in decision making

  G. Impact of multijurisdictional tax issues on federal taxation (including consideration of local, state, and multinational tax issues)

  H. Tax research and communication

      1.   Authoritative hierarchy

      2.   Communications with or on behalf of clients

IV. Federal Taxation of Property Transactions (12%–16%)

  A. Types of assets

  B. Basis and holding periods of assets

  C. Cost recovery (depreciation, depletion, and amortization)

  D. Taxable and nontaxable sales and exchanges

  E. Amount and character of gains and losses, and netting process

  F. Related party transactions

  G. Estate and gift taxation

      1.   Transfers subject to the gift tax

      2.   Annual exclusion and gift tax deductions

3. Determination of taxable estate
4. Marital deduction
5. Unified credit

V. Federal Taxation of Individuals (13%–19%)
   A. Gross income
      1. Inclusions and exclusions
      2. Characterization of income
   B. Reporting of items from pass-through entities
   C. Adjustments and deductions to arrive at taxable income
   D. Passive activity losses
   E. Loss limitations
   F. Taxation of retirement plan benefits
   G. Filing status and exemptions
   H. Tax computations and credits
   I. Alternative minimum tax

VI. Federal Taxation of Entities (18%–24%)
   A. Similarities and distinctions in tax treatment among business entities
      1. Formation
      2. Operation
      3. Distributions
      4. Liquidation
   B. Differences between tax and financial accounting
      1. Reconciliation of book income to taxable income
      2. Disclosures under Schedule M-3
   C. C corporations
      1. Determination of taxable income/loss
      2. Tax computations and credits, including alternative minimum tax
      3. Net operating losses
      4. Entity/owner transactions, including contributions and distributions
      5. Earnings and profits
      6. Consolidated returns
   D. S corporations
      1. Eligibility and election
      2. Determination of ordinary income/loss and separately stated items
      3. Basis of shareholder's interest
      4. Entity/owner transactions, including contributions and distributions
      5. Built-in gains tax
   E. Partnerships
      1. Determination of ordinary income/loss and separately stated items
      2. Basis of partner's/member's interest and basis of assets contributed to the partnership
      3. Partnership and partner elections
      4. Transactions between a partner and the partnership
      5. Treatment of partnership liabilities
      6. Distribution of partnership assets
      7. Ownership changes and liquidation and termination of partnership
   F. Trusts and estates
      1. Types of trusts
      2. Income and deductions
      3. Determination of beneficiary's share of taxable income
   G. Tax-exempt organizations
      1. Types of organizations
      2. Obtaining and maintaining tax-exempt status
      3. Unrelated business income

References—Regulation Ethics, Professional and Legal Responsibilities, and Business Law
• AICPA Code of Professional Conduct • AICPA Statements on Standards for Tax Services • Revised Model Business Corporation Act • Revised Uniform Limited Partnership Act • Revised Uniform Partnership Act • Securities Act of 1933 • Securities Exchange Act of 1934 • Sarbanes-Oxley Act of 2002 • Uniform Commercial Code • Current textbooks covering business law, auditing, accounting, and ethics • *Federal Taxation*: Internal Revenue Code of 1986, as amended, and Regulations • Treasury Department Circular 230 • Other administrative pronouncements • Case law • AICPA Model Tax Curriculum • Current Federal tax textbooks

BUSINESS ENVIRONMENT AND CONCEPTS (BEC)

The Business Environment and Concepts section tests knowledge and skills necessary to demonstrate an understanding of the general business environment and business concepts. The topics in this section include knowledge of corporate governance; economic concepts essential to understanding the global business environment and its impact on an entity's business strategy and financial risk management; financial management processes; information systems and communications; strategic planning; and operations management. In addition to demonstrating knowledge and understanding of these topics, candidates are required to apply that knowledge in performing audit, attest, financial reporting, tax preparation, and other professional responsibilities as certified public accountants.

Business Environment and Concepts Content Specification Outline

I. Corporate Governance (16%–20%)
    A. Rights, duties, responsibilities, and authority of the board of directors, officers, and other employees
        1. Financial reporting
        2. Internal control (including COSO or similar framework)
        3. Enterprise risk management (including COSO or similar framework)
    B. Control environment
        1. Tone at the top—establishing control environment
        2. Monitoring control effectiveness
        3. Change control process

II. Economic Concepts and Analysis (16%–20%)
    A. Changes in economic and business cycles—economic measures/indicators
    B. Globalization and local economies
        1. Impacts of globalization on companies
        2. Shifts in economic balance of power (e.g. capital) to/from developed from/to emerging markets
    C. Market influences on business strategies
    D. Financial risk management
        1. Market, interest rate, currency, liquidity, credit, price, and other risks
        2. Means for mitigating/controlling financial risks

III. Financial Management (19%–23%)
    A. Financial modeling, projections, and analysis
        1. Forecasting and trends
        2. Financial and risk analysis
        3. Impact of inflation/deflation
    B. Financial decisions
        1. Debt, equity, leasing
        2. Asset and investment management
    C. Capital management, including working capital
        1. Capital structure
        2. Short-term and long-term financing
        3. Asset effectiveness and/or efficiency
    D. Financial valuations (e.g. fair value)
        1. Methods for calculating valuations
        2. Evaluating assumptions used in valuations
    E. Financial transaction processes and controls

IV. Information Systems and Communications (15%–19%)
    A. Organizational needs assessment
        1. Data capture
        2. Processing
        3. Reporting
        4. Role of information technology in business strategy
    B. Systems design and other elements
        1. Business process design (integrated systems, automated, and manual interfaces)
        2. Information technology control objectives
        3. Role of technology systems in control monitoring
        4. Operational effectiveness
        5. Segregation of duties
        6. Policies
    C. Security
        1. Technologies and security management features
        2. Policies
    D. Internet—implications for business
        1. Electronic commerce
        2. Opportunities for business process reengineering
        3. Roles of Internet evolution on business operations and organization cultures
    E. Types of information system and technology risks
    F. Disaster recovery and business continuity

V. Strategic Planning (10%–14%)
    A. Market and risk analysis
    B. Strategy development, implementation, and monitoring
    C. Planning techniques
        1. Budget and analysis
        2. Forecasting and projection
        3. Coordinating information from various sources for integrated planning

VI. Operations Management (12%–16%)
    A. Performance management and impact of measures on behavior
        1. Financial and nonfinancial measures
        2. Impact of marketing practices on performance
        3. Incentive compensation
    B. Cost measurement methods and techniques
    C. Process management
        1. Approaches, techniques, measures, and benefits to process management–driven businesses
        2. Roles of shared services, outsourcing, and offshore operations, and their implications on business risks and controls
        3. Selecting and implementing improvement initiatives
        4. Business process reengineering
        5. Management philosophies and techniques for performance improvement, such as Just in Time (JIT), Quality, Lean, Demand Flow, Theory of Constraints, and Six Sigma
    D. Project management
        1. Project planning, implementation, and monitoring
        2. Roles of project managers, project members, and oversight or steering groups
        3. Project risks, including resource, scope, cost, and deliverables

References—Business Environment and Concepts
    • The Committee of Sponsoring Organizations of the Treadway Commission (COSO): Internal Control—Integrated Framework, Enterprise Risk Management; Sarbanes-Oxley Act of 2002: Title III, Corporate Responsibility, Title IV, Enhanced Financial Disclosures, Title VIII, Corporate and Criminal Fraud Accountability • Current Business Periodicals • Current Textbooks on: Accounting Information Systems, Budgeting and Measurement, Corporate Governance, Economics, Enterprise Risk Management Finance,

Management, Management Information Systems, Managerial Accounting, Production Operations, Project Management

CBTe—EXAM CHANGES EFFECTIVE 01/01/2011

Summary of 01/01/2011 CSO Changes

Auditing and Attestation (AUD)

Special note: This section will now include ethics and independence testing, previously a part of the REG section. However, the REG section will continue to test ethics and responsibilities as pertaining exclusively to tax practice.

Area I
- Current: Plan the Engagement (22%–28%)
- New: Engagement Acceptance and Understanding the Assignment (12%–16%)

Area II
- Current: Internal Control (12%–18%)
- New: Understanding the Entity and Its Environment (including Internal Control) (16%–20%)

Area III
- Current: Obtain and Document Information (32%–38%)
- New: Performing Audit Procedures and Evaluating Evidence (16%–20%)

Area IV
- Current: Review and Evaluate Work Performed (8%–12%)
- New: Evaluating Audit Findings, Communications and Reporting (16%–20%)

Area V
- Current: Communications and Reporting (12%–18%)
- New: Accounting and Review Service Engagements (12%–16%)

Area VI
- Current: N/A
- New: Professional Responsibilities (including Ethics and Independence) (16%–20%)

Financial Accounting and Reporting (FAR)

Special note: The testing of IFRS will be added to the FAR section of the exam.

Area I
- Current: Concepts and Standards for Financial Statements (17%–23%)
- New: Conceptual Framework, Standards, Standard Setting, and Presentation of Financial Statements (17%–23%)

Area II
- Current: Typical Items in Financial Statements (27%–33%)
- New: Financial Statement Accounts: Recognition, Measurement, Valuation, Calculation, Presentation, and Disclosures (27%–33%)

Area III
- Current: Specific Types of Transactions (27%–33%)
- New: Specific Transactions, Events, and Disclosures (27%–33%)

Area IV
- Current: Governmental Accounting and Reporting (8%–12%)
- New: Governmental Accounting and Reporting (8%–12%)

Area V
- Current: Not-for-Profit Accounting and Reporting (8%–12%)
- New: Not-for-Profit (Nongovernmental) Accounting and Reporting (8%–12%)

Regulation (REG)

Special notes: REG will now test ethics and responsibilities only as pertaining to tax practice. General ethics and independence testing has been moved to the AUD section. Business structure topics currently included in the BEC section will be added to the business law area of REG.

Area I
- Current: Ethics and Professional and Legal Responsibilities (15%–20%)
- New: Ethics, Professional, and Legal Responsibilities (15%–19%)

Area II
- Current: Business Law (20%–25%)
- New: Business Law (17%–21%)

Area III
- Current: Federal Tax Procedures and Accounting Issues (8%–12%)
- New: Federal Tax Process, Procedures, Accounting, and Planning (11%–15%)

Area IV
- Current: Federal Taxation of Property Transactions (8%–12%)
- New: Federal Taxation of Property Transactions (12%–16%)

Area V
- Current: Federal Taxation of Individuals (12%–18%)
- New: Federal Taxation of Individuals (13%–19%)

Area VI
- Current: Federal Taxation of Entities (22%–28%)
- New: Federal Taxation of Entities (18%–24%)

Business Environment and Concepts (BEC)

Special notes: Business structure topics have been relocated to the REG section. Further content additions include a new corporate governance topic, and a redefined information systems topic presented from a business entity manager's perspective.

Area I
- Current: Business Structure (17%–23%)
- New: Corporate Governance (16%–20%)

Area II
- Current: Economic Concepts (8%–12%)
- New: Economic Concepts and Analysis (16%–20%)

Area III
- Current: Financial Management (17%–23%)
- New: Financial Management (19%–23%)

Area IV
- Current: Information Technology (22%–28%)
- New: Information Systems and Communication (15%–19%)

Area V
- Current: Planning and Measurement (22%–28%)
- New: Strategic Planning (10%–14%)

Area VI
- Current: N/A
- New: Operations Management (12%–16%)

AUDITING AND ATTESTATION SECTION

Following is the new information that will now be tested on the Audit portion of the CPA Exam. Some of the information is newly tested information, and other material was tested previously on the CPA exam but is now being moved from other sections to the Audit section.

The Content and Skills Specifications for the Auditing and Attestation section of the CPA exam are similar to the current content specifications; however, the topics of ethics and independence and responsibilities under the Sarbanes-Oxley Act have been moved from the Regulation section of the exam to the Auditing and Attestation section.

New areas that have been added to the Content and Skills Specifications for the Audit exam include ethics and independence standards of the International Federation of Accountants, the Government Accountability Office, and the Department of Labor. Auditing standards of the International Federation of Accountants has also been added.

NEW MATERIAL—AUDITING AND ATTESTATION SECTION

International Ethics Standards for Accountants

The International Ethics Standards Board for Accountants (IESBA) is a standard-setting body within the International Federation of Accountants (IFAC) that issues ethical standards for accountants throughout the world. This group has issued the *Code of Ethics for Professional Accountants,* which is similar to the *Code of Professional Conduct* issued by the AICPA for accountants in the United States. The IESBA code is similar to the AICPA code and has three parts:

- Part A—Framework applies to all professional accountants.
- Part B—Applies to professional accountants in public practice.
- Part C—Applies to professional accountants in business.

Part A—Framework

Section 110—Integrity. Professional accountants should be straightforward and honest in all professional and business relationships. Integrity implies fair dealing and truthfulness. The accountant should not be associated with reports or other communications where the accountant believes the information contains a materially false or misleading statement, contains statements or information furnished recklessly, or omits or obscures information required to be included where such omission or obscurity would be misleading.

Section 120—Objectivity. Professional accountants should not compromise their professional or business judgment.

Section 130—Professional competence and due care. Professional accountants should maintain professional knowledge and skill at the level required to ensure that clients or employers receive competent professional service and to act diligently in accordance with applicable technical and professional standards.

Section 140—Confidentiality. Professional accountants should refrain from disclosing confidential information unless there is a legal or professional obligation to do so, and using confidential information for personal advantage.

Section 150—Professional behavior. Professional accountants should comply with laws and regulations and avoid actions that would discredit the profession. In marketing services the professional accountant shall be honest and truthful.

Part B—Accountants in Public Practice

Section 200—Professional accountants in public practice. This section of the code begins with a framework that presents threats to ethical behavior and safeguards to help mitigate these threats.

Section 210—Professional appointment. Before accepting a new client, a professional accountant should determine whether acceptance would create any threats to compliance with fundamental principles.

Section 220—Conflicts of interest. A professional accountant should take reasonable steps to indentify circumstances that could pose a conflict of interest.

Section 230—Second opinions. When asked to provide a second opinion on applicable accounting, auditing, reporting or other standards to specific circumstances or transactions, a professional accountant should evaluate the significance of threats and apply necessary safeguards.

Section 240—Fees and other types of remuneration. Commissions, referral fees, fees that are not adequate, and contingent fees may create threats to compliance with professional standards. Therefore, the professional accountant should make sure that necessary safeguards are in effcct around fee determination.

Section 250—Marketing professional services. Solicitation of new work through advertising or other forms of marketing may create a threat to compliance with fundamental principles. The accountant in public practice should not bring the profession in disrepute when marketing professional services. Assertions in marketing should be honest and truthful.

Section 260—Gifts and hospitality. Gifts and hospitality from a client may create a threat to independence. The accountant must evaluate the significance of the threat and apply necessary safeguards.

Section 270—Custody of client assets. A professional accountant in public practice shall not assume custody of client monies or other assets unless permitted by law.

Section 280—Objectivity—All services. A professional accountant shall determine when providing professional services whether there are threats to objectivity. If so, the accountant should apply necessary safeguards.

Section 290—Independence—Audit and review engagements. The international ethics rules regarding independence in audit and review engagements are similar to the AICPA rules. Both require the concepts of independence in mind and in appearance. However, the international ethics rules have fewer definitive prohibitions. Instead, the international standards rely on the conceptual framework approach of:

1. Identify threats to independence.
2. Evaluate the significance of the threats identified.
3. Apply safeguards, when necessary, to eliminate the threats or reduce them to an acceptable level.
   When evaluating whether to accept or continue a particular engagement or to assign a particular individual to the engagement team, the firm should identify any threats to independence. If the threats are not at an acceptable level, the firm should consider whether applying appropriate safeguards will reduce them to an acceptable level. If not, the firm should not accept or continue the engagement or not assign the particular individual to the engagement team. The firm should document these considerations and the conclusion. Threats to independence arise from self-interest, self-review, advocacy, familiarity, or

intimidation. Like the AICPA *Code of Professional Conduct,* the international ethics rules indicate these types of threats can arise from:

- Financial interests in the client.
- Having certain business relationships with the client.
- Serving as a director, officer, or employee of the client.
- Performing certain nonassurance services to the client.

Safeguards are of two categories: (1) those created by the profession, legislation, or regulation, and (2) those implemented by the firm in the work environment. An example of a safeguard in the first category is legislation that prohibits the performance of certain nonassurance services for audit clients. As an example in the second category, the audit firm may decide not to assign a particular individual to an audit engagement to mitigate a threat to independence.

Section 291—Independence for other assurance services. These requirements are similar to those established by the AICPA in the United States. They relate to maintaining independence from the parties making the assertion on which the accountant is providing assurance.

Part C—Professional Accountants in Business

The rules that apply to professional accountants in business relate to these areas:

- Potential conflicts
- Preparation and reporting on information
- Acting with sufficient expertise
- Financial interests
- Inducements

Independence Standards of the Governmental Accountability Office (GAO)

The GAO has separate independence standards for audits performed in accordance with generally accepted government auditing standards (GAGAS). Overall, the standards state:

In all matters relating to the audit work, the audit organization and the individual auditor, whether government or public, must be free from personal, external, and organizational impairments to independence, and must avoid the appearance of such impairments of independence.

Impairments of independence are personal, external, and organizational.

1. Personal impairments result from relationships or beliefs that might bias the auditors in performing the audit work. Examples include:
   a. Immediate family or close family member who is director or officer of the audited entity or is an employee in a position to exert direct and significant influence over the entity or the program under audit.
   b. Financial interest that is direct, or is significant/material though indirect, in the audit entity or program.
   c. Responsibility for managing an entity or making decisions that could affect operations of the entity or program being audited (e.g., serving as a director, officer, or other senior position of the entity).
   d. Auditing an entity and program for which the auditors (1) maintained accounting records, (2) authorized, executed or consummated transactions, or (3) maintained bank accounts.
   e. Preconceived ideas toward individuals, groups, organizations, or objectives of a particular program that could bias the audit.
   f. Biases, including political, ideological, or social convictions.
   g. Seeking employment during the conduct of the audit with the organization being audited.
   Audit firms should have policies and procedures to identify such impairments and resolve them on a timely basis.
2. External impairments, which occur when auditors are deterred from acting objectively or performing an effective audit. Examples include external interference resulting from unreasonable restrictions on time for completion of the audit, restrictions on access to records, threats to replace the auditor, or unreasonable pressure to reduce audit time to reduce audit costs.
3. Organizational impairments result from reporting responsibilities or other functions that the auditors perform that may affect their independence or performance of an effective audit. For external auditors, such impairments may result from performing nonaudit services. Audit organizations that perform such

services must evaluate whether providing the services creates impairment either in fact or appearance. The overreaching principles in making this evaluation are:

a. Auditors must not perform nonaudit services that involve performing management functions or making management decisions.

b. Auditors must not audit their own work or provide nonaudit services in situations in which the nonaudit services are significant or material to the subject matter of the audit.

Department of Labor Independence Requirements

Employee benefit plans must be audited in accordance with the Employee Retirement Security Act of 1974 (ERISA), as enforced by the Department of Labor (DOL). For purposes of auditing these plans, the DOL has issued guidelines to determine whether the accountant is independent.

An accountant is not independent with respect to the plan if:

1. During the period of professional engagement, at the date of the opinion, or during the period covered by the financial statements, the accountant or his or her firm or a member thereof
   a. Had, or was committed to acquire, any direct financial interest or any material indirect financial interest in the plan or plan sponsor;
   b. Was connected as a promoter, underwriter, investment advisor, voting trustee, director, officer, or employee of the plan or plan sponsor except that a firm will not be deemed not independent if a former officer or employee of the plan or plan sponsor is employed by the firm and such individual has completely disassociated himself or herself from the plan or plan sponsor and does not participate in auditing financial statements of the plan covering any period of his or her employment by the plan or plan sponsor.
2. An accountant or a member of an accounting firm maintains financial records for the employee benefit plan.

However, an accountant may permissibly engage in or have members of his or her firm engage in certain activities that will not have the effect of removing recognition of independence. For example, an accountant will not fail to be recognized as independent if:

1. At or during the period of his or her professional engagement the accountant or his or her firm is retained or engaged on a professional basis by the plan sponsor. However, the accountant must not violate the prohibitions in (1) and (2) preceding.
2. The rendering of services by an actuary associated with the accountant or his or her firm shall not impair the accountant's or the firm's independence.

International Auditing and Assurance Standards

International auditing standards are developed by the International Auditing and Assurance Standards Board (IAASB) of the International Federation of Accountants (IFAC), a worldwide organization of approximately 160 national accounting bodies (e.g., the AICPA). IFAC was established to help foster a coordinated worldwide accounting profession with harmonized standards. Its boards also establish ethical and quality control standards for accounting professionals and accounting firms. International auditing standards are issued as a series of statements referred to as *International Standards on Auditing.*

The pronouncements of the IAASB do not override the auditing standards of its members. Rather, they are meant to help develop consistent worldwide professional standards. Members from countries that do not have their own standards may adopt IAASB standards as their own; members from countries that already have standards are encouraged to compare them to IAASB standards and to seek to eliminate any material inconsistencies. The following represent areas that a report commissioned by the European Commission (the executive organization of the European Union) suggests there are substantive differences between international and US PCAOB auditing standards:

1. International standards do not require an audit of internal control, while PCAOB standards do so require.
2. International standards do not allow reference to another audit firm involved in a portion of the audit while PCAOB standards allow the principal auditor to so report (i.e., percentages or dollars audited by the other auditor are reported and the opinion is based in part on the report of the other auditor).
3. International standards for documentation are less detailed than PCAOB standards, leaving more to professional judgment.

4. International standards in the area of going concern include a time horizon of at least, but not limited to 12 months while PCAOB standards limit the foreseeable future for a going concern consideration to up to 12 months.
5. International standards are based on a risk assessment approach (obtaining a broad understanding of an entity and its environment in order to identify where there may be risks of material misstatements) while the PCAOB standards currently are not. This difference will soon disappear as the PCAOB is in the process of adopting such standards (as has the AICPA Auditing Standards Board).

Additional differences not included in the above report as substantive differences include those listed in the next table.

Topic	International	U.S. Standards (both AIPCA and PCAOB)
Confirmation of accounts receivable	Not required. In making a determination on whether to confirm, the auditor should consider the assessed risk of material misstatement at the assertion level and how the audit evidence from other planned audit procedures will reduce the risk of material misstatement at the assertion level to an acceptably low level.	Confirmation is presumptively required unless accounts receivable are immaterial, the use of confirmations would be ineffective, or the combined assessed level of inherent and control risk is low.
Fraud	Auditors should obtain a written representation from management that it has disclosed to the auditor the results of its assessment of the risk of fraud.	Not required. However, various representations on fraud are obtained (management's knowledge of its responsibility, management's knowledge of fraud, allegations of fraud).
Illegal acts	The auditor's concern is with whether laws and regulations may materially affect the financial statements. No explicit distinction is made between direct and indirect effect illegal acts.	The audit obtains reasonable assurance of detection of illegal acts that have a direct and material effect on financial statement amounts; if evidence about possible illegal acts with an indirect effect comes to the auditor's attention, it is considered.
Sending letter of audit inquiry to lawyers	Only required when an auditor "assesses a risk of material misstatement."	Presumptively required.
Reviewing predecessor auditor's workpapers for evidence on beginning balances	The standard states that this may provide sufficient appropriate audit evidence on opening balances.	This statement is not included in standards.
Audit report modification for consistency related to changes in accounting principles	Not required.	Audit reports are modified for changes with a material effect on the financial statements.
Inclusion of an emphasis of a matter paragraph in an audit report	Preferably after the opinion paragraph.	No such statement (may be before or after opinion paragraph).
Providing location the auditor practices in an audit report	Required.	Not required.
Dating the audit report for a subsequent event	When management amends financial statements for a subsequent event, the auditor should perform necessary procedures and change the date of the audit report to no earlier than the date the financial statements were accepted as amended.	Auditors may "dual date" report (see Section A.2. of Reporting Module).

Switching from auditing standards to accounting standards, candidates should know that the International Financial Reporting Standards (IFRS) are developed by the International Accounting Standards Board (IASB). These standards represent an alternative financial reporting framework to U.S. generally accepted accounting principles (GAAP). When a client follows IFRS it has an effect on the audit process because of the differences between IFRS and U.S. GAAP. Apart from some specific differences in rules, IFRS are considered to be more principle-based than U.S. GAAP. Therefore, IFRS generally require the application of more judgment.

QUESTIONS ON THE NEW AUDITING AND ATTESTATION MATERIAL

1. In relation to the AICPA *Code of Professional Conduct*, the IFAC *Code of Ethics for Professional Accountants*:
    a. Has more outright prohibitions.
    b. Has fewer outright prohibitions.
    c. Has no outright prohibitions.
    d. Applies only to professional accountants in business.

2. Based on the IFAC *Code of Ethics for Professional Accountants*, threats to independence arise from all of the following **except**:
    a. Self-interest.
    b. Advocacy.
    c. The audit relationship.
    d. Intimidation.

3. If an audit firm discovers threats to independence with respect to an audit engagement, the IFAC *Code of Ethics for Professional Accountants* indicates that the firm should:
    a. Immediately resign from the engagement.
    b. Notify the appropriate regulatory body.
    c. Document the issue.
    d. Evaluate the significance of the threats and apply appropriate safeguards to reduce them to an acceptable level.

4. With respect to the acceptance of contingent fees for professional services, the IFAC *Code of Ethics for Professional Accountants* indicates that the accounting firm:
    a. Should not accept contingent fees.
    b. Should establish appropriate safeguards around acceptance of a contingent fee.
    c. Should accept contingent fees only for assurance services other than audits of financial statements.
    d. Should accept contingent fees if it is customary in the country.

5. With regard to marketing professional services, the IFAC *Code of Ethics for Professional Accountants* indicates that:
    a. Direct marketing is prohibited.
    b. Marketing is allowed if lawful.
    c. Marketing should be honest and truthful.
    d. Marketing of audit services is prohibited.

6. Independence standards of the GAO for audits in accordance with generally accepted government auditing standards describe three types of impairments of independence. Which of the following is **not** one of these types of impairments?
    a. Personal.
    b. Organizational.
    c. External.
    d. Unusual.

7. In accordance with the independence standards of the GAO for performing audits in accordance with generally accepted government auditing standards, which of the following is **not** an example of an external impairment of independence?
    a. Reducing the extent of audit work due to pressure from management to reduce audit fees.
    b. Selecting audit items based on the wishes of an employee of the organization being audited.
    c. Bias in the items the auditors decide to select for testing.
    d. Influence by management on the personnel assigned to the audit.

8. Under the independence standards of the GAO for performing audits in accordance with generally accepted government auditing standards, which of the following are overreaching principles for determining whether a nonaudit service impairs independence?
    I. Auditors must not perform nonaudit services that involve performing management functions or making management decisions.
    II. Auditors must not audit their own work or provide nonaudit services in situations in which the nonaudit services are significant or material to the subject matter of the audit.
    III. Auditors must not perform nonaudit services that require independence.
        a. I only.
        b. I and II only.
        c. I, II, and III.
        d. II and III only.

9. Which of the following bodies enforce the audit requirements of the Employee Retirement Security Act of 1974 (ERISA) with respect to employee benefit plans?
    a. Department of Labor.
    b. Department of Pension Management.
    c. Securities and Exchange Commission.
    d. Public Company Accounting Oversight Board.

10. The requirement for independence by the auditor regarding audits of employee benefit plans apply to the plan as well as:
    a. Investment companies doing business with the plan.
    b. Members of the plan.
    c. The plan sponsor.
    d. The actuary firm doing services for the plan.

11. What body establishes international auditing standards?
    a. Public Company Accounting Oversight Board.
    b. International Federation of Accountants.
    c. World Bank.
    d. International Assurance Body.

12. Which of the following is **not** true about international auditing standards?
    a. International auditing standards do not require an audit of internal control.

    b. International auditing standards do not allow reference to division of responsibilities in the audit report.
    c. International auditing standards require obtaining an attorney's letter.
    d. International auditing standards are based on a risk assessment approach.

13. Which of the following is **not** true about international auditing standards?
    a. Audit report modification for consistency in the application of accounting principles is required.
    b. Confirmation of accounts receivable is not required.
    c. The location in which the auditor practices must be disclosed in the audit report.
    d. International auditing standards do not require an audit of internal control.

ANSWER EXPLANATIONS FOR THE NEW AUDITING AND ATTESTATION MATERIAL

1. **(b)** The requirement is to identify the characteristic that differs between the two sets of ethical standards. Answer (b) is correct because the IFAC Code has fewer outright prohibitions than the AICPA Code. Answers (a) and (c) are incorrect because the IFAC Code has fewer outright prohibitions. Answer (d) is incorrect because the IFAC Code applies to all professional accountants.

2. **(c)** The requirement is to identify the item that is not a threat to independence. Answer (c) is correct because the audit relationship, in itself, is not a threat to independence. Answers (a), (b), and (d) are incorrect because they all represent types of threats to independence.

3. **(d)** The requirement is to identify the appropriate course of action when threats to independence are discovered. Answer (d) is correct because the firm should evaluate the significance of the threats and apply safeguards, if necessary, to reduce them to an acceptable level. Answer (a) is incorrect because the firm would resign only if appropriate safeguards could not reduce the threats to an acceptable level, or it is required based on a prohibition. Answer (b) is incorrect because the firm would not notify a regulatory body at this point. Answer (c) is incorrect

because the firm would document the issue, but only after it is resolved.

4. **(b)** The requirement is to identify what the IFAC *Code of Ethics for Professional Accountants* provides with respect to contingent fees. Answer (b) is correct because the IFAC Code indicates that if the contingent fee presents a threat to apply fundamental principles, the firm should establish appropriate safeguards. Answer (a) is incorrect because a contingent fee may be accepted if threats can be reduced to an acceptable level. Answers (c) and (d) are incorrect because the IFAC Code does not contain these provisions.

5. **(c)** The requirement is to identify the IFAC Code provision regarding marketing. Answer (c) is correct because the IFAC Code indicates the marketing must be honest and truthful. Answers (a) and (d) are incorrect because no particular form of marketing is prohibited. Answer (b) is incorrect because marketing must be honest and truthful as well as legal.

6. **(d)** The requirement is to identify the impairment that is not one of the three types of impairments described in the GAO standards. Answer (d) is correct because an unusual impairment is not one of the types of impairments described in the GAO standards. Answers (a), (b) and (c) are incorrect

because they are the three types of impairments described in the GAO standards.

7. **(c)** The requirement is to identify the example that does not represent an external impairment of independence. Answer (c) is correct because this item is an example of a personal impairment of independence. Answers (a), (b), and (d) are incorrect because they are all examples of external impairments of independence.

8. **(b)** The requirement is to identify the overreaching principles for identifying whether nonaudit services impair independence. Answer (b) is correct because I and II are the two principles. Answer (a) is incorrect because II is also an overreaching principle. Answer (c) is incorrect because III is not an overreaching principle. Answer (d) is incorrect because I is an overreaching principle and III is not.

9. **(a)** The requirement is to identify the body that enforces the audit requirements of ERISA. Answer (a) is correct because the Department of Labor is responsible for enforcing the audit requirements. Answer (b) is incorrect because the Department of Pension Management does not exist. Answers (c) and (d) are incorrect because the SEC and the PCAOB deal with auditing requirements for entities with publicly traded securities (issuers).

10. **(c)** The requirement is to identify the party that independence standards also apply to when performing an audit of an employee benefit plan. Answer (c) is correct because the Department of Labor rules also apply to independence from the plan and the plan sponsor. Answers (a), (b), and (d) are incorrect because the independence standards do not apply to these parties.

11. **(b)** The requirement is to identify the body that establishes international auditing standards. Answer (b) is correct because the International Auditing and Assurance Standards Board of the International Federation of Accountants establishes international auditing standards. Answer (a) is incorrect because the Public Company Accounting Oversight Board establishes standards for the audit of public companies in the United States. Answers (c) and (d) are incorrect because these bodies do not establish auditing standards.

12. **(c)** The requirement is to identify the item that is not true about international auditing standards. Answer (c) is correct because international auditing standards require obtaining an attorney's letter only if the auditors assess a risk of material misstatement. Answers (a), (b), and (d) are incorrect because they are all true about international auditing standards.

13. **(a)** The requirement is to identify the item that is not true about international auditing standards. Answer (a) is correct because international auditing standards do not require a modification of the audit report for consistency in the application of accounting principles. Answers (b), (c), and (d) are incorrect because they are true about international auditing standards.

EXAMPLES OF THE NEW TASK-BASED SIMULATIONS—AUDITING AND ATTESTATION

The simulations in the Auditing and Assurance section of this manual will also help you review for the new smaller task-based simulations because many of the new task-based simulations are like single parts of the ones currently used.

QUESTIONS

Task-Based Simulation 1
    (From Wiley Module 1)
    Green, CPA, is considering audit risk, including fraud risk, at the financial statement level in planning the audit of National Federal Bank (NFB) Company's financial statements for the year ended December 31, 2005. Audit risk at the financial statement level is influenced by the risk of material misstatements, which may be indicated by a combination of factors related to management, the industry, and the entity. In assessing such factors, Green has gathered the following information concerning NFB's environment.

Company Profile
    NFB is a federally insured bank that has been consistently more profitable than the industry average by marketing mortgages on properties in a prosperous rural area, which has experienced considerable growth in recent years. NFB packages its mortgages and sells them to large mortgage investment trusts. Despite recent volatility of interest rates, NFB has been able to continue selling its mortgages as a source of new lendable funds.

NFB's board of directors is controlled by Smith, the majority stockholder, who also acts as the chief executive officer. Management at the bank's branch offices has authority for directing and controlling NFB's operations and is compensated based on branch profitability. The internal auditor reports directly to Harris, a minority shareholder, who also acts as chairman of the board's audit committee.

The accounting department has experienced little turnover in personnel during the five years Green has audited NFB. NFB's formula consistently underestimates the allowance for loan losses, but its controller always has been receptive to Green's suggestions to increase the allowance during each engagement.

Recent Developments

During 2005, NFB opened a branch office in a suburban town 30 miles from its principal place of business. Although this branch is not yet profitable due to competition from several well-established regional banks, management believes that the branch will be profitable by 2007.

Also, during 2005, NFB increased the efficiency of its accounting operations by installing a new, sophisticated computer system.

Assume you are preparing for the audit personnel discussion of potential risks of material misstatement due to fraud for the NFB audit. While any matters below might be discussed, indicate by marking the appropriate four highest risks based on the information contained in the simulation description and requirements of professional standards.

	Risk	*High-risk item*
1.	Computer fraud risk	○
2.	Risk related to management override of internal control	○
3.	Fraud by branch management	○
4.	Fraud by accounting personnel	○
5.	Misstatement of accounting estimates	○
6.	Fraud by loan processing clerks	○
7.	Fraud by internal auditors	○
8.	The risk of fraudulent misstatement of revenues	○

Task-Based Simulation 2
(From Wiley Module 2)

Research

On the Adams audit, your firm discovered certain immaterial audit adjustments that the client's management chose not to record. Management has now asked you not to communicate anything regarding these omitted entries to the audit committee—after all, they are immaterial.

1. Which section of the Professional Standards addresses this issue?
   a. AU
   b. PCAOB
   c. AT
   d. AR
   e. ET
   f. BL
   g. CS
   h. QC
2. Enter the exact section number and paragraphs that address communicating these uncorrected misstatements to the audit committee.

Task-Based Simulation 3
(From Wiley Module 3)

Items 1 through 7 represent audit objectives for the investments and accounts receivable. To the right of each set of audit objectives is a listing of possible audit procedures for that account. For each audit objective, select the audit procedure that would primarily respond to the objective. Select only one procedure for each audit objective. A procedure may be selected only once or not at all.

Audit procedures for investments
A. Trace opening balances in the subsidiary ledger to prior year's audit workpapers.
B. Determine that employees who are authorized to sell investments do not have access to cash.
C. Examine supporting documents for a sample of investment transactions to verify that prenumbered documents are used.
D. Determine that any impairments in the price of investments have been recorded properly.
E. Verify that transfers from the current to the noncurrent investment portfolio have been recorded properly.
F. Obtain positive confirmations as of the balance sheet date of investments held by independent custodians.
G. Trace investment transactions to minutes of the board of directors meetings to determine that transactions were properly authorized.

Audit objectives for investments	(A)	(B)	(C)	(D)	(E)	(F)	(G)
1. Investments are properly described and classified in the financial statements.	○	○	○	○	○	○	○
2. Recorded investments represent investments actually owned at the balance sheet date.	○	○	○	○	○	○	○
3. Trading investments are properly valued at fair market value at the balance sheet date.	○	○	○	○	○	○	○

Audit procedures for accounts receivable
A. Analyze the relationship of accounts receivable and sales, and compare it with relationships for preceding periods.
B. Perform sales cutoff tests to obtain assurance that sales transactions and corresponding entries for inventories and cost of goods sold are recorded in the same and proper period.
C. Review the aged trial balance for significant past due accounts.
D. Obtain an understanding of the business purpose of transactions that resulted in accounts receivable balances.
E. Review loan agreements for indications of whether accounts receivable have been factored or pledged.
F. Review the accounts receivable trial balance for amounts due from officers and employees.
G. Analyze unusual relationships between monthly accounts receivable balances and monthly accounts payable balances.

Audit objectives for accounts receivable	(A)	(B)	(C)	(D)	(E)	(F)	(G)
4. Accounts receivable represent all amounts owed to the entity at the balance sheet date.	○	○	○	○	○	○	○
5. The entity has legal right to all accounts receivable at the balance sheet date.	○	○	○	○	○	○	○
6. Accounts receivable are stated at net realizable value.	○	○	○	○	○	○	○
7. Accounts receivable are properly described and presented in the financial statements.	○	○	○	○	○	○	○

ANSWER EXPLANATIONS FOR THE NEW TASK-BASED SIMULATIONS

Solution to Task-Based Simulation 1

	Risk	*High-risk item*
1.	Computer fraud risk	○
2.	Risk related to management override of internal control	●
3.	Fraud by branch management	●
4.	Fraud by accounting personnel	○
5.	Misstatement of accounting estimates	●
6.	Fraud by loan processing clerks	○
7.	Fraud by internal auditors	○
8.	The risk of fraudulent misstatement of revenues	●

Solution to Task-Based Simulation 2

  1. a

  2. | AU | 380 | 40–41 |

Solution to Task-Based Simulation 3

  1. (**E**) The verification of transfers from the current to the noncurrent investment portfolio will provide assurance that the investments are properly classified in the financial statements.

  2. (**F**) Positive confirmation replies as of the balance sheet date for investments held by independent custodians will provide assurance that the recorded investments are in fact owned by the audit client.

  3. (**D**) Because trading investments should be valued at fair market value, determining whether any impairments in the price of investments have been recorded will provide assurance that investments are properly valued.

  4. (**B**) Performance of sales cutoff tests will provide assurance that sales transactions and the related receivables are recorded in the proper period. Thus, sales cutoff tests will provide assurance that all amounts owed to the entity at the balance sheet date are recorded in that period.

  5. (**E**) A review of loan agreements, paying special attention to accounts receivable that have been factored, will provide assurance as to whether the entity has a legal right to all accounts receivable at the balance sheet date.

  6. (**C**) An analysis of the aged trial balance for significant past due accounts will provide evidence with respect to accounts that may be uncollectible. Accordingly, the procedure will address the net realizable value of accounts receivable.

  7. (**F**) Because material amounts due from officers and employees should be segregated from other receivables, a review of the trial balance for amounts due from officers and employees will provide assurance that accounts receivable are properly described and presented in the financial statements.

RESHUFFLED MATERIAL—AUDITING AND ATTESTATION SECTION

This represents material that was previously being tested on the Uniform CPA Exam but was covered in areas other than Audit.

This section came from Wiley Module 21, Professional Responsibilities, which was previously tested in the Regulation Section.

Professional Responsibilities

This module presents requirements relating to a CPA's professional responsibilities related to ethics, including independence, as well as certain other responsibilities. The module begins with the AICPA *Code of Professional Conduct,* which consists of two sections: (1) Principles (the framework) and (2) Rules (governing performance of professional services). Integrated with these two sections are many related interpretations and rules that are also examined. The remainder of the module includes coverage of a number of other areas related to a CPA's professional responsibilities with which you should be familiar.

You should expect a significant number of questions from the AICPA *Code of Professional Conduct* and somewhat fewer from each of the other areas. Also expect a simulation question in which you must show your research skills relating to finding particular information in the AICPA *Code of Professional Conduct* (codified using ET prefaces).

Study Program for the Professional Responsibilities Module

  A. AICPA Requirements
     1. *Code of Professional Conduct*—General
     2. *Code of Professional Conduct*—Principles
     3. *Code of Professional Conduct*—Rules, Interpretations, and Rulings
     4. Responsibilities in Consulting Services
     5. Responsibilities in Personal Financial Planning
  B. Sarbanes-Oxley Act of 2002
  C. Public Company Accounting Oversight Board
  D. Other
     1. Securities and Exchange Commission (SEC) Overview
     2. Government Accountability Office (GAO)
     3. Department of Labor (DOL)

The primary reference here is the AICPA *Code of Professional Conduct*. This module incorporates an outline of its key provisions. However, you should access it electronically to gain a familiarity to allow you to respond efficiently to a simulation research question.

A. AICPA Requirements

1. *Code of Professional Conduct*—General
   a. The code is applicable to all AICPA members, not merely those in public practice.
   b. Compliance with the code depends primarily on members' understanding and voluntary actions and only secondarily on:
      (1) Reinforcement by peers.
      (2) Public opinion.
      (3) Disciplinary proceedings.
         (a) Possible disciplinary proceedings include from joint trial board panel **admonishment, suspension** (for up to two years), or **expulsion** from AICPA, or acquittal.
   c. The code provides **minimum** levels of acceptable conduct relating to all services performed by CPAs, unless wording of a standard specifically excludes some members.
      (1) For example, some standards do not apply to CPAs not in public practice.
   d. Overall structure of the code goes from very generally worded standards to more specific and operational rules.
      (1) Interpretations and rulings remaining from the prior code are even more specific.
   e. The Principles section consists of six articles:
      I. Responsibilities
      II. The Public Interest
      III. Integrity
      IV. Objectivity and Independence
      V. Due Care
      VI. Scope and Nature of Services

2. *Code of Professional Conduct*—Principles
   a. Outline of six Articles in Section 1 of the code:
      Article I—Responsibilities. In carrying out their responsibilities as professionals, members should exercise sensitive professional and moral judgments in all their activities.
      Article II—The Public Interest. Members should accept the obligation to act in a way that will serve the public interest, honor the public trust, and demonstrate commitment to professionalism.
      (1) A distinguishing mark of a professional is acceptance of responsibility to the public.
         (a) The accounting profession's public consists of clients, credit grantors, governments, employers, investors, business and financial community, and others.
         (b) In resolving conflicting pressures among groups an accountant should consider the public interest (the collective well-being of the community).
      Article III—Integrity. To maintain and broaden public confidence, members should perform all professional responsibilities with the highest sense of integrity.
      (1) Integrity can accommodate the inadvertent error and honest difference of opinion, but it cannot accommodate deceit or subordination of principle.
      (2) Integrity
         (a) Is measured in terms of what is right and just.
         (b) Requires a member to observe **principles of objectivity, independence, and due care**.
      Article IV—Objectivity and Independence. A member should maintain objectivity and be free of conflicts of interest in discharging professional responsibilities. A member in public practice should be independent in fact and appearance when providing auditing and other attestation services.
      (1) Overall
         (a) Objectivity is a state of mind.
            1] Objectivity imposes obligation to be impartial, intellectually honest, and free of conflicts of interest.
            2] Independence precludes relationships that may appear to impair objectivity in rendering attestation services.
         (b) Regardless of the service performed, members should protect integrity of their work, maintain objectivity, and avoid any subordination of their judgment.

(2) Members in public practice require maintenance of objectivity and independence (includes avoiding conflict of interest).

    (a) Attest services—require independence in fact and in appearance

(3) Members **not in public practice**:

    (a) Are unable to maintain appearance of independence but must maintain objectivity.

    (b) When employed by others to prepare financial statements or to perform auditing, tax, or consulting services, must remain objective and candid in dealings with members in public practice.

Article V—Due Care. A member should observe the profession's technical and ethical standards, strive continually to improve competence and the quality of services, and discharge professional responsibility to the best of the member's ability.

(1) Competence is derived from both education and experience.

(2) Each member is responsible for assessing his/her own competence and for evaluating whether education, experience, and judgment are adequate for the responsibility taken.

Article VI—Scope and Nature of Services. A member in public practice should observe the Principles of the *Code of Professional Conduct* in determining the scope and nature of services to be provided.

(1) Members should:

    (a) Have in place appropriate internal quality control procedures for services rendered.

    (b) Determine whether scope and nature of other services provided to an audit client would create a conflict of interest in performance of audit.

    (c) Assess whether activities are consistent with role as professionals.

3. *Code of Professional Conduct*—Rules, Interpretations, and Rulings

  a. Combined outline of Section 2 of the code (rules) integrated with interpretation and rulings.

    ET Section 100.01—Conceptual Framework for AICPA Independence Standards. The conceptual framework describes the risk-based approach to analyzing independence that is used by the AICPA Professional Ethics Executive Committee (PEEC). A member is not independent if there is an unacceptable risk to his/her independence. Risk is unacceptable if the relationship would compromise (or would be perceived as compromising by an informed third party) the member's professional judgment.

(1) In using this framework, the member should identify and evaluate threats (both individually and in the aggregate) to independence. Types of threats include:

    (a) *Self-review threat.* Reviewing evidence that results from the member's own work (e.g., preparing source documents for an audit client).

    (b) *Advocacy threat.* Actions promoting the client's interests or position (e.g., promoting a client's securities).

    (c) *Adverse interest threat.* Actions or interests between the member and the client that are in opposition (e.g., litigation between the client and the member).

    (d) *Familiarity threat.* Members having a close or longstanding relationship with client or knowing individuals or entities who performed nonattest services for the client (e.g., a member of the attest engagement team whose spouse is in a key position at the client).

    (e) *Undue influence threat.* Attempts by a client's management (or others) to coerce the member or exercise excessive influence over the member (e.g., threat to replace the member over a disagreement regarding an accounting principle).

    (f) *Financial self-interest threat.* Potential benefit to a member from a financial interest in, or some financial relationship with, an attest client (e.g., having a direct financial interest in the client).

    (g) *Management participation threat.* Assuming the role of management or performing management functions for the attest client (e.g., serving as an officer of the client).

(2) After considering the threats to independence, the member should consider the safeguards that mitigate or eliminate threats to independence. The three types of safeguards include:

    (a) Safeguards created by the profession, legislation, or regulation (e.g., required continuing education on independence and ethics).

    (b) Safeguards implemented by the client (e.g., an affective governance structure, including an active audit committee).

    (c) Safeguards implemented by the firm (e.g., quality controls for attest engagements).

Rule 101 Independence. A member in public practice shall be independent in the performance of professional services as required by standards promulgated by designated bodies.

Interpretation 101-1. Independence is impaired if:

(1) During the period of the professional engagement, a covered member:

    (a) Had or was committed to acquire any direct or material indirect financial interest in the client.

    (b) Was a trustee of any trust or executor or administrator of any estate if such trust or estate had or was committed to acquire any direct or material indirect financial interest in the client.

    (c) Had a joint closely held investment that was material to the covered member.

    (d) Except as specifically permitted in Interpretation 101-5, had any loan to or from the client, any officer or director of the client, or any individual owning 10% or more of the client's outstanding equity securities or other ownership interests.

(2) During the period of the professional engagement, a partner or professional employee of the firm, his/her immediate family, or any group of such persons acting together owned more than 5% of a client's outstanding equity securities or other ownership interests.

(3) During the period covered by the financial statements or during the period of the professional engagement, a partner or professional employee of the firm was simultaneously associated with the client as a:

    (a) Director, officer, or employee, or in any capacity equivalent to that of a member of management;

    (b) Promoter, underwriter, or voting trustee; or

    (c) Trustee for any pension or profit-sharing trust of the client.

Application of the Independence Rules to a Covered Member's Immediate Family

(1) Except as stated in the following paragraph, a covered member's immediate family is subject to Rule 101 [ET Section 101.01], and its interpretations and rulings.

(2) The exceptions are that independence would not be considered to be impaired solely as a result of the following:

    (a) An individual in a covered member's immediate family was employed by the client in a position other than a key position.

    (b) In connection with his/her employment, an individual in the immediate family of one of the following covered members participated in a retirement, savings, compensation, or similar plan that is sponsored by a client or that invests in a client (provided such plan is normally offered to all employees in similar positions):

        1] A partner or manager who provides 10 or more hours of nonattest services to the client; or

        2] Any partner in the office in which the lead attest engagement partner primarily practices in connection with the attest engagement.

(3) For purposes of determining materiality under Rule 101 [ET Section 101.01], the financial interests of the covered member and his/her immediate family should be aggregated.

Application of the Independence Rules to Close Relatives

(1) Independence would be considered to be impaired if:

    (a) An individual participating on the attest engagement team has a close relative who had:

        1] A key position with the client; or

        2] A financial interest in the client that

            a] The individual or partner knows or has reason to believe was material to the close relative; or

            b] Enabled the close relative to exercise significant influence over the client.

    (b) An individual in a position to influence the attest engagement or any partner in the office in which the lead attest engagement partner primarily practices in connection with the attest engagement has a close relative who had:

        1] A key position with the client; or

        2] A financial interest in the client that:

            a] The individual or partner knows or has reason to believe was material to the close relative; and

            b] Enabled the close relative to exercise significant influence over the client.

Important Definitions

(1) **Covered member.** A covered member is:
   (a) An individual on the attest engagement team;
   (b) An individual in a position to influence the attest engagement;
   (c) A partner or manager who provides nonattest services to the attest client beginning once he/she provides 10 hours of nonattest services to the client within any fiscal year;
      1] The firm signs the report on the financial statements for the fiscal year during which those services were provided; or
      2] He/she no longer expects to provide 10 or more hours of nonattest services to the attest client on a recurring basis;
   (d) A partner in the office in which the lead attest engagement partner primarily practices in connection with the attest engagement;
   (e) The firm, including the firm's employee benefit plans; or
   (f) An entity whose operating, financial, or accounting policies can be controlled (as defined by generally accepted accounting principles [GAAP] for consolidation purposes) by any of the individuals or entities described in (a) through (e) or by two or more such individuals or entities if they act together.

(2) **Individual in a position to influence the attest engagement.** An individual in a position to influence the attest engagement is one who:
   (a) Evaluates the performance or recommends the compensation of the attest engagement partner;
   (b) Directly supervises or manages the attest engagement partner, including all successively senior levels above that individual through the firm's chief executive;
   (c) Consults with the attest engagement team regarding technical or industry-related issues specific to the attest engagement; or
   (d) Participates in or oversees, at all successively senior levels, quality control activities, including internal monitoring, with respect to the specific attest engagement.

(3) **Period of the professional engagement.** The period of the professional engagement begins when a member either signs an initial engagement letter or other agreement to perform attest services or begins to perform an attest engagement for a client, whichever is earlier. The period lasts for the entire duration of the professional relationship (which could cover many periods) and ends with the formal or informal notification, either by the member or the client, of the termination of the professional relationship or by the issuance of a report, whichever is later. Accordingly, the period does not end with the issuance of a report and recommence with the beginning of the following year's attest engagement.

(4) **Key position.** A key position is a position in which an individual:
   (a) Has primary responsibility for significant accounting functions that support material components of the financial statements;
   (b) Has primary responsibility for the preparation of the financial statements; or
   (c) Has the ability to exercise influence over the contents of the financial statements, including when the individual is a member of the board of directors or similar governing body, chief executive officer, president, chief financial officer, chief operating officer, general counsel, chief accounting officer, controller, director of internal audit, director of financial reporting, treasurer, or any equivalent position.

(5) **Close relative.** A close relative is a parent, sibling, or nondependent child.

(6) **Immediate family.** Immediate family is a spouse, spousal equivalent, or dependent (whether related or not).

Interpretation 101-2. A firm's independence is considered to be impaired if a partner or professional employee leaves the firm and is subsequently employed by or associated with a client in a key position, unless all of the following conditions are met:

(1) Amounts due to the former partner or professional employee for his/her previous interest in the firm and unfunded benefits are not material to the firm, and the amounts of payments are fixed;

(2) The former partner or professional employee is not in a position to influence the accounting firm's operations or financial policies;

(3) The former partner or professional employee is not associated with the firm (e.g., provides consulting services to the firm, the individual's name is included in the firm directory, etc.);

(4)   The ongoing attest engagement team considers the risk of reduced audit effectiveness resulting from the fact that the partner or professional employee has prior knowledge of the audit plan;

(5)   The firm assesses whether the existing attest engagement team members have appropriate experience and stature to deal effectively with the former partner or employee if significant interaction will occur; and

(6)   The subsequent attest engagement is reviewed to determine whether the team members maintained the appropriate level of skepticism when evaluating the representations of the former partner or employee.

Interpretation 101-3. When a CPA performs nonattest services for an attest client, it **may or may not** impair independence.

(1)   This interpretation requires compliance with regulatory independence rules by regulators such as the SEC, the General Accounting Office (GAO), and the Department of Labor (DOL).

(2)   The CPA must not perform management functions or make management decisions for attest clients.

(3)   Client must:
   (a)   Make management decisions and perform management functions.
   (b)   Designate a competent employee, preferably in senior management, to oversee services.
   (c)   Evaluate adequacy and results.
   (d)   Accept responsibility for results.
   (e)   Establish and maintain internal controls.

(4)   The CPA must establish in writing understanding with client (board of directors, audit committee, or management) regarding:
   (a)   Engagement objectives.
   (b)   Services to be performed.
   (c)   Client's acceptance of its responsibilities.
   (d)   CPA's responsibilities.
   (e)   Any limitation of the engagement.

(5)   General activities that impair independence:
   (a)   Authorizing, executing, or consummating transactions.
   (b)   Preparing source documents.
   (c)   Having custody of assets.
   (d)   Supervising employees.
   (e)   Determining recommendations to be implemented.
   (f)   Reporting to the board of directors on behalf of management.
   (g)   Serving as stock transfer agent, registrar, or general counsel.

(6)   Independence is impaired by the performance of appraisal, valuation, and actuarial services if the results are material to the financial statements and the service involves a significant degree of subjectivity.

(7)   Performing internal audit services for a client impairs independence unless the client understands its responsibility for internal control and designates an officer to manage the internal audit function.

(8)   The Sarbanes-Oxley Act of 2002 places additional restrictions on nonattest services for public company audit clients.

Interpretation 101-4. A CPA who is a director of a nonprofit organization where board is large and representative of community leadership is **not** lacking independence if:

(1)   Position is purely honorary.

(2)   Position is identified as honorary on external materials.

(3)   CPA participation is restricted to use of name.

(4)   CPA does not vote or participate in management affairs.

Interpretation 101-5. Loans from financial institution clients and related terminology.

(1)   Independence is not impaired by certain "grandfathered" and other loans from financial institution clients.
   (a)   Grandfathered loans that are permitted (home mortgages, other secured loans, loans immaterial to CPA) that were obtained:
      1]   Prior to January 1, 1992, under standards then in effect;

        2] From a financial institution for which independence was not required, and the financial institution subsequently became an attest client;

        3] Obtained from a financial institution for which independence was not required, and the loan was sold to an attest client; or

        4] Obtained by a CPA prior to becoming a member of CPA firm of which the financial institution is an attest client.

        Note: All of the above must be kept current and not renegotiated after the above dates. Also, the collateral on other secured loans must equal or exceed the remaining loan balance.

  (b) Other permitted loans from a financial institution attest client:

        1] Automobile loans and leases collateralized by automobile.

        2] Loans of surrender value under an insurance policy.

        3] Borrowings fully collateralized by cash deposits at same financial institution (e.g., "passbook loans").

        4] Aggregate outstanding balances from credit card and overdraft accounts that are reduced to $10,000 on a current basis.

(2) Terminology

  (a) Loan—Financial transactions that generally provide for repayment terms and a rate of interest.

  (b) Financial institution—An entity that makes loans to the general public as part of its normal business operations.

  (c) Normal lending procedures, terms, and requirements—Comparable to those received by other borrowers during period, when considering:

        1] Amount of loan and collateral.

        2] Repayment terms.

        3] Interest rate, including "points."

        4] Closing costs.

        5] General availability of such loans to public.

Interpretation 101-6. Effect of threatened litigation

(1) Client-CPA actual or threatened litigation:

  (a) Commenced by present management alleging audit deficiencies, impairs.

  (b) Commenced by auditor against present management for fraud, deceit impairs.

  (c) Expressed intention by present management alleging deficiencies in audit work impairs if auditor believes **strong possibility** of claim.

  (d) Immaterial not related to audit **usually** does **not** impair (i.e., billing disputes).

(2) Litigation by client security holders or other third parties generally does not impair unless material client-CPA cross-claims develop.

(3) If independence is impaired, CPA should disassociate and/or disclaim an opinion for lack of independence.

Interpretation 101-7. (Deleted)

Interpretation 101-8. A CPA's financial interests in nonclients may impair independence when those nonclients have financial interests in the CPA's clients.

Interpretation 101-9. (Deleted)

Interpretation 101-10. Describes members' duties for independence when auditing entities included in governmental financial statements.

(1) Generally, auditor of a material fund type, fund account group, or component unit of entity that should be disclosed in notes of general-purpose financial statements, but is not auditing primary government, should be independent with respect to those financial statements and primary government.

(2) Also should be independent if, although funds and accounts are separately immaterial, they are material in the aggregate.

Interpretation 101-11. Modified application of Rule 101 for certain engagements to issue restricted-use reports under the Statements on Standards for Attestation Engagements (SSAE).

(1) Rule 101: Independence and its interpretations and rulings apply to all attest engagements. However, for purposes of performing engagements to issue reports under the SSAE that are restricted to identified parties, only the following covered members, and their immediate

families, are required to be independent with respect to the responsible party[1] in accordance with Rule 101:

(a) Individuals participating on the attest engagement team;

(b) Individuals who directly supervise or manage the attest engagement partner; and

(c) Individuals who consult with the attest engagement team regarding technical or industry-related issues specific to the attest engagement.

(2) In addition, independence would be considered to be impaired if the firm had a financial relationship covered by Interpretation 101-1.A with the responsible party that was material to the firm.

(3) In cases where the firm provides nonattest services to the responsible party that are proscribed under Interpretation 101-3 and that do not directly relate to the subject matter of the attest engagement, independence would not be considered to be impaired.

(4) In circumstances where the individual or entity that engages the firm is not the responsible party or associated with the responsible party, individuals on the attest engagement team need not be independent of the individual or entity but should consider their responsibilities under Interpretation 102-2 with regard to any relationships that may exist with the individual or entity that engages them to perform these services.

(5) This interpretation does not apply to an engagement performed under the Statement on Auditing Standards or Statement on Standards for Accounting and Review Services or to an examination or review engagement performed under the SSAE.

Interpretation 101-12. Independence is impaired if, during professional engagement or while expressing an opinion, member's firm had any material cooperative arrangement with client.

(1) Cooperative arrangement exists when member's firm and client participate jointly in business activity such as:

(a) Joint ventures to develop or market a product or service.

(b) Arrangements to provide services or products to a third party.

(c) Arrangements to combine services or products of the member's firm with those of client to market them with references to both parties.

(d) Arrangements under which member firm or client act as distributor of other's products or services.

(2) Joint participation with client is not a cooperative arrangement and is thus allowed if all of the following three conditions are present.

(a) Participation of the firm and client are governed by separate agreements.

(b) Neither firm nor client assumes any responsibility for the other.

(c) Neither party is an agent of the other.

Interpretation 101-13. (Deleted)

Interpretation 101-14. If a firm is organized in an alternative practice structure, in which the attest function is part of a larger organization that leases the staff to the attest function, the independence provisions of the AICPA *Code of Professional Conduct* must be adhered to by all staff and management on attest engagement and every individual who is a direct superior of attest partners or managers. Indirect superiors of attest partners and managers cannot have any relationships prohibited by Interpretation 101-1A.

Interpretation 101-15. This interpretation provides definitions of direct and indirect financial interests that may impair independence.

(1) A **financial interest** is an ownership interest in an equity or a debt security issued by an entity, including derivatives directly related to the interest.

(2) A **direct financial interest** is:

(a) One owned directly by an individual or entity, under control of the individual or entity, or beneficially owned through an investment vehicle;

(b) Under the control of an individual or entity; or

(c) Beneficially owned through an investment vehicle, estate, trust or other intermediary when the beneficiary

---

[1] As defined in the SSAE.

    1] Controls the intermediary, or

    2] Has the authority to supervise or participate in the intermediary's investment decisions.

Rule 102 Integrity and Objectivity. In performance of **any** professional service, a member shall

    (a) Maintain objectivity and integrity;

    (b) Avoid conflicts of interest; and

    (c) Not knowingly misrepresent facts or subordinate judgment.

    (1) In tax matters, resolving doubt in favor of client does not, by itself, impair integrity or objectivity.

Interpretation 102-1. Knowingly making or permitting false and misleading entries in an entity's financial statements or records is a violation.

Interpretation 102-2. A conflict of interest may occur if a member performing a professional service has a **significant relationship** with another person, entity, product, or service that **could be viewed** as impairing the member's objectivity.

    (1) If the member believes that the professional service can be performed with objectivity, and if the relationship is disclosed to and consent is obtained from the client, employer, or other appropriate parties, the rule does not prohibit performance of the professional service.

    (2) Nothing in this interpretation overrides Rule 101 (on independence), its interpretations, and rulings.

Interpretation 102-3. When a member deals with his/her employer's external accountant, the member must be candid and not knowingly misrepresent facts or knowingly fail to disclose material facts.

Interpretation 102-4. If a member and his/her supervisor have a disagreement concerning the preparation of financial statements or the recording of transactions, the member should:

    (1) Allow the supervisor's position if that position is an acceptable alternative with authoritative support and/or does not result in a material misstatement.

    (2) Report the problem to higher levels in firm if supervisor's position could cause material misstatements in records.

    (3) Consider quitting firm if after reporting the problem to upper management, action is not taken. Consider reporting this to regulatory authorities and external accountant.

Interpretation 102-5. Those involved in educational services, such as teaching full- or part-time at a university, teaching professional education courses, or engaged in research and scholarship, are subject to Rule 102.

Interpretation 102-6. Sometimes members are asked by clients to act as advocates in support of clients' position on tax services, consulting services, accounting issues, or financial reporting issues. Member is still subject to Rule 102. Member is also still subject to Rules 201, 202, and 203. Member is also subject to Rule 101 for professional services requiring independence.

Note: *While CPA candidates should read the rulings to better understand the ethics rules and interpretations, it is **not** necessary to memorize them; consider them to be illustrations. Gaps in sequence are due to deleted sections.*

Rule 101, 102 Ethics Rulings
Independence and Integrity Ethics Rulings

2. A member may join a trade association that is a client, without impairing independence but may not serve in a capacity of management.

8. Extensive accounting and consulting services, including interpretation of statements, forecasts, and so on, do not impair independence.

9. Independence is impaired if the member cosigns checks or purchase orders or exercises general supervision over budgetary controls.

10. The independence of an elected legislator (a CPA) in a local government is impaired with respect to that governmental unit.

11. Mere designation as executor or trustee, without actual services in either capacity, does not impair independence, but actual service does.

12. If a member is a trustee of a foundation, independence is impaired.

14. Independence of a member serving as director or officer of a local United Way or similar organization is not impaired with respect to a charity receiving funds from that organization unless the organization exercises managerial control over that charity.

16. Independence is impaired if a member serves on the board of a nonprofit social club if the board

has ultimate responsibility for the affairs of the club.

17. The acquisition of equity or debt securities as a condition for membership in a country club does not normally impair independence; serving on the club's governing board or taking part in its management does impair independence.

19. Independence is impaired if a member serves on a committee administering a client's deferred compensation program.

20. Membership on governmental advisory committees does not impair independence with respect to that governmental unit.

21. A member serving as director of an enterprise would not be independent with respect to the enterprise's profit sharing and retirement trust.

29. A member's independence is impaired when owning bonds in a municipal authority.

31. A member's ownership of an apartment in a co-op apartment building would impair the member's and the firm's independence.

38. A member serving with a client bank in a cofiduciary capacity, with respect to a trust, does not impair independence with respect to the bank or trust department (if the estate's or trust's assets were not material).

41. Independence is not impaired when a member's retirement plan is invested and managed by an insurance company in a separate account, not a part of the general assets of the insurance company.

48. A university faculty member cannot be independent to a student senate fund because the student senate is a part of the university that is the member's employer.

52. Independence is impaired when prior year fees for professional services, whether billed or unbilled, remain unpaid for more than one year prior to the date of the report.

60. If a member audits an employee benefit plan, independence is impaired with respect to the employer if a partner or professional employee of the firm had significant influence over such employer, was in a key position with the employer, or was associated with the employer as a promoter, underwriter, or voting trustee.

64. Independence with respect to a fund-raising foundation is impaired if a member serves on the board of directors of the entity for whose benefit the foundation exists (unless position is purely honorary).

65. Member who is **not** in public practice may use CPA designation in connection with financial statements and correspondence of member's employer. May also use CPA designation on business cards if along with employment title. Member may **not** imply independence from employer. Member cannot state that transmittal is in conformity with GAAP.

67. If a client financial institution merely services a member's loan, independence is not impaired.

69. A member with a material limited partnership interest is not independent of other limited partnerships that have the same general partner.

70. Maintaining state or federally insured deposits (e.g., checking accounts, savings accounts, certificates of deposit) in a financial institution does not impair independence; uninsured deposits do not impair independence if the uninsured amounts are immaterial.

71. CPA Firm A is not independent of an entity audited by Firm B. CPA Firm B may only use Firm A personnel in a manner similar to internal auditors without impairing Firm B's independence.

72. A member (and the member's firm) are not independent if the member serves on the advisory board of a client unless the advisory board (1) is truly advisory, (2) has no authority to make or appear to make management decisions, and (3) membership is distinct with minimal, if any, common membership with management and the board of directors.

74. A member must be independent to issue an audit opinion or a review report but need not be independent to issue a compilation report. (Such lack of independence is disclosed.)

75. Membership in a credit union does not impair audit independence if (1) the member qualifies as a credit union member on grounds other than by providing professional services, (2) the member does not exert significant influence over the credit union, (3) the member's loans (if any) from credit union are normal (see Interpretation 101-1), and (4) the conditions of Ruling 70 have been met.

81. A member's investment in a limited partnership impairs independence with respect to the limited partnership; when the investment is material, independence is impaired with respect to both the general partner of the limited partnership and any subsidiaries of the limited partnership.

82. When a member is the campaign treasurer for a mayoral candidate, independence is impaired with respect to the candidate's campaign organization, but independence is not impaired with respect to the candidate's political party or the municipality.

85. A member may serve as a bank director, but this is generally not desirable when he/she has clients that are bank customers; performing both

services is allowed, however, if the relationship is disclosed and acceptable to all appropriate parties. Revealing confidential client information without client permission is a violation of the code, even when the failure to disclose such information may breach the member's fiduciary responsibility as a director.

91. Independence is not impaired when a member has an "operating lease" from a client made under normal terms; independence is impaired by a "capital lease" from a client unless the "loan" related to the lease qualifies as "grandfathered."

92. A material joint investment in a vacation home with an officer, director, or principal stockholder of an attest client will impair independence.

93. When a member serves as a director or officer for the United Way or a similar organization and that organization provides funds to local charities that are the member's clients, a conflict of interest will not be considered to exist if the relationship is disclosed and consent is obtained from the appropriate parties.

94. Independence is not impaired if client in the engagement letter agrees to release, indemnify, defend, and hold harmless the member from any liability and costs from misrepresentations of management.

95. An agreement by the member and a client to use alternative dispute resolution techniques in lieu of litigation before a dispute arises does not impair independence.

96. A commencement of an alternative dispute resolution does not impair independence unless the member's and client's positions are materially adverse so that the proceedings are similar to litigation, such as binding arbitration.

98. A loan from a nonclient who is a subsidiary of a client does impair independence. A loan from a nonclient parent does not impair independence with respect to a client subsidiary if the subsidiary is not material to the parent.

99. If a member is asked by a company to provide personal financial planning or tax services for its executives and the member may give the executives recommendations adverse to the company, before accepting and while doing this work, the member should consider Rule 102 on Integrity and Objectivity and Rule 301 on Confidential Client Information. The member can perform the work if he/she believes it can be done with objectivity.

100. A member who was independent when his/her report was issued may resign the report or consent to its use at a later date when his/her independence is impaired if no postaudit work is performed while impaired.

102. If a member indemnifies client for damages, losses or costs arising from lawsuits, claims, or settlements relating directly or indirectly to clients acts, this impairs independence.

103. A member or a firm would be considered independent when providing extended audit services for a client providing the services are performed in compliance with Interpretation 101-13.

106. Independence would be impaired if a member or the firm had significant influence over an entity that has significant influence over the client.

107. A covered member's participation in a health and welfare plan sponsored by a client would impair independence with respect to the client sponsor and the plan. However, if the covered member's participation results from permitted employment of the covered member's immediate family, independence would not be considered impaired.

110. A covered member is associated with an entity in a position that allows him/her to exercise significant influence over the entity. If the entity has a loan to or from a client. Independence would be impaired unless the loan is specifically permitted under Interpretation 101-5.

111. The performance of investment management or custodial services for an employee benefit plan would impair independence with respect to the plan. Independence would also be impaired with respect to the client sponsor of a defined benefit plan if the assets under management or in the custody of the member are material.

112. Rule 102, Integrity and Objectivity, requires the member to disclose to the client that the member uses a third-party service provider to perform certain of the services for the client.

113. Objectivity is impaired if a member receives a gift or entertainment from a client, unless the gift or entertainment is reasonable in the circumstances.

114. Objectivity is impaired if a covered member offers gifts or entertainment to an attest client, unless the gift or entertainment is clearly insignificant to the recipient.

Public Company Accounting Oversight Board (PCAOB) Independence Standards. The PCAOB adopted the AICPA *Code of Professional Conduct* as its interim ethical standards on April 16, 2003. Since then the PCAOB has adopted several additional independence standards. These standards apply to public accounting firms registered with the PCAOB when they are auditing an issuer (a public company).

(1) A registered public accounting firm must comply with all rules and standards of the PCAOB and also those set forth in the rules and regulations of the SEC under the federal securities laws.

(2) A registered public accounting firm is not independent of its audit client if the firm provides any service or product to the client for a contingent fee or a commission, or receives from the audit client a contingent fee or commission.

(3) A registered public accounting firm is not independent of its audit client if the firm provides any nonaudit service to the audit client related to marketing, planning, or opining in favor of:

    (a) A *confidential transaction* (a tax transaction that is offered to a client under conditions of confidentiality and for which the client pays the public accounting firm a fee), or

    (b) *Aggressive tax position transaction* initially recommended by the public accounting firm.

(4) A registered public accounting firm is not independent of its audit client if the firm provides any tax service to a person in a financial reporting oversight role at the audit client, or an immediate family member of such person, unless:

    (a) The person is in a financial reporting oversight role only because he/she serves as a member of the board of directors or similar body;

    (b) The person is in a financial reporting oversight role at the audit client only because of the person's relationship to an affiliate of the entity being audited; and

        1] The affiliate's financial statements are not material to the consolidated financial statements; or

        2] The affiliate is audited by another public accounting firm; or

    (c) The person was not in a financial reporting oversight role at the audit client before a hiring or some other change in employment and the tax services were

        1] Provided pursuant to an engagement in process prior to the change in employment; and

        2] Completed on or before 180 days after the change in employment.

(5) A registered public accounting firm must get preapproval from the audit committee to perform for an audit client any permissible tax service.

(6) A registered public accounting firm must communicate with the audit committee all relationships between the firm and the audit client that may reasonably be thought to bear on independence.

Rule 201 General Standards. Member must comply with the following standards for all professional engagements:

(1) Only undertake professional services that one can reasonably expect to complete with professional competence.

(2) Exercise due professional care.

    (a) Member may need to consult with experts to exercise due care.

(3) Adequately plan and supervise engagements.

(4) Obtain sufficient relevant data to afford a reasonable basis for conclusions and recommendations.

Interpretation 201-1. Competence to complete an engagement includes:

(1) Technical qualifications of CPA and staff.

(2) Ability to supervise and evaluate work.

(3) Knowledge of technical subject matter.

(4) Capability to exercise judgment in its application.

(5) Ability to research subject matter and consult with others.

Interpretations 201-2, 3, 4. (Deleted)

Rule 202 Compliance with Standards. A member who performs auditing, review, compilation, consulting services, tax, or other services shall comply with standards promulgated by bodies designated by Council.

Note: *The designated bodies are:*

(1) *Financial Accounting Standards Board for accounting principles for businesses.*

(2) *Governmental Accounting Standards Board for accounting principles for state and local governmental entities.*

(3) *Public Company Accounting Oversight Board for auditing, attestation, quality control, ethics and independence standards for companies covered by the Sarbanes-Oxley Act.*

(4) *International Accounting Standards Board for international accounting standards.*

(5) *AICPA designated bodies:*
  (a) *Accounting and Review Services Committee.*
  (b) *Auditing Standards Board.*
  (c) *Management Consulting Services Executive Committee.*
  (d) *Tax Executive Committee.*
  (e) *Forensic and Valuation Executive Committee.*

Rule 203 Accounting Principles. Member cannot provide positive or negative assurance that financial statements are in conformity with GAAP (FASB, GASB, and FASAB statements) if statements contain departures from GAAP having a material effect on statements taken as a whole except when unusual circumstances would make financial statements following GAAP misleading.

(1) When unusual circumstances require a departure from GAAP, CPA must disclose in report the departure, its effects (if practicable), and reasons why compliance would result in a misleading statement.

Interpretation 203-1. CPAs are to allow departure from Authoritative Standards (without giving qualified or adverse opinion) only when results of applying will be misleading.

Examples of possible circumstances justifying departure are:
(a) New legislation.
(b) New form of business transaction.

Interpretation 203-2. FASB, GASB, and FASAB Interpretations are covered by Rule 203.

Interpretation 203-3. (Deleted)

Interpretation 203-4. Rule 203 also applies to communications by employees such as reports to regulatory authorities, creditors, and auditors.

Rule 201, 202, 203 Ethics Rulings

8. A member selecting subcontractors for consulting services engagements is obligated to select subcontractors on the basis of professional qualifications, technical skills, and so on.

9. A member should be in a position to supervise and evaluate work of a specialist in his/her employ.

10. If a member prepares financial statements as a stockholder, partner, director, or employee of an entity, any transmittal should indicate the member's relationship and should not imply independence. If transmittal indicates financial statements are in accordance with GAAP, Rule 203 must be met. If financial statements are on member's letterhead, member should disclose lack of independence.

11. Rule 203 applies to members performing litigation support services.

12. The CPA firm must provide adequate oversight of all services performed by a third-party provider for the firm's clients to ensure that the provider complies with professional standards.

Rule 301 Confidential Client Information. Member in public practice shall not disclose confidential client information without client consent except for:
(1) Compliance with Rule 202 and 203 obligations.
(2) Compliance with enforceable subpoena or summons.
(3) AICPA review of professional practice.
(4) Initiating complaint or responding to inquiry made by a recognized investigative or disciplinary body.

Interpretation 301-1. (Deleted)

Interpretation 301-2. (Deleted)

Interpretation 301-3. A member who is considering selling his/her practice, or merging with another CPA, may allow that CPA to review confidential client information without the specific consent of the client.
(1) The member should take appropriate precautions (e.g., obtain a written confidentiality agreement) so that the prospective purchaser does not disclose such information.

Note: *This exception relates only to a review in conjunction with a purchase or merger. It **does not** apply to the review of workpapers **after** a CPA has purchased another's practice. AU 315, discussed in detail later in this module, requires that the successor who wishes to review predecessor auditor workpapers should request the client to authorize the predecessor to make such workpapers available.*

Rule 302 Contingent Fees.

(1) A member in public practice shall not:
  - (a) Perform for a contingent fee any professional services when the member or member's firm also performs any of the following services for that client:
    - 1] Audits or reviews of financial statements.
    - 2] Compilations when the member is independent and expects that a third party may use the financial statements.
    - 3] Examinations of prospective financial information.
  - (b) Prepare an original or amended tax return or claims for a tax refund for a contingent fee for any client.
(2) Solely for purposes of this rule, (a) fees fixed by courts or other public authorities, or (b) in tax matters, fees determined based on the results of a judicial proceeding or findings of governmental agency, are not regarded as contingent and are therefore permitted.

Interpretation 302-1. Contingent fees in tax matters.

(1) A contingent fee **would be permitted** in various circumstances in which the amounts due are not clear; examples are:
  - (a) Representing a client in an examination by a revenue agent.
  - (b) Filing amended tax returns based on a tax issue that is the subject of a test case **involving a different taxpayer** or where the tax authority is developing a position.
  - (c) Representing a taxpayer in getting a private ruling.
(2) A contingent fee **would not be permitted** for preparing an amended tax return for a client claiming a refund that is clearly due to the client because of an inadvertent omission.

Rule 301, 302 Ethics Rulings

1. A member may utilize outside computer services to process tax returns as long as there is no release of confidential information.
2. With client permission, a member may provide P&L percentages to a trade association.
3. A CPA withdrawing from a tax engagement due to irregularities on the client's return should urge successor CPA to have client grant permission to reveal reasons for withdrawal.
6. A member may be engaged by a municipality to verify taxpayer's books and records for the purpose of assessing property tax. The member must maintain confidentiality.
7. Members may reveal the names of clients without client consent unless such disclosure releases confidential information.
14. A member has a responsibility to honor confidential relationships with nonclients. Accordingly, members may have to withdraw from consulting services engagements where the client will not permit the member to make recommendations without disclosing confidential information about other clients or nonclients.
15. If the member has conducted a similar consulting services study with a negative outcome, the member should advise potential clients of the previous problems providing that earlier confidential relationships are not disclosed. If the earlier confidential relationship may be disclosed (through client knowledge of other clients), the member should seek approval from the first client.

16. In divorce proceedings, a member who has prepared joint tax returns for the couple should consider both individuals to be clients for purposes of requests for confidential information relating to prior tax returns. Under such circumstances, the CPA should consider reviewing the legal implications of disclosure with an attorney.
17. A contingent fee or a commission is considered to be "received" when the performance of the related services is complete and the fee or commission is determined.
18. Identical to Ruling 85 under Rule 101.
19. A member's spouse may provide services to a member's attest client for a contingent fee and may refer products or services for a commission.
20. When a member learns of a potential claim against him/her, the member may release confidential client information to member's liability carrier used solely to defend against claim.
21. Identical to Ruling 99 under Rule 102.
23. A member may disclose confidential client information to the member's attorney or a court in connection with actual or threatened litigation.
24. A member's fee for investment advisory services for an attest client that is based on a percentage of the portfolio would be considered contingent and a violation of Rule 302, unless:
  - a. The fee is determined as a specified percentage of the portfolio;
  - b. The dollar amount of the portfolio is determined at the beginning of each quarterly

period (or longer) and is adjusted only for additions or withdrawals by the client; and

c. The fee arrangement is not renewed with the client more frequently than on a quarterly basis.

25. A member who provides for a contingent fee investment advisory service, or refers for a commission products or services to the owners, officers, or employees of an attest client, would not violate Rule 302 with respect to the client.

Rule 501 Acts Discreditable. A member shall not commit an act discreditable to the profession.

    Interpretation 501-1. Retention of client records after client has demanded them is discreditable.

(1) A CPA may keep analyses and schedules prepared by the client for the CPA and need not make them available to the client.

(2) A CPA may keep workpapers with information not reflected in the client's books (adjusting, closing, consolidating entries, etc.) until payment of fees due is received.

Interpretation 501-2. Discrimination on basis of race, color, religion, sex, age, or national origin is discreditable.

Interpretation 501-3. In audits of governmental grants, units, or other recipients of governmental monies, failure to follow appropriate governmental standards, procedures, and so on, is discreditable.

Interpretation 501-4. Negligently making (or permitting or directing another to make) false or misleading journal entries is discreditable.

Interpretation 501-5. When a governmental body, commission, or other regulatory agency has requirements beyond those required by GAAS, members are required to follow them.

(1) Failure to follow these requirements is considered an act discreditable to the profession, unless the member discloses in the report that such requirements were not followed and the reasons therefor.

Interpretation 501-6. Member who solicits or discloses May 1996 or later Uniform CPA Examination question(s) and/or answer(s) without AICPA written authorization has committed an act discreditable to profession in violation of Rule 501.

Interpretation 501-7. A member who fails to comply with applicable federal, state, or local laws and regulations regarding the timely filing of his/her personal tax returns or the timely remittance of all payroll and other taxes collected on behalf of others has committed an act discreditable to the profession.

Interpretation 501-8. In some engagements, government regulators prohibit indemnification or limitation of liability agreements. If the CPA engages in such agreements when they are prohibited, he/she has committed an act discreditable to the profession.

Rule 502 Advertising and Other Forms of Solicitation. In public practice, the member shall not seek to obtain clients by false, misleading, deceptive advertising or other forms of solicitation.

Interpretation 502-1. (Deleted)

Interpretation 502-2. Advertising that is false, misleading, or deceptive is prohibited, including advertising that:

(1) Creates false or unjustified expectations.

(2) Implies ability to influence a court, tribunal, regulatory agency or similar body or official.

(3) Contains unrealistic estimates of future fees.

(4) Would lead a reasonable person to misunderstand or be deceived.

Interpretations 502-3, 4. (Deleted)

Interpretation 502-5. CPA may render services to clients of third parties as long as all promotion efforts are within code.

Rule 503 Commissions and Referral Fees.

(1) A member in public practice may not accept a commission for recommending a product or service to a client when the member or member's firm also performs any of the following services for that client:

    (a) Audits or reviews of financial statements.

    (b) Compilations when the member is independent and expects that a third party may use the financial statements.

    (c) Examinations of prospective financial information.

(2) A member who receives a commission [not prohibited in (1) above] shall disclose that fact to the client.

(3) A member who accepts a referral fee for recommending or referring any service of a CPA to any person or entity, or who pays a referral fee to obtain a client, must disclose such acceptance or payment to the client.

Rule 504. (Deleted)

Rule 505 Form of Practice and Name. Member may practice public accounting in form of proprietorship, partnership, professional corporation, and so on and may not practice under a misleading name.

(1) May include past partners.

(2) An individual may practice in name of a former partnership for up to two years (applies when all other partners have died or withdrawn).

(3) A firm name may include a fictitious name or indicate specialization if name is not misleading.

(4) Firm may not designate itself as member of AICPA unless all partners or shareholders are members.

(5) Appendix B to *Code of Professional Conduct* allows non-CPA ownership of CPA firms under certain conditions.

    (a) 66 2/3% (supermajority) of ownership (both voting rights and financial interest) must belong to CPAs. Non-CPA owners must be involved in own principal occupation, not practice accounting, and not hold selves out as CPAs.

    (b) CPAs must have ultimate responsibility in firm, not non-CPAs.

    (c) Non-CPA owners must abide by AICPA *Code of Professional Conduct*, CPE requirements, and hold a baccalaureate degree.

    (d) Non-CPAs not eligible to be members of AICPA.

Interpretation 505-1. (Deleted)

Interpretation 505-2. Applicability of rules to members who operate a separate business that provides accounting services.

(1) A member in public practice who participates in the operation of a separate business that performs accounting, tax, and similar services must observe all of the Rules of Conduct.

(2) A member not otherwise in the practice of public accounting must observe the Rules of Conduct if the member holds out as a CPA and performs for a client any professional services included in public accounting.

Interpretation 505-3. CPAs with attest practices that are organized as alternative practice structures must remain financially and otherwise responsible for the attest work.

Rule 591 Ethics Rulings and Other Responsibilities
Ethics Rulings

Due to rescinding the advertising and solicitation prohibition, the majority of the ethics rulings have been suspended.

2. A member may permit a bank to collect notes issued by a client in payment of fees.

3. A CPA employed by a firm with non-CPA practitioners must comply with the Rules of Conduct. If a partner of such a firm is a CPA, the CPA is responsible for all persons associated with the firm to comply with the rules of conduct.

33. A member who is a course instructor has the responsibility to determine that the advertising materials promoting the course are within the bounds of Rule 502.

38. A member who is controller of a bank may place his/her CPA title on bank stationery and in paid advertisements listing the officers and directors of the bank.

78. CPAs who are also attorneys may so indicate on their letterhead.

108. Members interviewed by the press should observe the *Code of Professional Conduct* and not provide the press with any information for publication that the member could not publish himself.

117. A member may be a director of a consumer credit company if he/she is not the auditor.

134. Members who share offices, employees, and so on may not indicate a partnership exists unless a partnership agreement is in effect.

135. CPA firms that are members of an association cannot use letterhead that indicates a partnership rather than an association.

136. Where a firm consisting of a CPA and a non-CPA is dissolved, and an audit is continued to be serviced by both, the audit opinion should be signed by both individuals, such that a partnership is not indicated.

137. The designation "nonproprietary partner" should not be used to describe personnel as it may be misleading.

138. A member may be a partner of a firm of public accountants when all other personnel are not

certified and at the same time practice separately as a CPA.

140. A partnership practicing under the name of the managing partner who is seeking election to high office may continue to use the managing partner's name plus "and Company" if the managing partner is elected and withdraws from the partnership.

141. A CPA in partnership with a non-CPA is ethically responsible for all acts of the partnership and those of the non-CPA partner.

144. A CPA firm may use an established firm name in a different state even though there is a difference in the roster of partners.

145. Newly merged CPA firms may practice under a title that includes the name of a previously retired partner from one of the firms.

176. A CPA firm's name, logo, and so on, may be imprinted on newsletters and similar publications if the CPA has a reasonable basis to conclude that the information is not fake, misleading, or deceptive.

177. Performing centralized billing services for a doctor is a public accounting service and must be conducted in accordance with the code.

179. CPA firms that are members of an association (for purposes of joint advertising, training, etc.) should practice in their own names, although they may indicate membership in the association.

183. A CPA firm may designate itself "Accredited Personal Financial Specialists" on its letterhead and in marketing materials if all partners or shareholders of the firm currently have the AICPA-awarded designation.

184. Identical to Ruling 18 under Rule 302.

185. A member may purchase a product from a supplier and resell it to a client at a profit without disclosing the profit to the client.

186. A member may contract for support services from a computer-hardware maintenance servicer and bill them to a client at a profit without disclosing the profit to the client.

187. Identical to Ruling 19 under Rule 302.

188. When a member refers products to clients through distributors and agents, the member may not perform for those clients the services described in Rule 503 [part (1) of the outline of Rule 503].

189. When individuals associated with a client entity have an internal dispute, and have separately asked a member for client records, the member need only supply them once, and to the individual who previously has been designated or held out as the client's representative.

190. A member who is in a partnership with non-CPAs may sign reports with the firm name and below it affix his/her own signature with the designation "Certified Public Accountant," providing it is clear that the partnership is not being held out as composed entirely of CPAs.

191. If a member (not an owner) of a firm is terminated, he/she may not take copies of the firm's client files without the firm's permission.

192. A member who provides for a contingent fee investment advisory services, or refers for a commission products or services to the owners, officers, or employees of an attest client would not violate Rule 302 or Rule 503 with respect to the client.

4. Responsibilities in Consulting Services
   a. In January 1991, a new series of pronouncements on consulting services, Statements on Standards for Consulting Services (SSCS), became effective. This series of pronouncements replaces the three Statements on Standards for Management Advisory Services. These standards apply to CPAs in public practice who provide consulting services.
   b. Outline of SSCS 1 Definitions and Standards
      (1) Comparison of consulting and attest services:
          (a) **Attest services**—Practitioner expresses a conclusion about the reliability of a written assertion that is the responsibility of another party (the asserter).
          (b) **Consulting services**—Practitioner develops the findings, conclusions, and recommendations presented, generally only for the use and benefit of the client; the nature of the work is determined solely by agreement between the practitioner and the client.
          (c) Performance of consulting services **for an attest client** requires that the practitioner maintain independence and does not in and of itself impair independence.
              Note: While one must remain objective in performing consulting services, independence is not required unless the practitioner also performs attest (e.g., audit) services for that client.
      (2) Definitions
          (a) **Consulting services practitioner**—A CPA holding out as a CPA (i.e., a CPA in public practice) while engaged in the performance of a consulting service for a client.

    (b) **Consulting process**—Analytical approach and process applied in a consulting service.

    (c) This definition **excludes** services subject to other AICPA technical standards on auditing (SAS), other attest services (SSAE), compilations and reviews (SSARS), most tax engagements, and recommendations made during one of these engagements as a direct result of having performed these excluded services.

    (d) **Consulting services**—Professional services that employ the practitioner's technical skills, education, observations, experiences, and knowledge of the consulting process.

(3) Types of consulting services:

    (a) **Consultations**—Provide counsel in a short time frame, based mostly, if not entirely, on existing personal knowledge about the client.

      1] Examples: reviewing and commenting on a client business plan, suggesting software for further client investigation.

    (b) **Advisory services**—Develop findings, conclusions, and recommendations for client consideration and decision making.

      1] Examples: Operational review and improvement study, analysis of accounting system, strategic planning assistance, information system advice.

    (c) **Implementation services**—Place an action plan into effect.

      1] Examples: Installing and supporting computer system, executing steps to improve productivity, assisting with mergers.

    (d) **Transaction services**—Provide services related to a specific client transaction, generally with a third party.

      1] Examples: Insolvency services, valuation services, information related to financing, analysis of a possible merger or acquisition, litigation services.

    (e) **Staff and other support services**—Provide appropriate staff and possibly other support to perform tasks specified by client.

      1] Examples: Data processing facilities management, computer programming, bankruptcy trusteeship, controllership activities.

    (f) **Product services**—Provide client with a product and associated support services.

      1] Examples: Sale, delivery, installation, and implementation of training programs, computer software, and systems development.

(4) Standards for Consulting Services

    (a) General Standards of Rule 201 of *Code of Professional Conduct*:

      1] Professional competence.

      2] Due professional care.

      3] Planning and supervision.

      4] Sufficient relevant data.

    (b) Additional standards established for this area (under Rule 202 of *Code of Professional Conduct*):

      1] Client interest. Must serve client interest while maintaining **integrity** and **objectivity**.

      2] Understanding with client. Establish either in **writing or orally**.

      3] Communication with client. Inform client of any conflicts of interest, significant reservations about engagement, significant engagement findings.

    (c) Professional judgment must be used in applying SSCS.

      1] Example: Practitioner not required to decline or withdraw from a consulting engagement when there are mutually agreed on limitations with respect to gathering relevant data.

5. Responsibilities in Personal Financial Planning

   a. Definition, scope, and standards of personal financial planning.

    (1) Personal financial planning engagements are only those that involve developing strategies and making recommendations to assist a client in defining and achieving personal financial goals.

    (2) Personal financial planning engagements involve all of following:

      (a) Defining engagement objectives.

      (b) Planning specific procedures appropriate to engagement.

      (c) Developing basis for recommendations.

      (d) Communicating recommendations to client.

      (e) Identifying tasks for taking action on planning decisions.

     (3) Other engagements may also include:
        (a) Assisting client to take action on planning decisions.
        (b) Monitoring client's progress in achieving goals.
        (c) Updating recommendations and helping client revise planning decisions.
     (4) Personal financial planning does not include services that are limited to, for example:
        (a) Compiling personal financial statements.
        (b) Projecting future taxes.
        (c) Tax compliance, including, but not limited to, preparation of tax returns.
        (d) Tax advice or consultations.
     (5) CPA should act in conformity with AICPA *Code of Professional Conduct.*
        (a) Rule 102, Integrity and Objectivity.
           1] A member shall maintain objectivity and integrity, be free of conflicts of interest, and not knowingly misrepresent facts or subordinate his/her judgment to others.
        (b) Rule 201:
           1] A member shall undertake only those professional services that member can reasonably expect to be completed with professional competence, shall exercise due professional care in the performance of professional services, shall adequately plan and supervise performance of professional services, and shall obtain sufficient relevant data to afford a reasonable basis for conclusions or recommendations.
        (c) Rule 301, Confidential Client Information.
           1] Member in public practice shall not disclose any confidential client information without specific consent of client.
        (d) Rule 302, Contingent Fees.
           1] Rules must be followed.
     (6) When a personal financial planning engagement includes providing assistance in preparation of personal financial statements or financial projections, the CPA should consider applicable provisions of AICPA pronouncements, including:
        (a) Statements on Standards for Accounting and Review Services.
        (b) Statement on Standards for Attestation Engagements Financial Forecasts and Projections.
        (c) Audit and Accounting Guide for Prospective Financial Information.
        (d) Personal Financial Statements Guide.
     (7) The CPA should document his/her understanding of scope and nature of services to be provided.
        (a) Consider engagement letter.
     (8) Personal financial planning engagement should be adequately planned.
     (9) Engagement's objectives form basis for planning engagement.
        (a) Procedures should reflect materiality and cost-benefit considerations.
    (10) Relevant information includes understanding of client's goals, financial position, and available resources for achieving goals.
        (a) External factors (such as inflation, taxes, and investment markets) and nonfinancial factors (such as client attitudes, risk tolerance, spending habits, and investment preferences) are also relevant information.
        (b) Relevant information also includes reasonable estimates furnished by client's advisors or developed by CPA.
    (11) Recommendations ordinarily should be in writing and include summary of client's goals and significant assumptions and description of any limitations on work performed.
    (12) Unless otherwise agreed, CPA is not responsible for additional services, for example:
        (a) Assisting client to take action on planning decisions.
        (b) Monitoring progress in achieving goals.
        (c) Updating recommendations and revising planning decisions.
  b. Working with other advisors.
     (1) If CPA does not provide a service needed to complete an engagement, he/she should restrict scope of engagement and recommend that client engage another advisor.
     (2) If client declines to engage another advisor, CPA and client still may agree to proceed with engagement.

    c. Implementation engagement functions and responsibilities.

       (1) Implementation engagements involve assisting client to take action on planning decisions developed during personal financial planning engagement.

       (2) Implementation includes activities such as selecting investment advisors, restructuring debt, creating estate documents, establishing cash reserves, preparing budgets, and selecting and acquiring specific investments and insurance products.

       (3) When undertaking implementation engagement, CPA should apply existing professional standards and published guidance.

B. Sarbanes-Oxley Act of 2002

  1. Title 1—Authorizes establishment of Public Company Accounting Oversight Board.

    a. Consists of five members:

       (1) Two members must be or have been CPAs.

       (2) Three members cannot be or cannot have been CPAs.

       (3) None of the board members may receive pay or profits from CPA firms.

    b. Board regulates CPA firms ("registrants") that audit SEC registrants ("issuers").

       (1) Main functions are to:

          (a) Register and conduct inspections of public accounting firms (this replaces peer reviews).

          (b) Set or adopt standards on auditing, quality control, independence, or preparation of audit reports (as per below, PCAOB adopted AICPA standards on an interim basis as of April 16, 2003).

       (2) Details—PCAOB:

          (a) Enforces compliance with professional standards, securities laws relating to accountants and audits.

          (b) May regulate nonaudit services CPA firms perform for clients.

          (c) Performs investigations and disciplinary proceedings on registered public accounting firms.

          (d) May perform any other duties needed to promote high professional standards and to improve auditing quality.

    c. Accounting firms must have second partner review and approve each audit report.

    d. Accounting firms must report on an audit of internal control in addition to the audit of the financial statements for issuers.

    e. Most CPA workpapers must be saved for seven years.

    f. Material additional services of auditors must receive preapproval by audit committee, and fees for those services must be disclosed to investors.

  2. Title II—Auditor Independence.

    a. The act lists several specific service categories that the issuer's public accounting firm cannot legally perform:

       (1) Bookkeeping or other services relating to financial statements or accounting records.

       (2) Financial information systems design and/or implementation.

       (3) Appraisal services.

       (4) Internal audit outsourcing services.

       (5) Management functions.

       (6) Actuarial services.

       (7) Investment or broker-dealer services.

       (8) Certain tax services, such as tax planning for potentially abusive tax shelters.

         Note that the act does not restrict auditors from performing these services to nonaudit clients or to private companies. Also, the act permits the auditor to perform nonaudit services not specifically prohibited (e.g., tax services) when approved by issuer's audit committee.

    b. The audit partner for the job and the audit partner who reviews the audit can do the audit services for only five consecutive years.

       (1) If public company has hired employee of an audit firm to be its chief executive officer, chief financial officer, or chief audit officer within previous year, that audit firm cannot audit the company.

   c. The audit firm should report critical accounting policies, alternative treatments of transactions, and so on, and other material written communications between the accounting firm and management to the audit committee.

3. Title III—Section 303.

   a. It is unlawful for any officer or director to take any action to fraudulently influence, coerce, manipulate, or mislead any public accountant engaged in the performance of the audit.

4. Title IV.

   a. Section 404 is particularly important to the overall process of CPA reporting on internal control (IC).

     (1) It in essence led to CPA reporting on client internal control by establishing the following:

       (a) It is management's responsibility to establish adequate internal control.

       (b) Management must assess its IC.

       (c) The CPA firm attests to management's assessment of IC.

   b. Section 406 requires that every issuer shall report whether it has adopted a code of ethics for senior financial officers.

   c. CEOs and CFOs of most large companies are now required to certify financial statements filed with SEC.

     (1) They certify that the information "fairly presents in all material respects the financial statements and result of operations" of the company.

C. Public Company Accounting Oversight Board

1. On April 16, 2003, the PCAOB adopted the following AICPA standards as its interim standards to be used on an initial transitional basis:

   a. Auditing Standards Board Standards (through SAS 95).

   b. Attestation Standards.

   c. Quality Control Standards.

   d. Ethics Standards 101 (Independence) and 102 (Integrity and objectivity) and several standards issued by the Independence Standards Board.

2. The PCAOB has broad authority to oversee the public accounting profession by establishing rules in the above areas; in addition, it:

   a. Registers public accounting firms that audit issuers companies.

   b. Performs inspections of the practices of registered firms.

   c. Conducts investigations and disciplinary proceedings of registered firms.

   d. Sanctions registered firms.

3. Inspections performed by the PCAOB:

   a. The Sarbanes-Oxley Act requires that the PCAOB perform inspections of CPA firms that include at least the following three general components:

     (1) An inspection and review of selected audit and review engagements.

     (2) An evaluation of the sufficiency of the quality control system of the CPA firm and the manner of documentation and communication of the system.

     (3) Performance of such other testing of the audit, supervisory, and quality control procedures as are considered necessary.

   b. Although inspections performed by the PCAOB staff meet the AICPA's practice review requirement for the public auditing practices of CPA firms, they differ from peer reviews conducted by CPA firms. Inspections generally focus on selected quality control issues and also may consider other aspects of practice management, such as how partner compensation is determined. Most of the inspection process is focused on evaluating a CPA firm's performance on a sample of individual audit and review engagements. In selecting the engagements for inspection, the PCAOB staff uses a risk assessment process to identify those engagements that have a higher risk of lack of compliance with professional standards. When an audit is selected, the inspection focuses on the high-risk aspects of that engagement, such as revenue recognition and accounting estimates. When a lack of compliance with professional standards is identified, the PCAOB staff attempts to determine the cause, which may lead to identification of a defect in the firm's quality control system.

    c. Each inspection results in a written report that is transmitted to the SEC and appropriate regulatory authorities. Also included is a letter of comments by the PCAOB inspectors, and any responses by the CPA firm. While the contents of most of the reports are made available to the public, discussion of criticisms of a firm's quality control system are not made public unless the firm does not address the criticism within 12 months.

D. Other

    1. Securities and Exchange Commission (SEC).

      a. The mission of the SEC is to protect investors, maintain fair, orderly, and efficient markets, and facilitate capital formation.

      b. The SEC has the authority to establish standards relating to financial accounting, auditing, and CPA professional conduct when involved with public-company financial statements

        (1) Some of those standards differ from AICPA requirements.

        (2) Currently, the SEC works with the PCAOB in this area.

      c. PCAOB pronouncements require SEC approval.

      d. Historically, SEC independence rules have been more restrictive than those than the AICPA in areas such as:

        (1) The SEC requirements make clear that performing bookkeeping services impairs audit independence; this is allowed under AICPA rules (thereby, only for nonpublic clients).

        (2) The SEC (and PCAOB) have required companies to disclose audit and nonaudit fees earned by CPA firms.

    2. Government Accountability Office (GAO)

      a. The GAO's mission is to support Congress in meeting its constitutional responsibilities and to help improve the performance and ensure the accountability of the federal government.

      b. Work includes:

        (1) Auditing agency operations to determine whether federal funds are being spent efficiently and effectively.

        (2) Investigating allegations of illegal and improper activities.

        (3) Reporting on how well government programs meet their objectives.

        (4) Performing policy analyses and outlining various options for Congress.

        (5) Issuing legal decision and opinions.

      c. The GAO develops additional requirements for audits of organizations that receive federal financial assistance.

        (1) These are included in *Government Auditing Standards,* referred to as the "Yellow Book." (The *Government Auditing Standards* outline follows the PCAOB outlines.)

      d. GAO independence requirements:

        (1) In all matters relating to audit work, the audit organization and the individual auditor must be free of personal, external, and organizational impairments to independence, and must avoid the appearance of such impairments of independence. Many are similar to AICPA restrictions.

        (2) Some are more restrictive in some areas than those of the AICPA; examples are:

          (a) CPA firm cannot allow personnel working on nonattest engagements also to work on the audit.

          (b) *Government Auditing Standards* places restrictions on the nature of nonattest services to be performed for an audit client.

            1] Nonattest services must be deemed not significant or material to the subject matter of the audit.

    3. Department of Labor (DOL)

      a. The DOL's mission involves fostering and promoting the welfare of job seekers, wage earners, and retirees of the United States.

      b. The DOL conducts financial and performance audits following *Government Auditing Standards* relating to its mission, including audits of:

        (1) Compliance with applicable laws and regulations.

        (2) Evaluation of economy and efficiency of operations.

        (3) Evaluation of effectiveness in achieving program results.

c. Employee benefit plans must be audited in accordance with the Employee Retirement Security Act of 1974 (ERISA), as enforced by DOL. Independence requirements are in general similar to those of the AICPA, except that:
   (1) Accountant or firm may be engaged on a professional basis by the plan sponsor and the accountant may serve as an actuary.
d. In some circumstances (e.g., definition of "member" for purposes of those who must maintain independence within a CPA firm), DOL requirements differ from AICPA requirements—in such cases, they are generally more restrictive.

QUESTIONS ON PROFESSIONAL RESPONSIBILITIES

Multiple-Choice Questions (1–39)

1. Which of the following best describes what is meant by the term "generally accepted auditing standards"?
   a. Rules acknowledged by the accounting profession because of their universal application.
   b. Pronouncements issued by the Auditing Standards Board.
   c. Measures of the quality of the auditor's performance.
   d. Procedures to be used to gather evidence to support financial statements.

2. For which of the following can a member of the AICPA receive an automatic expulsion from the AICPA?
   I. Member is convicted of a felony.
   II. Member files his/her own fraudulent tax return.
   III. Member files fraudulent tax return for a client knowing that it is fraudulent.
      a. I only.
      b. I and II only.
      c. I and III only.
      d. I, II, and III.

3. Which of the following is an example of a safeguard implemented by the client that might mitigate a threat to independence?
   a. Required continuing education for all attest engagement team members.
   b. An effective corporate governance structure.
   c. Required second partner review of an attest engagement.
   d. Management selection of the CPA firm.

4. Which of the following is a "self-review" threat to member independence?
   a. An engagement team member has a spouse that serves as CFO of the attest client.
   b. A second partner review is required on all attest engagements.

c. An engagement team member prepares invoices for the attest client.
d. An engagement team member has a direct financial interest in the attest client.

5. According to the standards of the profession, which of the following circumstances will prevent a CPA performing audit engagements from being independent?
   a. Obtaining a collateralized automobile loan from a financial institution client.
   b. Litigation with a client relating to billing for consulting services for which the amount is immaterial.
   c. Employment of the CPA's spouse as a client's director of internal audit.
   d. Acting as an honorary trustee for a not-for-profit organization client.

6. The profession's ethical standards most likely would be considered to have been violated when a CPA represents that specific consulting services will be performed for a stated fee and it is apparent at the time of the representation that the:
   a. Actual fee would be substantially higher.
   b. Actual fee would be substantially lower than the fees charged by other CPAs for comparable services.
   c. CPA would not be independent.
   d. Fee was a competitive bid.

7. According to the ethical standards of the profession, which of the following acts is generally prohibited?
   a. Issuing a modified report explaining a failure to follow a governmental regulatory agency's standards when conducting an attest service for a client.
   b. Revealing confidential client information during a quality review of a professional practice by a team from the state CPA society.
   c. Accepting a contingent fee for representing a client in an examination of the client's federal tax return by an IRS agent.

d. Retaining client records after an engagement is terminated prior to completion and the client has demanded their return.

8. According to the profession's ethical standards, which of the following events may justify a departure from a Statement of the Governmental Accounting Standards Board?

	New legislation	Evolution of a new form of business transaction
a.	No	Yes
b.	Yes	No
c.	Yes	Yes
d.	No	No

9. May a CPA hire for the CPA's public accounting firm a non-CPA systems analyst who specializes in developing computer systems?
   a. Yes, provided the CPA is qualified to perform each of the specialist's tasks.
   b. Yes, provided the CPA is able to supervise the specialist and evaluate the specialist's end product.
   c. No, because non-CPA professionals are not permitted to be associated with CPA firms in public practice.
   d. No, because developing computer systems is not recognized as a service performed by public accountants.

10. Stephanie Seals is a CPA who is working as a controller for Brentwood Corporation. She is not in public practice. Which statement is true?
   a. She may use the CPA designation on her business cards if she also puts her employment title on them.
   b. She may use the CPA designation on her business cards as long as she does not mention Brentwood Corporation or her title as controller.
   c. She may use the CPA designation on company transmittals but not on her business cards.
   d. She may not use the CPA designation because she is not in public practice.

11. According to the standards of the profession, which of the following activities would most likely **not** impair a CPA's independence?
   a. Providing advisory services for a client.
   b. Contracting with a client to supervise the client's office personnel.
   c. Signing a client's checks in emergency situations.
   d. Accepting a luxurious gift from a client.

12. Which of the following reports may be issued only by an accountant who is independent of a client?
   a. Standard report on an examination of a financial forecast.
   b. Report on consulting services.
   c. Compilation report on historical financial statements.
   d. Compilation report on a financial projection.

13. According to the standards of the profession, which of the following activities may be required in exercising due care?

	Consulting with experts	Obtaining specialty accreditation
a.	Yes	Yes
b.	Yes	No
c.	No	Yes
d.	No	No

14. Larry Sampson is a CPA and is serving as an expert witness in a trial concerning a corporation's financial statements. Which of the following is (are) true?
   I. Sampson's status as an expert witness is based on his specialized knowledge, experience, and training.
   II. Sampson is required by AICPA ruling to present his position objectively.
   III. Sampson may regard himself as acting as an advocate.
      a. I only.
      b. I and II only.
      c. I and III only.
      d. III only.

15. According to the ethical standards of the profession, which of the following acts is generally prohibited?
   a. Purchasing a product from a third party and reselling it to a client.
   b. Writing a financial management newsletter promoted and sold by a publishing company.
   c. Accepting a commission for recommending a product to an audit client.
   d. Accepting engagements obtained through the efforts of third parties.

16. To exercise due professional care, an auditor should:
   a. Critically review the judgment exercised by those assisting in the audit.
   b. Examine all available corroborating evidence supporting managements assertions.

c. Design the audit to detect all instances of illegal acts.

d. Attain the proper balance of professional experience and formal education.

17. Kar, CPA, is a staff auditor participating in the audit engagement of Fort, Inc. Which of the following circumstances impairs Kar's independence?

a. During the period of the professional engagement, Fort gives Kar tickets to a football game worth $75.

b. Kar owns stock in a corporation that Fort's 401(k) plan also invests in.

c. Kar's friend, an employee of another local accounting firm, prepares Fort's tax returns.

d. Kar's sibling is director of internal audit at Fort.

18. On June 1, 2008, a CPA obtained a $100,000 personal loan from a financial institution client for whom the CPA provided compilation services. The loan was fully secured and considered material to the CPA's net worth. The CPA paid the loan in full on December 31, 2009. On April 3, 2009, the client asked the CPA to audit the client's financial statements for the year ended December 31, 2009. Is the CPA considered independent with respect to the audit of the client's December 31, 2009 financial statements?

a. Yes, because the loan was fully secured.

b. Yes, because the CPA was not required to be independent at the time the loan was granted.

c. No, because the CPA had a loan with the client during the period of a professional engagement.

d. No, because the CPA had a loan with the client during the period covered by the financial statements.

19. Which of the following statements is (are) correct regarding a CPA employee of a CPA firm taking copies of information contained in client files when he/she leaves the firm?

I. A CPA leaving a firm may take copies of information contained in client files to assist another firm in serving that client.

II. A CPA leaving a firm may take copies of information contained in client files as a method of gaining technical expertise.

a. I only.

b. II only.

c. Both I and II.

d. Neither I nor II.

20. Which of the following statements is correct regarding an accountant's workpapers?

a. The accountant owns the workpapers and generally may disclose them as he/she sees fit.

b. The client owns the workpapers but the accountant has custody of them until his/her bill is paid in full.

c. The accountant owns the workpapers but generally may not disclose them without the client's consent or a court order.

d. The client owns the workpapers but, in the absence of the accountant's consent, may not disclose them without a court order.

21. Which of the following is an authoritative body designated to promulgate attestation standards?

a. Auditing Standards Board.

b. Governmental Accounting Standards Board.

c. Financial Accounting Standards Board.

d. General Accounting Office.

22. According to the profession's standards, which of the following would be considered consulting services?

	Advisory services	Implementation services	Product services
a.	Yes	Yes	Yes
b.	Yes	Yes	No
c.	Yes	No	Yes
d.	No	Yes	Yes

23. According to the standards of the profession, which of the following events would require a CPA performing a consulting services engagement for a nonaudit client to withdraw from the engagement?

I. The CPA has a conflict of interest that is disclosed to the client, and the client consents to the CPA continuing the engagement.

II. The CPA fails to obtain a written understanding from the client concerning the scope of the engagement.

a. I only.

b. II only.

c. Both I and II.

d. Neither I nor II.

24. Which of the following services may a CPA perform in carrying out a consulting service for a client?

I. Analysis of the client's accounting system.

II. Review of the client's prepared business plan.

III. Preparation of information for obtaining financing.
   a. I and II only.
   b. I and III only.
   c. II and III only.
   d. I, II, and III.

25. Under the Statements on Standards for Consulting Services, which of the following statements best reflects a CPA's responsibility when undertaking a consulting services engagement? The CPA must:
   a. Not seek to modify any agreement made with the client.
   b. Not perform any attest services for the client.
   c. Inform the client of significant reservations concerning the benefits of the engagement.
   d. Obtain a written understanding with the client concerning the time for completion of the engagement.

26. Which of the following services is a CPA generally required to perform when conducting a personal financial planning engagement?
   a. Assisting the client to identify tasks that are essential in order to act on planning decisions.
   b. Assisting the client to take action on planning decisions.
   c. Monitoring progress in achieving goals.
   d. Updating recommendations and revising planning decisions.

27. In relation to the AICPA *Code of Professional Conduct*, the IFAC *Code of Ethics for Professional Accountants*:
   a. Has more outright prohibitions.
   b. Has fewer outright prohibitions.
   c. Has no outright prohibitions.
   d. Applies only to professional accountants in business.

28. Based on the IFAC *Code of Ethics for Professional Accountants,* threats to independence arise from all of the following except:
   a. Self-interest.
   b. Advocacy.
   c. The audit relationship.
   d. Intimidation.

29. If an audit firm discovers threats to independence with respect to an audit engagement, the IFAC *Code of Ethics for Professional Accountants* indicates that the firm should:
   a. Immediately resign from the engagement.
   b. Notify the appropriate regulatory body.

   c. Document the issue.
   d. Evaluate the significance of the threats and apply appropriate safeguards to reduce them to an acceptable level.

30. With respect to the acceptance of contingent fees for professional services, the IFAC *Code of Ethics for Professional Accountants* indicates that the accounting firm:
   a. Should not accept contingent fees.
   b. Should establish appropriate safeguards around acceptance of a contingent fee.
   c. Should accept contingent fees only for assurance services other than audits of financial statements.
   d. Should accept contingent fees if it is customary in the country.

31. With regard to marketing professional services, the IFAC *Code of Ethics for Professional Accountants* indicates that:
   a. Direct marketing is prohibited.
   b. Marketing is allowed if lawful.
   c. Marketing should be honest and truthful.
   d. Marketing of audit services is prohibited.

32. Independence standards of the GAO for audits in accordance with generally accepted government auditing standards describe three types of impairments of independence. Which of the following is **not** one of these types of impairments?
   a. Personal.
   b. Organizational.
   c. External.
   d. Unusual.

33. In accordance with the independence standards of the GAO for performing audits in accordance with generally accepted government auditing standards, which of the following is **not** an example of an external impairment of independence?
   a. Reducing the extent of audit work due to pressure from management to reduce audit fees.
   b. Selecting audit items based on the wishes of an employee of the organization being audited.
   c. Bias in the items the auditors decide to select for testing.
   d. Influence by management on the personnel assigned to the audit.

34. Under the independence standards of the GAO for performing audits in accordance with

generally accepted government auditing standards, which of the following are overreaching principles for determining whether a nonaudit service impairs independence?

I. Auditors must not perform nonaudit services that involve performing management functions or making management decisions.

II. Auditors must not audit their own work or provide nonaudit services in situations in which the nonaudit services are significant or material to the subject matter of the audit.

III. Auditors must not perform nonaudit services that require independence.

    a. I only.
    b. I and II only.
    c. I, II and III.
    d. II and III only.

35. Which of the following bodies enforce the audit requirements of the Employee Retirement Security Act of 1974 (ERISA) with respect to employee benefit plans?
    a. Department of Labor.
    b. Department of Pension Management.
    c. Securities and Exchange Commission.
    d. Public Company Accounting Oversight Board.

36. The requirement for independence by the auditor regarding audits of employee benefit plans apply to the plan as well as:
    a. Investment companies doing business with the plan.
    b. Members of the plan.
    c. The plan sponsor.
    d. The actuary firm doing services for the plan.

37. What body establishes international auditing standards?
    a. Public Company Accounting Oversight Board.
    b. International Federation of Accountants.
    c. World Bank.
    d. International Assurance Body.

38. Which of the following is **not** true about international auditing standards?
    a. International auditing standards do not require an audit of internal control.
    b. International auditing standards do not allow reference to division of responsibilities in the audit report.
    c. International auditing standards require obtaining an attorney's letter.
    d. International auditing standards are based on a risk assessment approach.

39. Which of the following is **not** true about international auditing standards?
    a. Audit report modification for consistency in the application of accounting principles is required.
    b. Confirmation of accounts receivable is not required.
    c. The location in which the auditor practices must be disclosed in the audit report.
    d. International auditing standards do not require an audit of internal control.

EXAMPLES OF THE NEW TASK-BASED SIMULATIONS—PROFESSIONAL RESPONSIBILITY SIMULATIONS

Task-Based Simulation 1

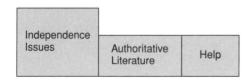

    Assume that you are analyzing relationships for your firm to identify situations in which an auditor's independence may be impaired. For each of the following numbered situations, determine whether the auditor (a covered member in the situation) is considered to be independent. If the auditor's independence would **not** be impaired select "No." If the auditor's independence would be impaired select "Yes."

	Yes	No
1. The auditor is a cosigner of a client's checks.	○	○
2. The auditor is a member of a country club that is a client.	○	○
3. The auditor owns a large block of stock in a client but has placed it in a blind trust.	○	○
4. The auditor placed her checking account in a bank that is her client. The account is fully insured by a federal agency.	○	○
5. The client has not paid the auditor for services for the past two years.	○	○
6. The auditor is leasing part of his building to a client.	○	○
7. The auditor joins, as an ordinary member, a trade association that is also a client.	○	○
8. The auditor has an immaterial, indirect financial interest in the client.	○	○

Task-Based Simulation 2

Independence and Various Services	Authoritative Literature	Help

The director of the audit committee of Hanmei Corp., a nonissuer (nonpublic) company, has indicated that the company may be interested in engaging your firm to perform various professional services. Consider each of the following potential services **by itself**, and determine whether a CPA firm may provide such a service. If a CPA firm may provide the service, fill in the circle under the first or second column of replies based on whether independence is required. If the service may not be provided, fill in the circle under "May Not Provide." For each service you should have only one reply.

Service	May provide, independence is required	May provide, independence is not required	May not provide
1. Provide an opinion on whether financial statements are prepared following the cash basis of accounting.	○	○	○
2. Compile a forecast for the coming year.	○	○	○
3. Compile the financial statements for the past year and issue a publicly available report.	○	○	○
4. Apply certain agreed-on procedures to accounts receivable for purposes of obtaining a loan, and express a summary of findings relating to those procedures.	○	○	○
5. Review quarterly information, and issue a report that includes limited assurance.	○	○	○
6. Perform an audit of the financial statements on whether they are prepared following generally accepted accounting principles.	○	○	○
7. Perform a review of a forecast the company has prepared for the coming year.	○	○	○
8. Compile the financial statements for the past year but not issue a report since the financial statements are only for the company's use.	○	○	○
9. Calculate the client's taxes and fill out the appropriate tax forms.	○	○	○
10. Design a new payroll system for Hanmei and base billings on Hanmei's actual savings for the next three years.	○	○	○

Task-Based Simulation 3

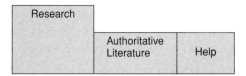

Covered Member   You work with a CPA firm as an assistant. The senior on the XYZ audit has asked you to determine whether you are eligible to work on the XYZ audit since he knows that you own 100 shares of XYZ worth $700 in total. He has asked you to research the following:

1. He thinks that he recalls the issue relates to whether you are or are not a "covered member." He would like you to find the definition of a covered member in the professional standards. What section and paragraph addresses the definition of a covered member?
2. Regardless of what you find, he would like you to determine whether a covered member may have such an immaterial financial investment in an audit client. What section and paragraph addresses this issue?

Task-Based Simulation 4

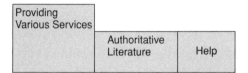

The firm of Willingham and Whiting (WW), CPAs, has had requests from a number of clients and prospective clients as to providing various types of services. Please reply as to whether the appropriate independence rules (AICPA and/or PCAOB) allow the following engagements with:

A—Allowable, given these facts.
N—Not allowable, given these facts.

(If both AICPA and PCAOB rules apply and one of them does not allow the services, answer "N.")

Case	Request	Public or nonpublic client	Allowable (A) or not allowable (NA)?
1.	Provide internal audit outsourcing as well as perform the audit.	Public	
2.	Prepare the corporate tax return as well as perform the audit.	Public	
3.	Prepare the corporate tax return as well as perform the audit.	Nonpublic	
4.	Provide bookkeeping services as well as perform the audit; WW will not determine journal entries, authorize transactions, prepare or modify source documents.	Nonpublic	
5.	Provide financial information systems design and implementation assistance; WW provides no attest services for that company.	Public	
6.	Serve on the board of directors of the company; WW provides no attest services for that company.	Public	
7.	Implement an off-the-shelf accounting package as well as perform the audit.	Nonpublic	
8.	Provide actuarial services related to certain liabilities as well as perform the audit; the subjectively determined liabilities relate to a material portion of the financial statements.	Nonpublic	
9.	Provide actuarial services related to certain liabilities as well as perform the audit; the subjectively determined liabilities relate to material portion of the financial statements.	Public	
10.	Corporate executives of an audit client want to have WW provide tax planning for themselves (not the company).	Public	

Task-Based Simulation 5

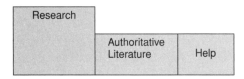

Payroll System Engagement   Michael Edlinger is president of Edlinger Corporation, a nonpublic manufacturer of kitchen cabinets. He has been approached by Marla Wong, a partner with Wong and Co., CPAs, who suggests that her firm can design a payroll system for Edlinger that will either save his corporation money or be free. More specifically, Ms. Wong proposes to design a payroll system for Edlinger on a contingent fee basis. She suggests that her firm's fee will be 25% of the savings in payroll for each of the next four years. After four years Edlinger will be able to keep all future savings. Edlinger Corporation's payroll system costs currently are approximately $200,000 annually, and the corporation has not previously been a client of Wong. Edlinger Corporation is audited by another CPA firm, and Wong & Co. provides no other services to Edlinger Corporation.

Selections
A. AU
B. PCAOB
C. AT
D. AR
E. ET
F. BL
G. CS
H. QC

	(A)	(B)	(C)	(D)	(E)	(F)	(G)	(H)
1. Which section of the Professional Standards addresses this issue and will be helpful in determining whether Wong & Co. may perform this engagement under these terms without violating professional requirements?	○	○	○	○	○	○	○	○

2. Provide the appropriate paragraph citation that addresses this issue.

3. Interpret your findings in parts 1 and 2 and conclude on whether Wong & Co. may perform this service without violating professional standards.

_____ Yes, this service may be performed without violating professional standards.

_____ No, this service may not be performed without violating professional standards.

Task-Based Simulation 6

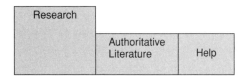

Professional Standards   You have worked with James & Co. CPAs for approximately four months. Jen Jefferson, who has just started with James & Co., has asked you to explain the nature of various professional standards to her. More specifically, she would like to have a better understanding of which standards to address, in which circumstances.

Select the appropriate title of standards for **1** through **10** below. Standards may be selected once, more than once, or not at all.

Title of Standards
A. AICPA Bylaws (BL)
B. *Code of Professional Conduct* (ET)
C. PCAOB Auditing Standards
D. Standards for Performing and Reporting on Peer Reviews (PR)

E. Statements on Auditing Standards (AU)
F. Statements on Quality Control Standards (SQCS)
G. Statements on Standards for Accounting and Review Services (SSARs)
H. Statements on Standards for Attestation Engagements (SSAE)
I. Statements on Standards for Consulting Services (CS)
J. Statements on Standards for Tax Services (TS)

Standards that provide guidance	(A)	(B)	(C)	(D)	(E)	(F)	(G)	(H)	(I)	(J)
1. For performance of a review of a nonpublic company's annual financial statements.	○	○	○	○	○	○	○	○	○	○
2. On whether a contingent fee may be billed to a client.	○	○	○	○	○	○	○	○	○	○
3. Related to firm requirements of CPA firms that are enrolled in an AICPA-approved practice-monitoring system.	○	○	○	○	○	○	○	○	○	○
4. For an examination of a client's financial forecast.	○	○	○	○	○	○	○	○	○	○
5. Relating to overall requirements when providing services for an advisory services engagement.	○	○	○	○	○	○	○	○	○	○
6. For the audit of a public company.	○	○	○	○	○	○	○	○	○	○
7. For the performance of an interim review of the quarterly financial statements of a nonpublic audit client.	○	○	○	○	○	○	○	○	○	○
8. For reporting on client pro forma financial information.	○	○	○	○	○	○	○	○	○	○
9. On whether an investment of a CPA impairs her independence with respect to a client.	○	○	○	○	○	○	○	○	○	○
10. On performing a compilation of a nonpublic company's quarterly statements.	○	○	○	○	○	○	○	○	○	○

MULTIPLE-CHOICE ANSWER EXPLANATIONS

A.2. Code of Professional Conduct—Principles

1. (**c**) The requirement is to identify the statement that best describes the meaning of generally accepted auditing standards. Answer (c) is correct because generally accepted auditing standards deal with measures of the quality of the performance of audit procedures (AU 150). Answer (d) is incorrect because procedures relate to acts to be performed, not directly to the standards. Answer (b) is incorrect because generally accepted auditing standards have been issued by predecessor groups as well as by the Auditing Standards Board. Answer (a) is incorrect because there may or may not be *universal* compliance with the standards.

2. (**d**) All of these can result in the automatic expulsion of the member from the AICPA. Answer (a) is incorrect because although the conviction of a felony can result in automatic expulsion, likewise can the other two. Answers (b) and (c) are incorrect because all three can result in automatic expulsion from the AICPA.

A.3. Code of Professional Conduct—Rules, Interpretations, and Rulings

3. (**b**) Answer (b) is correct because an effective corporate governance structure is a control that can be implemented by a client that increases independence of the attest team. Answer (a) is incorrect because it is a safeguard that is implemented by regulation or the CPA firm. Answer (c) is incorrect because it is a safeguard that is required by regulation or the CPA firm. Answer (d) is incorrect because it represents a threat rather than a safeguard.

4. (**c**) Answer (c) is correct because the team member would be reviewing his or her own work. Answer (a) is incorrect because this is an example of a familiarity threat. Answer (b) is incorrect because this is an example of a safeguard to threats to independence. Answer (d) is incorrect because this represents a financial self-interest threat to independence.

5. (**c**) According to the *Code of Professional Conduct*, Rule 101 regarding independence, a

spouse may be employed by a client if he/she does not exert significant influence over the contents of the client's financial statements. This is a key position as defined by the Interpretation of Rule 101.

6. (**a**) According to Rule 102 of the *Code of Professional Conduct*, in performing any professional service, a member shall maintain objectivity and integrity, avoid conflicts of interest, and not knowingly misrepresent facts. Answer (a) is correct as this would be knowingly misrepresenting the facts. Answers (b) and (d) are incorrect as these are not intentional misstatements. Answer (c) is incorrect because while one must remain objective while performing consulting services, independence is not required unless the CPA also performs attest services for that client.

7. (**d**) The requirement is to determine which act is generally prohibited. Answer (d) is correct because "If an engagement is terminated prior to completion, the member is required to return only client records" (ET 501). Answer (a) is incorrect because issuing a modified report explaining a failure to follow a governmental regulatory agency's standards when conducting an attest service is not prohibited. Answer (c) is incorrect because accepting a contingent fee is allowable when representing a client in an examination by a revenue agent of the client's federal or state income tax return (ET 302). Answer (b) is incorrect because revealing confidential client information during a quality review of a professional practice by a team from the state CPA society is not prohibited (ET 301).

8. (**c**) According to Rule 203 of the *Code of Professional Conduct*, CPAs are allowed to depart from a GASB Statement only when results of the standard would be misleading. Examples of possible circumstances justifying departure are new legislation and a new form of business transaction.

9. (**b**) The requirement is to determine whether a CPA may hire a non-CPA systems analyst and, if so, under what conditions. Answer (b) is correct because ET 291 allows such a situation when the CPA is qualified to supervise and evaluate the work of the specialist. Answer (a) is incorrect because the CPA need not be qualified to perform the specialist's tasks. Answer (c) is incorrect because non-CPA professionals are permitted to be associated with CPA firms in public practice.

Answer (d) is incorrect because nonprofessionals may be hired, and because developing computer systems is recognized as a service performed by public accountants.

10. (**a**) She may use the CPA designation on her business cards when she does not imply independence but shows her title and her employer. Therefore, answer (b) is incorrect. Answer (c) is incorrect because she may use the CPA designation on her business cards or company transmittals if she does not imply independence. Answer (d) is incorrect because under the above situations, she can use the CPA designation.

11. (**a**) The requirement is to determine the activity that would most likely **not** impair a CPA's independence. Accounting and consulting services do not normally impair independence because the member's role is advisory in nature (ET 191). Answers (b) and (c) are incorrect because management functions are being performed (ET 191). Answer (d) is incorrect because accepting a luxurious gift impairs a CPA's independence (ET 191).

12. (**a**) The requirement is to identify the type of report that may be issued only by an independent accountant. Answer (a) is correct because AT 101 requires an accountant be independent for all attestation engagements. An attestation engagement is one in which the accountant expresses a conclusion about the reliability of assertions which are the responsibility of another party. A standard report on an examination of a financial forecast requires the auditor to express an opinion, which requires an accountant to be independent. Answer (b) is incorrect because CS 100 indicates that consulting services are fundamentally different from the attestation function and therefore do not require independence of the accountant. Answers (c) and (d) are incorrect because AR 100 indicates that an accountant who is not independent is not precluded from issuing a report on a compilation of financial statements.

13. (**b**) Per ET 56, due care requires a member to discharge professional responsibilities with competence and diligence. Competence represents the attainment and maintenance of a level of understanding and knowledge that enables a member to render services with facility and acumen. It also establishes the limitations of a member's capabilities by dictating that

consultation or referral may be required when a professional engagement exceeds the personal competence of a member or a member's firm. Accordingly, answer (b) is correct as it may be required to consult with experts in exercising due care. Due care does not require obtaining specialty accreditation.

14. **(b)** Under ruling 101 under Rule of Conduct 102, when a CPA is acting as an expert witness, he/she should **not** act as an advocate but should give his/her position based on objectivity. The expert witness does this based on specialized knowledge, training, and experience.

15. **(c)** The requirement is to determine which act is generally prohibited. Answer (c) is correct because "a member in public practice shall not for a commission recommend or refer to a client any product or service, or for a commission recommend or refer any product or service to be supplied by a client, or receive a commission when the member or the member's firm perform for that client: (1) an audit of a financial statement; or (2) a compilation of a financial statement when the member expects that a third party will use the financial statement and the member's compilation report does not disclose a lack of independence; or (3) an examination of prospective financial information." Answer (a) is incorrect because a member may purchase a product and resell it to a client. Any profit on sale would not constitute a commission (ET 591).

16. **(a)** The principle of due care requires the member to observe the profession's technical and ethical standards, strive continually to improve competence and the quality of services, and discharge responsibility to the best of the member's ability. Answer (b) is incorrect as the auditor is not required to examine *all* corroborating evidence supporting management's assertions but rather to examine evidence on a scope basis based on his/her consideration of materiality and level of risk assessed. Answer (c) is incorrect as the auditor should be aware of the possibility of illegal acts, but an audit provides no assurance that all or any illegal acts will be detected. Answer (d) is not the best answer because competence is derived from both education and experience. The principle of due care requires the member to strive to improve competence; however, attaining the proper balance of professional experience and formal education is not a criterion for exercising due care.

17. **(d)** The fact that a close relative of Kar works for Fort impairs Kar's independence. Answer (a) is incorrect because the gift is of a token amount, which does not impair Kar's independence. Answer (b) is incorrect because a joint financial investment must be material to impair independence, and this would generally not occur with respect to a retirement plan. Answer (c) is incorrect because preparation of the client's tax return is not a service that impairs independence.

18. **(b)** Independence was not required at the time the loan was obtained, and because it is fully secured, it is grandfathered by 101-5. Answer (a) is incorrect because if the CPA is required to be independent, a mortgage loan would not be permitted even if it was fully secured. Answer (c) is incorrect because the CPA was not required to be independent of the client. Answer (d) is incorrect because the CPA was not required to be independent of the client.

19. **(d)** Both of the statements are incorrect; either would violate Rule 301 on confidential client information. Answer (a) is incorrect because statement I also is incorrect. Answer (b) is incorrect because statement II also is incorrect. Answer (c) is incorrect because statements I and II are both incorrect.

20. **(c)** Information in the CPA's workpapers is confidential and may not be disclosed except with the client's consent or by court order. Answer (a) is incorrect because disclosure of the information would generally violate Rule 301 on confidential client information. Answers (b) and (d) are incorrect because the CPA owns the workpapers.

21. **(a)** The requirement is to identify the listed authoritative body designated to promulgate attestation standards. Answer (a) is correct because only the Auditing Standards Board, the Accounting and Review Services Committee, and the Management Advisory Services Executive Committee have been authorized to promulgate attestation standards.

A.4. Responsibilities in Consulting Services

22. **(a)** Types of consulting services include consultations, advisory services, implementation services, transaction services, staff and other support services, and product services.

23. **(d)** According to the Statements on Standards for Consulting Services, independence is not

required for performance of consulting services unless the CPA also performs attest services for that client. However, the CPA must remain objective in performing the consulting services. Furthermore, the understanding with the client for performing the services can be established either in writing or orally.

24. (**d**) CS 100 indicates that the nature and scope of consulting services is determined solely by the practitioner and the client, typically in which the practitioner develops findings, conclusions, and recommendations for the client. All three services listed would fall under the definition of consulting services.

25. (**c**) The AICPA Statement on Standards for Consulting Services, Section 100, describes general standards for all consulting services, in addition to those established under the AICPA *Code of Professional Conduct*. Section 100 addresses the areas of client interest, understanding with the client, and communication with the client. Specifically, this section states that the accountant should inform the client of significant reservations concerning the scope or benefits of the engagement.

26. (**a**) Personal financial planning engagements are only those that involve developing strategies and making recommendations to assist a client in defining and achieving personal financial goals. Personal financial engagements involve all of the following:
    1. Defining engagement objectives.
    2. Planning specific procedures appropriate to engagement.
    3. Developing basis for recommendations.
    4. Communicating recommendations to client.
    5. Identifying tasks for taking action on planning decisions.
    Other engagements also may include but generally are not **required** to perform the following:
    1. Assisting client to take action on planning decisions.
    2. Monitoring client's progress in achieving goals.
    3. Updating recommendations and helping client revise planning decisions.

B.1. Common Law Liability to Clients

27. (**b**) The requirement is to identify the characteristic that differs between the two sets of ethical standards. Answer (b) is correct because

the IFAC Code has fewer outright prohibitions than the AICPA Code. Answers (a) and (c) are incorrect because the IFAC Code has fewer outright prohibitions. Answer (d) is incorrect because the IFAC Code applies to all professional accountants.

28. (**c**) The requirement is to identify the item that is not a threat to independence. Answer (c) is correct because the audit relationship, in itself, is not a threat to independence. Answers (a), (b), and (d) are incorrect because they all represent types of threats to independence.

29. (**d**) The requirement is to identify the appropriate course of action when threats to independence are discovered. Answer (d) is correct because the firm should evaluate the significance of the threats and apply safeguards, if necessary, to reduce them to an acceptable level. Answer (a) is incorrect because the firm would resign only if appropriate safeguards could not reduce the threats to an acceptable level, or it is required based on a prohibition. Answer (b) is incorrect because the firm would not notify a regulatory body at this point. Answer (c) is incorrect because the firm would document the issue, but only after it is resolved.

30. (**b**) The requirement is to identify what the IFAC *Code of Ethics for Professional Accountants* provides with respect to contingent fees. Answer (b) is correct because the IFAC Code indicates that if the contingent fee presents a threat to apply fundamental principles, the firm should establish appropriate safeguards. Answer (a) is incorrect because a contingent fee may be accepted if threats can be reduced to an acceptable level. Answers (c) and (d) are incorrect because the IFAC Code does not contain these provisions.

31. (**c**) The requirement is to identify the IFAC Code provision regarding marketing. Answer (c) is correct because the IFAC Code indicates the marketing must be honest and truthful. Answers (a) and (d) are incorrect because no particular form of marketing is prohibited. Answer (b) is incorrect because marketing must be honest and truthful as well as legal.

32. (**d**) The requirement is to identify the impairment that is not one of the three types of impairments described in the GAO standards. Answer (d) is correct because an unusual impairment is not one of the types of impairments described in the GAO standards. Answers (a), (b), and (c) are incorrect

because they are the three types of impairments described in the GAO standards.

33. **(c)** The requirement is to identify the example that does not represent an external impairment of independence. Answer (c) is correct because this item is an example of a personal impairment of independence. Answers (a), (b), and (d) are incorrect because they are all examples of external impairments of independence.

34. **(b)** The requirement is to identify the overreaching principles for identifying whether nonaudit services impair independence. Answer (b) is correct because I and II are the two principles. Answer (a) is incorrect because II is also an overreaching principle. Answer (c) is incorrect because III is not an overreaching principle. Answer (d) is incorrect because I is an overreaching principle and III is not.

35. **(a)** The requirement is to identify the body that enforces the audit requirements of ERISA. Answer (a) is correct because the Department of Labor is responsible for enforcing the audit requirements. Answer (b) is incorrect because the Department of Pension Management does not exist. Answers (c) and (d) are incorrect because the SEC and the PCAOB deal with auditing requirements for entities with publicly traded securities (issuers).

36. **(c)** The requirement is to identify the party that independence standards also apply to when performing an audit of an employee benefit plan. Answer (c) is correct because the Department of Labor rules also apply to independence from the plan and the plan sponsor. Answers (a), (b), and (d) are incorrect because the independence standards do not apply to these parties.

37. **(b)** The requirement is to identify the body that establishes international auditing standards. Answer (b) is correct because the International Auditing and Assurance Standards Board of the International Federation of Accountants establishes international auditing standards. Answer (a) is incorrect because the Public Company Accounting Oversight Board establishes standards for the audit of public companies in the United States. Answers (c) and (d) are incorrect because these bodies do not establish auditing standards.

38. **(c)** The requirement is to identify the item that is not true about international auditing standards. Answer (c) is correct because international auditing standards require obtaining an attorney's letter only if the auditors assess a risk of material misstatement. Answers (a), (b), and (d) are incorrect because they are all true about international auditing standards.

39. **(a)** The requirement is to identify the item that is not true about international auditing standards. Answer (a) is correct because international auditing standards do not require a modification of the audit report for consistency in the application of accounting principles. Answers (b), (c), and (d) are incorrect because they are true about international auditing standards.

SOLUTIONS TO SIMULATIONS

Task-Based Simulation 1

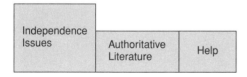

1. **(Y)** Since the auditor is a cosigner on a client's check, the auditor could become liable if the client defaults. This relationship impairs the auditor's independence.
2. **(N)** Independence is not impaired because membership in the country club is essentially a social matter.
3. **(Y)** An auditor may not hold a direct financial interest in a client. Putting it in a blind trust does not solve the impairment of independence.
4. **(N)** If the auditor places his/her account in a client bank, this does not impair independence if the accounts are state or federally insured. If the accounts are not insured, independence is not impaired if the amounts are immaterial.

5. **(Y)** The auditor's independence is impaired when prior years' fees for professional services remain unpaid for more than one year.
6. **(Y)** The auditor's independence is impaired when he/she leases space out of a building he/she owns to a client.
7. **(N)** When the auditor does not serve in management, he/she may join a trade association who is a client.
8. **(N)** Independence is impaired for direct financial interests and material, indirect financial interests but not for immaterial, indirect financial interests.

Task-Based Simulation 2

Independence and Various Services	Authoritative Literature	Help

Service	May provide, independence is required	May provide, independence is not required	May not provide
1. Provide an opinion on whether financial statements are prepared following the cash basis of accounting	●	○	○
2. Compile a forecast for the coming year.	○	●	○
3. Compile the financial statements for the past year and issue a publicly available report.	○	●	○
4. Apply certain agreed-on procedures to accounts receivable for purposes of obtaining a loan, and express a summary of findings relating to those procedures.	●	○	○
5. Review quarterly information and issue a report that includes limited assurance.	●	○	○
6. Perform an audit of the financial statements on whether they are prepared following generally accepted accounting principles.	●	○	○
7. Perform a review of a forecast the company has prepared for the coming year.	○	○	●
8. Compile the financial statements for the past year but not issue a report since the financial statements are only for the company's use.	○	●	○
9. Calculate the client's taxes and fill out the appropriate tax forms.	○	●	○
10. Design a new payroll system for Hanmei and base billings on Hanmei's actual savings for the next three years.	○	●	○

Task-Based Simulation 3

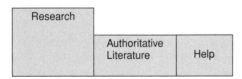

Research		
	Authoritative Literature	Help

1. ET 92.06
2. ET 101.02

Task-Based Simulation 4

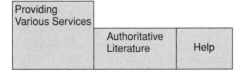

Providing Various Services		
	Authoritative Literature	Help

1. Not allowable (PCAOB requirements prohibit)
2. Allowable
3. Allowable
4. Allowable
5. Allowable (Because no attest services are provided, the PCAOP allows this.)
6. Not allowable
7. Allowable
8. Not allowable (AICPA rules prohibit this when amounts are subjectively determined and material.)
9. Not allowable (Both AICPA and PCAOB rules prohibit this when amounts are subjectively determined and material.)
10. Not allowable

Task-Based Simulation 5

Research		
	Authoritative Literature	Help

1. ET
2. ET 302.01
3. Yes

Task-Based Simulation 6

Research		
	Authoritative Literature	Help

Standards that provide guidance	(A)	(B)	(C)	(D)	(E)	(F)	(G)	(H)	(I)	(J)
1. For performance of a review of a nonpublic company's annual financial statements.	○	○	○	○	○	○	●	○	○	○
2. On whether a contingent fee may be billed to a client.	○	●	○	○	○	○	○	○	○	○
3. Related to firm requirements of CPA firms that are enrolled in an AICPA-approved practice-monitoring system.	○	○	○	○	○	●	○	○	○	○
4. For an examination of a client's financial forecast.	○	○	○	○	○	○	○	●	○	○
5. Relating to overall requirements when providing services for an advisory services engagement.	○	○	○	○	○	○	○	○	●	○
6. For the audit of a public company.	○	○	●	○	○	○	○	○	○	○
7. For the performance of an interim review of the quarterly financial statements of a nonpublic audit client.	○	○	○	○	●	○	○	○	○	○
8. For reporting on client pro forma financial information.	○	○	○	○	○	○	○	●	○	○
9. On whether an investment of a CPA impairs her independence with respect to a client.	○	●	○	○	○	○	○	○	○	○
10. On performing a compilation of a nonpublic company's quarterly statements.	○	○	○	○	○	○	●	○	○	○

RESHUFFLED MATERIAL—AUDITING AND ATTESTATION SECTION

This represents material that was previously being tested on the Uniform CPA Exam, but was covered in areas other than Audit.

This section came from Wiley Module 22, section C, Federal Security Acts, which was previously tested in the Regulation Section.

Sarbanes-Oxley Act of 2002

1. New federal law that contains many reforms that affect this module, Module 21, and other selected modules.
   a. Act also directs the SEC to conduct several studies and to promulgate regulations for corporations, accounting profession, other professions, directors, and officers that are expected to affect issues for CPA exam.
      (1) New laws and new regulations are expected from this for at least the next few years—each new piece of information will be available when relevant for your preparation for CPA exam.
2. Act covers all public companies.
3. Section 906 certification provision of act requires that each periodic report that contains financial reports of the issuer must be accompanied with written statement of CEO or CFO that certifies that reports comply fully with relevant securities laws and also fairly present the financial condition of company in all material aspects.
   a. Any officer who makes certification while knowing it does not comply with SEC requirements can be fined up to $1,000,000 or imprisoned for up to 10 years, or both.
      (1) Officers can be fined for up to $5,000,000 or imprisoned for up to 20 years, or both, for willful violation of this certification requirement.
      (2) The SEC is now permitted to freeze payments to officers and directors during investigation of wrongdoings.
      (3) The SEC may now prevent unfit individuals from serving as officers or directors of public companies.
   b. CEO and CFO must give up any bonuses, incentive-based pay and profits on sales of stock that they received during 12-month period before financial statements are required to be restated because of omissions or misstatements of material facts.
4. Section 302 certification makes officers responsible for maintaining effective internal controls and requires principal executive and financial officers to disclose all significant internal control deficiencies to issuer's auditors and audit committee.
   a. Management must now evaluate any changes in internal control methods.
   b. New rules prohibit officers and directors of an issuer or their agents from fraudulently influencing or coercing auditors to render financial statements materially misleading.
5. Act amends Securities Exchange Act of 1934 to make it illegal for issuer to give various types of personal loans to or for any executive officer or director.
6. CEO and CFO must give up any bonus, any compensation that is equity based or incentive based, or any profit from sale of corporation's securities during period when corporation was required to restate financial statements due to wrongdoings.
   a. CEO and CFO must give up these bonuses and profits even if wrongdoings were not by them but also if they were by any other officer or employee.
   b. Act now requires that any wrongdoing officer give up profits from stock sales or bonuses received due to stock being overpriced because of false information.
      (1) Act allows not only that improper gains be recovered but also any remedy needed to protect investors.
7. Attorneys required to report to chief legal counsel or CEO such things as material violations of securities laws or breach of fiduciary duties.
   a. Attorneys must report this to audit committee (or another committee) or board of directors if counsel or CEO does not take action.
8. Companies must disclose material off-balance-sheet liabilities and transactions.
   a. Amendments require management disclosure of information needed by users of financial statements to better understand off-balance-sheet arrangements involving such things as their business purpose, market risk, credit risk, liquidity, or other material effects.
9. Pro forma information disclosed to public in financial reports, press releases, and so on must not contain any untrue statement of a material fact or omit any material fact.
   a. Pro forma information must also be reconciled with financial statements prepared in accordance with GAAP.

10. The SEC now requires that reports by insiders that disclose their securities holdings must be filed electronically with the SEC to result in earlier public notification and wider public availability of this information.
    a. Issuers having corporate Web sites also must post such information quickly.
11. New rules require disclosures, both financial and nonfinancial, to aid public in assessing risk better pertaining to companies (e.g., disclosing off-balance-sheet financing).
    a. Also, aid in purpose of act to produce reports under Securities Acts that are timely and reliable.

3 FINANCIAL ACCOUNTING AND REPORTING SECTION

Following is the new information that will now be tested on the Financial Accounting and Reporting section of the CPA Exam.

The Content and Skills Specifications for the Financial and Reporting section of the CPA exam are similar to the current content specifications, with these exceptions:

1. International financial reporting standards are now included in the specifications. This material is summarized below.
2. SEC reporting requirements are now included in the specifications. This material is summarized below.

NEW MATERIAL—FINANCIAL ACCOUNTING AND REPORTING SECTION

International Financial Reporting Standards (IFRS)

A. Introduction

The International Accounting Standards Committee (IASC) issued International Accounting Standards (IAS) from 1973 to 2001. In addition, the IASC created a Standing Interpretations Committee (SIC) that provided further interpretive guidance on accounting issues not addressed in the standards. In 2001, the International Accounting Standards Board (IASB) replaced the IASC. The IASB adopted the existing International Accounting Standards (IAS) and interpretations issued by the Standing Interpretations Committee (SIC). Since 2001, the IASB is responsible for issuing International Financial Reporting Standards (IFRS), and the International Financial Reporting Interpretations Committee (IFRIC) is responsible for issuing interpretations of the standards. Therefore, the current international accounting guidelines are contained in the IAS and IFRS pronouncements, together with SIC and IFRIC interpretations.

It is often said that U.S. GAAP employs a "rules"-based approach. In other words, the standards are usually explicit as to precise rules that must be followed for recognition, measurement, and financial statement presentation. IFRS, however, is considered a "principles"-based approach because it attempts to set general principles for recognition, measurement, and reporting, and allows professional judgment in applying these principles. This principles-based approach should focus on a true and fair view or a fair representation of the financial information.

In 2002, the FASB and the IASB agreed to work toward convergence in the accounting standards. Therefore, you will find some IFRS accounting treatments identical, some similar, and others different from U.S. GAAP. An effective study strategy is to study U.S. GAAP and then learn the significant differences between U.S. GAAP and IFRS. This compare/contrast strategy will help the candidate to remember which method is U.S. GAAP and which method is IFRS. As you study this module, notice the differences in the following areas:

1. **Vocabulary or definition differences.** Although the concepts of U.S. GAAP and IFRS are similar, vocabulary and definitions are often somewhat different.
2. **Recognition and measurement differences.** Differences may exist in when and how an item is recognized in the financial statements. Alternative methods may be acceptable in U.S. GAAP whereas only one method may be allowed for IFRS (or vice versa). In some instances, either IFRS or U.S.

GAAP may not require an item be recognized in the financial statements. In addition, the amount recognized (measurement of the item) may be different in the two sets of standards.

3. **Presentation and disclosure differences.** "Presentation" refers to the presentation of items on the financial statements whereas "disclosure" refers to the additional information contained in the notes to financial statements. Again, differences exist as to whether an item must be presented in the financial statements or disclosed in the footnotes as well as the types of information that must be disclosed.

The table below highlights the major accounting differences between U.S. GAAP and IFRS.

B. Basic Concepts

The IASB *Framework for the Preparation and Presentation of Financial Statements* establishes the underlying concepts for preparing financial statements. This framework addresses the objectives of financial statements, underlying assumptions, qualitative characteristics of financial statement information, definitions, recognition, measurement, and capital maintenance concepts.

Major Differences—IFRS versus U.S. GAAP

U.S. GAAP	IFRS
Financial Statement Presentation	
No specific requirement regarding comparative information.	Requires comparative information for prior year.
Comprehensive income may be presented within the statement of changes in shareholders' equity and changes in equity may be presented in the notes.	Requires a separate statement of comprehensive income and statement of changes in equity.
Presentation of certain items as extraordinary is required.	Extraordinary items are not allowed.
Revenue Recognition	
Construction contracts are accounted for using the percentage-of-completion method if certain criteria are met. Otherwise, the completed contract method is used.	Construction contracts are accounted for using the percentage-of-completion method if certain criteria are met. Otherwise, revenue recognition is limited to the costs incurred. The completed contract method is not allowed.
Consolidated Financial Statements	
No exemption from consolidating subsidiaries in general-purpose financial statements.	Under certain restrictive situations, a subsidiary (normally required to be consolidated) may be exempt from the requirement.
Noncontrolling interest measured at fair value.	Noncontrolling interest may be measured either at fair value or the proportionate share of the value of the identifiable assets and liabilities of the acquiree.
Monetary Current Assets and Current Liabilities	
Short-term obligations expected to be refinanced can be classified as noncurrent if the entity has the intent and ability to refinance.	Short-term obligations expected to be refinanced can be classified as noncurrent only if the entity has entered into an agreement to refinance prior to the balance sheet date.
Contingencies that are probable and can be reasonably estimated are accrued.	Contingencies that are probable and measurable are considered provisions and accrued.
Inventory	
LIFO cost flow assumption is an acceptable method.	The LIFO cost flow assumption is not allowed.
Inventories are valued at lower of cost of market (between a floor and a ceiling).	Inventories are valued at lower of cost or net realizable value.
Any impairment write-downs create a new cost basis; previously recognized impairment losses are not reversed.	Previously recognized impairment losses are reversed.
Fixed Assets	
Revaluation not permitted.	Revaluation of assets is permitted as an election for an entire class of assets but must be done consistently.
No separate accounting for investment property.	Separate accounting is prescribed for investment property versus property, plant, and equipment.
Unless the assets are "held for sale," they are valued using the cost model.	Investment property may be measured at fair value.

(Continued)

Major Differences—IFRS versus U.S. GAAP (*Continued*)

U.S. GAAP	IFRS
Biological assets are not a separate category.	Biological assets are a separate category and not included in property, plant, and equipment.
There is no requirement to account for separate components of an asset.	If the major components of an asset have significantly different patterns of consumption or economic benefits, the entity must allocate the costs to the major components and depreciate them separately.
Impairment losses are not reversed.	Impairment losses may be reversed in future periods.
Financial Investments	
Compound (hybrid) financial instruments are not split into debt and equity components unless certain requirements are met, but they may be bifurcated into debt and derivative components.	Compound financial interests (e.g., convertible bonds) are split into debt, equity, and, if applicable, derivative components.
Declines in fair value below cost may result in impairment loss solely based on a change in interest rate unless entity has the ability and intent to hold the debt untill maturity.	Generally, only evidence of a credit default results in impairment loss for an available-for-sale debt instrument.
When impairment is recognized through the income statement, a new cost basis is established, and such losses cannot be reversed.	Impairment losses in available-for-sale investments may be reversed in future periods.
Unless the fair value option is elected, loans and receivables are classified as either (1) held for investment, which is measured at amortized cost, or (2) held for sale, which is measured at lower of cost or fair value.	Loans and receivables are measured at amortized cost unless classified into the fair value through profit or loss category or the available-for-sale category, both of which are carried at fair value.
Leases	
Operating leased assets are never recorded on the balance sheet.	Assets held by lessee under operating leases may be capitalized on the balance sheet if they meet certain requirements.
A lease for land and building that transfers ownership to the lessee or contains a bargain purchase option would be classified as a capital lease regardless of the relative value of the land. If the fair value of the land at inception represents 25% or more of the total fair value, the lessee must consider the components separately when evaluating the lease.	When land and buildings are leased, elements of the lease are considered separately when evaluating the lease unless the amount for the land element is immaterial.
Income Taxes	
Deferred tax assets are recognized in full but valuation allowances reduce them to the amount that is more likely than not to be realized.	Deferred tax assets are recognized only to the extent it is probable that they will be realized.

Although the IASB *Framework* contains information similar to the Statement of Financial Accounting Concepts by the U.S. Financial Accounting Standards Board (FASB), three important differences exist:

1. Some terms and definitions are different.
2. The elements of financial statements are not identical.
3. The qualitative characteristics have several differences.

Candidates should become familiar with these subtle differences in the two sets of concepts.

The IASB *Framework* is not considered an accounting standard and therefore does not override any accounting treatment required by the International Accounting Standards (IAS) or International Financial Reporting Standards (IFRS). The *Framework* exists to assist in the development of future international accounting standards and to assist preparers in accounting for topics that do not have guidance in an existing standard.

According to the IASB *Framework*, the objective of financial statements is to provide information about the financial position, performance, and changes in financial position of an entity that is useful to a wide range of users. Users of financial information include investors, employees, lenders, suppliers, creditors, customers, governments, and the public. The underlying assumptions in financial statement are that they are prepared using the accrual basis of accounting and that the entity is a going concern.

The *Framework* sets forth four qualitative characteristics of financial statements:

1. Understandability
2. Relevance
3. Reliability
4. Comparability

Understandability. The concept of understandability requires that the information provided is readily understandable to users.

Relevance. Information has relevance when it can influence the user's economic decisions by helping them evaluate past, present, or future events. Relevance has certain attributes such as predictive value and a confirmatory role. (Note the change in vocabulary here: In U.S. GAAP, relevance has predictive value and feedback value.) In addition, IFRS includes materiality under the characteristic of relevance. Relevance is affected by the nature and materiality of the information. Information is considered material if its omission or misstatement could make a difference in a user's decision.

Reliability. Information is reliable if it is free from material error and bias, and it faithfully represents what it purports to represent. The attributes for reliability include faithful representation, substance over form, neutrality, prudence, and completeness. "Substance over form" indicates that transactions and events should be accounted for and presented in accordance with their substance and economic reality and not merely the legal form. "Neutrality" means that the information should be free from bias and that the information should not influence the user as to a predetermined result or outcome. "Prudence" is the inclusion of caution in exercising judgments needed to make estimates when there is uncertainty. Prudence requires that if judgment is used, assets or income should not be overstated and liabilities or expenses should not be understated. Prudence also requires that excessive provisions or reserves should not be used because in such cases, the financial statements would not be neutral. "Completeness" refers to not omitting information, because an omission would lead to false or misleading financial statements.

Comparability. The concept of comparability refers to the need for users to be able to compare financial statements of different entities to evaluate their financial position and performance. Comparability requires accounting policies to be disclosed and financial statements to have corresponding information for preceding periods (consistency).

The two constraints for relevant and reliable information are timeliness and the need to balance between cost and benefit. If information is not timely, it can lose relevance. The constraint of cost versus benefit provides that the benefits derived from the information should exceed the cost of providing it.

The most important distinctions in qualitative characteristics between the IASB *Framework* and FASB Concept Statements are the hierarchy of the characteristics and the terms used to describe them. Recall that in the FASB Concept Statements, the primary decision qualities were relevance and reliability. Relevance relied on predictive value, feedback value, and timeliness. With the IASB *Framework*, relevance relies on predictive and confirmatory value, as well as materiality. Under the FASB Concept Statements, reliability focused on verifiability, neutrality, and representational faithfulness. Under the IASB *Framework*, reliability focuses on faithful representation, substance over form, neutrality, prudence, and completeness. Finally, with the FASB Concept Statements, relevance and reliability were both impacted by comparability and consistency. With the IASB *Framework*, comparability focuses on identifying the accounting policies used and using the same policies in preceding periods. Although the term "consistency" is not overtly used in the IASB *Framework*, the concept of consistency is outlined under the heading "comparability."

The first table on the following page outlines the subtle differences in the FASB Concept Statements and the IASB *Framework*.

Another difference between IFRS and U.S. GAAP relates to the elements of financial statements. FASB SFAC 6 contains 10 elements of financial statements: assets, liabilities, equity, investments by owners, distributions by owners, comprehensive income, revenues, expenses, gains, and losses. The IASB *Framework* contains only **five elements**: assets, liabilities, equity, income, and expense. Notice that there are several significant vocabulary differences regarding the elements of financial statements. With U.S. GAAP, the term "income" is not a financial statement element. In U.S. GAAP, the term "income" is used to describe a calculation of some type (e.g., income from continuing operations, net income) or to designate a specific type of income such as interest income. However, with IFRS, the term "income" is a financial statement element, and the items that are considered "income" are revenues and gains. IFRS uses the term "profit" whereas U.S. GAAP uses the term "net income."

FASB Conceptual Framework	IASB *Framework*
Understandability	**Understandability**
Decision usefulness	—
Relevance: Predictive value Feedback value Timeliness	**Relevance:** Predictive value Confirmatory value Materiality
Reliability: Verifiability Neutrality Representational faithfulness	**Reliability:** Faithful representation Substance over form Neutrality Prudence Completeness
Comparability: Including Consistency	**Comparability:** Corresponding information in previous periods
Constraints: Benefits > Cost	**Constraints:** Timeliness Benefits > Cost Balance between qualitative characteristics

The IASB *Framework*'s formal definitions of the five elements are shown in the next table.

IASB *Framework*—Elements of Financial Statements

Asset	An asset is a resource controlled by the entity as a result of past events and from which future economic benefits are expected to flow to the entity.
Liability	A liability is a present obligation of the entity arising from past events, the settlement of which is expected to result in an outflow from the entity of resources embodying economic benefits.
Equity	Equity is the residual interest in the assets of the entity after deducting all its liabilities.
Income	Income is increases in economic benefits during the accounting period in the form of inflows or enhancements of assets or decreases of liabilities that result in increases in equity, other than those relating to contributions from equity participants.
Expenses	Expenses are decreases in economic benefits during the accounting period in the form of outflows or depletions of assets or incurrence of liabilities that result in decreases in equity, other than those relating to distributions to equity participants.

An important point to understand is that the definition of income includes both revenue and gains. Revenues arise in the normal course of business and are often referred to as sales, fees, interest, dividends, royalties, and rent. Gains are other items that meet the definition of income, which may or may not arise in the normal course of business. The IASB *Framework* indicates that gains are increases in economic benefits and are no different in nature from revenues. Therefore, they are not regarded as a separate element in the *Framework*. The *Framework* treats losses in the same way, as no different in nature from other expenses. However, the *Framework* also indicates that when gains or losses are reported in the income statement, they are usually displayed separately because this knowledge may be useful to the decision maker. Gains may be reported net of their related expenses, and losses may be reported net of their related income.

The IASB *Framework* provides for capital maintenance adjustments. When assets or liabilities are revalued or restated, and there is a corresponding increase or decrease to equity, the definition of income or expense may not be met. Therefore, certain items may be included in equity as revaluation reserves.

The IASB *Framework* defines "recognition" as the process of incorporating into the balance sheet or income statement an item that meets the definition of an element and satisfies the criteria for recognition. The two criteria for recognition are (1) it is probable that a future economic benefit will flow to the entity, and (2) the item has a cost or value that can be measured reliably.

The *Framework* also outlines various bases of measurement, such as historical cost, current cost, realizable (settlement) value, and present value. Current cost is the amount of cash or cash equivalent that would be paid if the same or equivalent asset was acquired currently. Realizable (settlement) value is the amount of cash that could be currently obtained by settling (e.g., selling) the asset in an orderly disposal. Although the measurement basis is commonly historical cost, certain accounts use different measurement methods.

1. Revenue Recognition   As indicated above, revenue is the gross inflow of economic benefits resulting from an entity's ordinary activities. These inflows must increase equity and not increase the contribution of owners or equity participants. Revenue is generated from the sale of goods, the rendering of services, and the use of an entity's assets by others. Various titles are used for revenue including sales, fees, interest, dividends, and royalties. Revenue is measured at the fair value of the consideration received or the receivable, net of trade discounts or rebates.

Revenue is recognized from the sale of goods if all five of the following criteria are met:

1. The significant risks and rewards of ownership of the goods are transferred to the buyer.
2. The entity does not retain either a continuing managerial involvement or control over the goods.
3. The amount of revenue can be measured reliably.
4. It is probable that economic benefits will flow to the entity from the transaction.
5. The costs incurred can be measured reliably.

Revenue can be recognized from rendering services when the outcome of rendering services can be estimated reliably. This method is often referred to as the percentage-of-completion method. Note that progress payments or advances from customers are not used to determine the state of completion. The outcomes can be estimated reliably if all the following criteria are met:

1. The amount of revenue can be measured reliably.
2. It is probable that economic benefits will flow to the entity.
3. The stage of completion at the end of the reporting period can be measured reliably.
4. The costs incurred and the costs to complete the transaction can be measured reliably.

If the outcomes cannot be estimated reliably, then revenue should be recognized using the cost recovery method. The cost recovery method recognizes revenue only to the extent that the expenses recognized are recoverable. Note that IFRS does not permit use of the completed contract method, which is allowed for U.S. GAAP.

Barter transactions are not recognized if the exchanged goods are similar in nature and value. If the goods are dissimilar, revenue is recognized at fair value of the goods received. If the fair value of the goods received cannot be measured, revenue is recognized at the fair value of goods or services given up.

Interest income is recognized using the effective interest method. Royalties should be accrued as provided for in the contractual agreement. Dividends should be recognized when the shareholder has a right to receive the dividend payment.

2. Error Correction   Accounting for error correction is similar to U.S. GAAP. A prior period error includes arithmetic mistakes, mistakes in applying accounting policies, and mistakes in recognition, measurement, presentation, or disclosures in the financial statements. IFRS requires the entity to correct the error by restating the comparative amounts for prior periods. If the error occurred before the earliest period presented, then the opening balances of assets, liabilities, and equity should be restated for the earliest period presented. Similar to U.S. GAAP, if it is impracticable to determine the periodic effects of the error, comparative information is restated from the earliest date practicable.

3. Accounting Changes   ***Change in accounting principle.*** The rules for accounting changes are also similar to U.S. GAAP. Accounting changes may occur only when a change is required by an IFRS or there is a voluntary change in accounting methods. In the case of a new IFRS pronouncement, the transition rules in the new IFRS statement should be followed. A voluntary change in accounting method may be made only if it provides reliable and more relevant information about the transactions, entity's financial position, performance, or cash flows. A voluntary change in accounting method is given retrospective application by applying the policy as if the new policy had always been applied. Retrospective application provides that the opening balances of equity is adjusted for the earliest period presented and that other amounts are disclosed for each prior period as if the new accounting policy had always been applied. If it is impracticable to determine the effects of the change, then the change may be applied on a prospective basis. Disclosures include the title of the IFRS requiring the change, the nature of the change, the amount of the adjustments to each financial statement line item, and effects on earnings per share.

Change in accounting estimate. A change in accounting estimate occurs due to uncertainties in measuring items on the financial statements. Changes in estimates include changes in estimates for bad debts, inventory obsolescence, the fair value of financial assets or liabilities, the useful life of a depreciable asset, or warranty obligations. A change in estimates is accounted for on a prospective basis in the period of the change (current period) and future periods.

4. Financial Statements   IAS 1 provides that a complete set of financial statements must be prepared annually. A complete set of financial statements includes a statement of financial position, a statement of comprehensive income, a statement of changes in equity, a statement of cash flows, and notes containing significant accounting policies and explanations. The headings on the financial statements should include the name of the entity, the title of the statement, and the date of the statement. The financial statements should present a "true and fair view" of the company. IFRS must be used unless there is a rare circumstance where the use of IFRS would produce misleading financial statements. Whenever an entity retrospectively applies an accounting policy, retrospectively restates its financial statements, or reclassifies items, three years of statements of financial position are required for comparative purposes. Presentation and classification of items on the financial statements should be consistent for the periods presented.

The accrual basis of accounting is used to prepare the financial statements, with the assumption that the entity is a going concern. Assets and liabilities may not be offset against each other unless specifically permitted by an IFRS. Similarly, income and expenses may not be offset unless specifically permitted. Offsets may be used for valuation purposes, such as contra accounts (allowance for uncollectible accounts or accumulated depreciation). Items on the financial statements should be presented separately for each material class of similar items. If an item is not material, it may be aggregated with other items.

Statement of Financial Position. Assets are classified as current and noncurrent. An asset is current if it is expected to be realized or held for consumption in the normal course of the entity's operating cycle, held primarily for trading purposes, expected to be realized within 12 months of the end of the period, or is cash or a cash equivalent that is not restricted. Noncurrent assets include tangible, intangible, operating, and financial assets that are long term, such as held-to-maturity investments, investment property, property and equipment, intangible assets, assets held for sale, and miscellaneous assets.

Liabilities are classified as current and noncurrent. A liability is current if it is expected to be settled in the normal course of business during the operating cycle, due to be settled within 12 months, held primarily for trading purposes, or does not have an unconditional right to defer settlement beyond 12 months. However, certain payables, such as trade payables and accruals for operating costs, are classified as current liabilities regardless of the settlement date.

Interest-bearing liabilities are classified based on whether they are due within 12 months. However, if an agreement to refinance the liability on a long-term basis is executed prior to the financial statement date, the liability may be classified as noncurrent. Note that this is different from U.S. GAAP, where if there is the intent and ability to refinance before the issuance of the financial statements, reclassification is permitted. An executed agreement prior to the balance sheet is not required. For IFRS, if the agreement to refinance is made after the balance sheet date, then the liability must be classified as current at the balance sheet date. Similar to U.S. GAAP, if a long-term debt becomes callable due to violation of a loan covenant, the liability must be classified as a current liability.

For shareholders' equity, the financial statements must disclose the number of shares of common stock authorized, issued, and outstanding. If there are preference shares (e.g., preferred stock), they must be reported separately, including the number of shares authorized, issued, and outstanding. Preference shares that are redeemable at the option of the holder must be classified as liabilities. Treasury shares repurchased are stated at cost and shown as a reduction to shareholders' equity. Accumulated other comprehensive income is reported in the shareholders' equity section of the balance sheet, and noncontrolling interests are disclosed as a separate item in the equity section of the balance sheet.

Although IAS 1 does not require a specific format for the statement of financial position, these 18 categories should be displayed:

1. Property, plant, and equipment
2. Investment property
3. Intangible assets
4. Financial assets
5. Investments accounted for using the equity method
6. Biological assets
7. Inventories
8. Trade and other receivables
9. Cash and cash equivalents

10. Total assets classified as held for sale and assets included in disposal groups classified as held for sale under IFRS 5
11. Trade and other payables
12. Provisions
13. Financial liabilities
14. Liabilities and assets for current tax
15. Deferred tax liabilities and deferred tax assets
16. Liabilities included in disposal groups classified as held for sale
17. Noncontrolling interest
18. Issued capital and reserves attributable to owners of the parent

Income Statement. IAS 1 requires that at a minimum, these eight items should be included on an income statement:

1. Revenue (referred to as income)
2. Finance costs (interest expense)
3. Share of profits and losses of associates and joint ventures accounted for using the equity method
4. Tax expense
5. Discontinued operations
6. Profit or loss
7. Noncontrolling interest in profit and loss
8. Net profit (loss) attributable to equity holders in the parent

If an entity acquires less than 100% of a subsidiary, the income statement should indicate the profit or loss attributable to the noncontrolling interest and the owners of the parent.

A significant difference between U.S. GAAP and IFRS is that IFRS does not permit the classification of items as "extraordinary items" on the income statement. Any gains or losses should be reported as income or expense. In addition, operating expenses may be classified either by nature or by function. Classification by nature is based on the character of the expense, such as salaries and wages, raw materials used, interest expense, tax expense, and depreciation of assets. Classification by function is based on the purpose of the expenditure such as manufacturing, distribution, or administration. If the entity classifies expenses by function, cost of sales must be stated separately from other expenses. (Note that in U.S. GAAP, expenses are classified by function, cost of goods sold, operating expenses, etc.). For IFRS, finance costs (interest expense) must be identified separately regardless of which classification scheme is used.

Operating expenses are normally classified as distribution costs (selling expenses) and general and administrative expenses. If an item is material in amount and of such a size, nature, or incidence that disclosure is important to understand the performance of the entity, then the item should be disclosed separately. Examples of those disclosures include write-downs of inventories; write-downs of plant, property, and equipment; restructuring costs; costs of litigation settlements; and reversals of provisions.

The treatment of discontinued operations is similar to U.S. GAAP. If an asset is classified as held for sale or is part of a disposal group, it is valued at the lower of carrying value or fair value less costs to sell. The write-down net of tax is included in discontinued operations in the income statement. For discontinued operations, three calculations are required:

1. The revenues, expenses, pretax profit or loss, and the related income tax expense are calculated.
2. The gain or loss on disposal or remeasurement is calculated with the related income tax expense.
3. The total of these two amounts is determined (net of tax) and must be disclosed on the income statement.

The footnote disclosures must include the pretax profit or loss, gain or loss on disposal, and tax effects as well as the net cash flows from operating, investing, and financing activities.

Statement of Comprehensive Income. The statement of comprehensive income may be presented in either one statement or in two statements. The two-statement approach presents a separate income statement and then presents a second statement, which begins with profit or loss and displays the components of comprehensive income. Items that are included in comprehensive income are changes in revaluation surplus for plant, property, and equipment; actuarial gains and losses on defined benefit plans; gains and losses from foreign currency translations; gains and losses on remeasuring available-for-sale financial assets; and the effective portion of gains and losses on hedging instruments in a cash flow hedge. Each component of comprehensive income should be stated separately on the statement of comprehensive income.

Statement of Cash Flows. The accounting rules for the statement of cash flows are similar to U.S. GAAP. For IFRS, cash flows include the inflows and outflows of both cash and cash equivalents. Cash equivalents include cash on hand, bank balances for immediate use, other demand deposits, and short-term investments with maturities of three months or less. Both the direct method and indirect method are acceptable methods for preparing the statement of cash flows. However, for the indirect method, operating activities may be presented using a modified approach. This modified indirect method shows revenues and expenses in operating activities and then reports the changes in working capital accounts.

As in U.S. GAAP, the statement of cash flows is divided into three parts: operating, investing, and financing activities. At the bottom of the statement of cash flows, a reconciliation must be made with the amounts in the statement of cash flows and the cash and cash equivalents reported in the statement of financial position.

The most significant difference between IFRS and U.S. GAAP is where certain items are presented on the statement of cash flows. For example, interest and dividends received may be reported on the statement of cash flows as operating or investing activities. Interest and dividends paid may be reported either in the operating activities or the financing activities sections. Although the entity has discretion on where interest and dividends are reported, it must be reported on a consistent basis. Cash from the purchase and sale of trading securities are classified as operating activities. Cash advances and loans (bank overdrafts) are also usually classified as operating activities. Taxes paid on income must be disclosed separately in operating activities. However, cash flows from certain taxes may be classified elsewhere if they are related to investing or financing activities. In addition, the effects of noncash transactions are not reported on the statement of cash flows. Instead, significant noncash activities must be disclosed in the notes to the financial statements.

C. Inventory

IFRS accounting for inventory differs from U.S. GAAP in three areas: cost flow assumption, valuation of inventory at year-end, and capitalization of interest.

With IFRS, the LIFO cost flow assumption is not permissible. Specific identification is required for inventory of goods that are not interchangeable or goods that are produced and segregated for specific projects. FIFO and weighted-average methods are acceptable methods under IFRS for other types of inventory. The retail method may be used only for certain industries. In addition, the gross profit method can be used to estimate ending inventory when a physical count is not possible. Inventories are carried at the lower of cost or net realizable value (LCNRV). An exception to LCNRV rule applies to agricultural inventories (biological assets) which are carried at fair value less costs to sell at the point of harvest.

Recall that in U.S. GAAP, lower of cost or market (LCM) is used to value inventories. "Market" is defined as replacement cost, subject to a ceiling and floor. The "ceiling" is net realizable value (NRV), and the "floor" is NRV less a less normal profit margin. Once inventory is written down, a loss may not be recovered. Although IFRS uses a similar valuation concept, IFRS values inventory at the lower of cost or net realizable value (LCNRV). Note that the calculations are different from U.S. GAAP. NRV is calculated as estimated selling price less estimated costs of completion and sale. Generally, LCNRV is applied on an item-by-item basis. However, under IFRS, if there are groups of items that have similar characteristics, they may be grouped for the application of LCNRV.

Assume the following facts for an inventory:

Historical cost	$100
Estimated selling price	90
Estimated costs to complete and sell	5
NRV	$ 85

To apply LCNRV to our example, you compare the cost of $100 to the estimated selling price less estimated costs to complete and sell ($90 – $5). NRV is $85. Therefore, the LCNRV is $85. The inventory would be written down to $85 with a corresponding expense on the income statement. If the inventory value at the end of Year 2 was $90, a recovery of the loss would be recorded by debiting Inventory and crediting an income account.

Note that if LCM were applied by U.S. standards, additional information would be needed. Specifically, U.S. GAAP would require the replacement cost, and the normal profit margin in order to arrive at the ceiling and the floor.

Rules for capitalization of interest are also different. U.S. GAAP allows no capitalization of interest for inventories that are routinely manufactured or otherwise produced in quantities on a repetitive basis. Similar to U.S. GAAP, IFRS does not allow interest or financing costs to be capitalized as an inventory cost if it is paid under normal credit terms. However, IFRS allows interest costs to be capitalized if there is a lengthy production period to prepare the goods for sale.

D. Fixed Assets

Some of the most significant differences between U.S. GAAP and IFRS exist in the area of accounting for fixed assets. Items that are classified as noncurrent assets under U.S. GAAP may be classified differently under IFRS. Specifically, noncurrent assets must be identified in categories such as: plant, property, and equipment; investment property; intangible assets; impairment of assets; and biological assets.

1. Plant, Property, and Equipment   Plant, property, and equipment (PPE) are tangible items that are expected to be used during more than one period and are used in the production or supply of goods or services, for rental to others, or for administrative purposes. Plant, property, and equipment are recorded at cost. Cost includes the purchase price net of discounts and rebates, the expenditures to bring the asset to its required location and condition, delivery and handling, site preparation, installation, assembly costs, professional fees, and the estimate of the cost of obligations required for the asset's disposal (decommissioning or site restoration). Similar to U.S. GAAP, costs of self-constructed assets include material, labor, and interest costs.

After an asset is initially recognized at cost, it is subsequently measured using either the cost model (CM) or the revaluation model (RM). Long-lived assets are divided into classes, and a decision is made for each class on which valuation method is applied. Note that a different valuation model can be used for different classes of assets but not individual assets within a class. Examples of classes of assets include land, equipment, motor vehicles, land and buildings, ships, aircraft, and furniture and fixtures.

The CM provides that the asset is carried at cost less an accumulated depreciation and less any accumulated impairment loss. The depreciation method chosen should reflect the pattern of economic benefits expected to be consumed. Straight-line, declining-balance, and units-of-production methods are acceptable depreciation methods. A change in depreciation method is considered a change in accounting estimate and is accounted for on a prospective basis.

Under the RM, the carrying amount of the asset is the fair value at the date of revaluation less any subsequent accumulated depreciation and subsequent accumulated impairment loss. The RM should be applied to assets whose value can be reliably measured. There is no rule regarding the frequency or date of revaluation; therefore, annual revaluations are not required. However, when revaluation is performed, it must be performed for the entire class of assets. Revaluation to fair value usually involves obtaining appraisals. When a class of assets is revalued, the asset account is written up or down, and the adjustment is recorded to the revaluation surplus account, which is reported in other comprehensive income for the period. If the revaluation model is used, accumulated depreciation can be adjusted proportionately, or the accumulated depreciation account can be eliminated and the asset shown net. When an asset is disposed of, a gain or loss is recognized and reported on the income statement. Any balance in the revaluation surplus account is transferred directly to retained earnings (not to profit or loss).

2. Investment Property   Investment property is defined as property held to earn rentals, for capital appreciation, or both. To qualify as investment property, it may not be used in the production or supply of goods or services or for administrative purposes, nor can it be held for sale in the ordinary course of business. Investment property includes land or a building and can be held by the owner or by a lessee under a financing lease. Examples of investment property also include land held for long-term appreciation, land held for an undetermined future use, buildings owned by the entity, or a vacant building held to be leased under an operating lease.

Investment property is recognized when it is probable that the future economic benefits of the property will flow to the entity and the cost of the property can be measured reliably. Investment property is measured at cost. After initial recognition, the investment property is measured under the fair value model (FVM) or the cost model (CM), with certain exceptions.

The FVM requires investment property to be measured at fair value. Changes in fair value are recognized in profit or loss in the period of the change. Notice that this is different treatment from for plant, property, and equipment, wherein the revaluation is recorded in other comprehensive income. If the FVM is used, no depreciation is recorded. The fair value is the price at which the property could be exchanged between knowledgeable parties in an arm's-length transaction.

The CM requires investment property to be carried on the balance sheet at cost less accumulated depreciation and less accumulated impairment losses. If an entity chooses the cost model, it must still disclose fair values in the notes to the financial statements.

Another difference between IFRS and U.S. GAAP involves investment property leased under operating leases. Under IFRS, an entity has the option to record investment property leased under an operating lease as an asset on the balance sheet if the lessee can reliably measure the fair value of the lease. Once this option is selected for one leased property, other investment property also must be accounted for using the fair value model.

Investment property does not include property used in the business, property being constructed or developed for others, property under construction that will be future investment property, and property held for sale in the normal course of business.

3. Intangible Assets   Intangible assets either have no physical substance or have a value that is not represented by its physical substance. Intangible assets are categorized as either identifiable or unidentifiable. An asset is identifiable if meets one of the two criteria: (1) It is based on contractual or legal rights, or (2) it can be separated from the entity, and sold, transferred, licensed, rented or exchanged. Notice this is similar to U.S. GAAP, where an identifiable intangible must meet the legal, contractual, or separability criteria. Identifiable intangibles include patents, copyrights, brand names, customer lists, trade names, computer software, formulae, licenses, and franchises.

Accounting for intangibles under IFRS depends on whether the intangible assets were acquired or internally developed. If the intangible assets were acquired, the intangible asset is recorded at cost. If the intangible assets were acquired in a business combination, newly identified intangibles are recognized at fair value separately from goodwill.

Internally generated intangibles must meet the definition of an identifiable asset (i.e. it must have future economic benefits and can be measured reliably). Although internally generated goodwill may provide future economic benefits, it cannot be measured reliably. Therefore, internally generated goodwill is not recognized as an asset. Similarly, expenditures on research may not result in probable future economic benefits; therefore, research expenditures are treated as an expense of the period. "Development" is the application of research findings for the production of new products or technology. Development costs may be recognized as an intangible asset if these six criteria are met:

1. Technological feasibility of completing the asset for use or sale has been achieved.
2. The entity intends to complete and use or sell the asset.
3. The entity has the ability to use or sell the asset.
4. The entity understands how the asset will generate probable future economic benefits.
5. Technical, financial, and other resources are available to complete development of the asset.
6. The entity has the ability to reliably measure the expenditures.

If all six conditions are not met, development costs should be expensed in the current period. Once development costs are expensed, they cannot be capitalized in the future.

Intangible assets may use either the cost model (CM) or the revaluation model (RM). Similar to plant, property, and equipment, the CM requires the asset to be recorded at its cost less any accumulated amortization or accumulated impairment losses. The RM requires that the fair value must be determined in an active market. Therefore, only intangible assets that are traded with active market prices may be valued using the revaluation model. The RM requires gains and losses on revaluation be recorded in other comprehensive income.

The useful life of an intangible asset is either finite or indefinite. Intangible assets with finite lives are amortized over the useful life; intangible assets with indefinite lives are not amortized but tested for impairment annually (at the reporting date).

4. Impairment of Assets   An entity should determine at each reporting date if there are conditions that would cause an asset to be impaired. Asset impairment exists if the carrying value of the asset is greater than its recoverable amount. The recoverable amount is the greater of the net selling price or its value in use. An impairment loss for an asset accounted for at historical cost is recognized as an expense of the current period. The loss may be included with depreciation expense or identified separately on the income statement. If the revaluation model was used, an impairment adjustment may be treated as a reversal of an upward revaluation. Once the entire revaluation account is eliminated, the excess charge is recognized in expense of the period. Hence, the revaluation account cannot have a debit balance.

Intangible assets with finite lives are tested for impairment when the asset's carrying value is more than its recoverable amount. However, if an intangible asset has an indefinite life, a test for impairment must be made annually.

If an intangible asset's carrying value is more than its recoverable amount, the asset is considered impaired. The recoverable amount is the greater of the net selling price (fair value less costs of disposal) or its value in use. The value in use is determined by estimating the future cash flows expected from the continued use of the asset and its disposal. Impairments for intangible assets carried at historical cost are recognized as charges against the current period profit or loss. If the revaluation method was used for long-lived assets, any increase in value was recorded in a revaluation account in other comprehensive income. Therefore, the impairment adjustment is used to reverse any previous revaluation adjustment. Once the revaluation account is reduced to zero, the impairment is then charged to expense of the period.

An important difference between U.S. GAAP and IFRS is that IFRS allows reversals of previously recognized impairments if the historical cost method is used. If the cost method is used, a reversal of impairment losses may be recognized in the income statement up to the amount of the impairments previously recognized. However, if the revaluation method is used, the recovery of impairments would be recognized in other comprehensive income.

5. Biological Assets Biological assets (agricultural assets) are living animals or plants and must be disclosed as a separate item on the balance sheet. Biological assets are recognized when a future economic benefit is probable, the entity controls the asset as a result of past events, and the cost or fair value can be measured reliably. Agricultural produce should be measured as fair value less costs to sell at harvest.

E. Monetary Current Assets and Current Liabilities
Normally, assets are reported as current and noncurrent, and liabilities are reported as current and noncurrent on the balance sheet. If a liquidity presentation provides more relevant and reliable information, then balance sheet items may be reported based on their liquidity without segregation. In a balance sheet segregated between current and noncurrent items, an asset is classified as current when (1) the entity expects to realize the asset or to consume or sell it within 12 months or the normal operating cycle, or (2) it holds the asset primarily for the purpose of trading. A liability is classified as current when (1) it expects to settle the liability within the normal operating cycle, (2) the liability will be settled within 12 months after the reporting period, or (3) it holds the liability for the purpose of trading.

IFRS defines the terms "financial assets" and "financial liabilities." A "financial asset" is any asset that is cash, an equity instrument of another entity, a contractual right to receive cash or another financial asset, a contractual right to exchange a financial instrument, or a contract that will be settled in the reporting entity's own equity instruments. A "financial liability" is any liability that is a contractual obligation to deliver cash or another financial asset, a contractual obligation to exchange financial instruments under potentially unfavorable conditions, or a contract that may be settled in the entity's own equity instruments. Financial assets and liabilities are reported at cost, with an option to report them at fair value.

There are two important areas where IFRS differ from U.S. GAAP. The first relates to short-term obligations expected to be refinanced. Under U.S. GAAP, short-term obligations expected to be refinanced may be reported in the noncurrent liability section of the balance sheet if the company has the intent and ability to refinance. However, IFRS requires obligations expected to be refinanced to be reported as current liabilities unless there is an agreement to refinance in place prior to the balance sheet date.

The second area in which the terminology and rules are different are "provisions" and "contingencies." Under IFRS, a "provision" is a liability that is uncertain in timing or amount. Provisions are made for items such as taxes payable, compensated absences, bad debts, warranties, and other estimated liabilities. A "contingency," however, depends on some future uncertainty or event.

A contingent asset is a possible asset that arises from past events that will be confirmed only by occurrence or nonoccurrence of uncertain future events that are not within the control of the reporting entity. As with U.S. GAAP, a contingent asset is not recognized, but it is disclosed if the economic benefits are probable.

Under IFRS, a contingent liability does not have the same definition as in the U.S. standards. Recall that under U.S. GAAP, the accounting for a contingency depends on whether the outcome is probable, reasonably possible, or remote, and on whether the contingency is measurable. In contrast, under IFRS if the outcome is probable and measurable, it is not considered a contingency. Instead, it classified as a "provision." Under IFRS, the term "contingency" is used to describe an event that is not recognized because it is not probable that an outflow will be required or the amount cannot be measured reliably. If an item qualifies as a contingency, the notes to the financial statements should include an estimate of the financial effect, an indication of the uncertainties, and the possibility of reimbursement. If the possibility of the event occurring is remote, no disclosure is required in the notes to the financial statements.

It should be noted that the "probable" threshold test for determining whether a provision should be made is "more likely than not," which is defined as a probability over 50%.

F. Borrowing Costs

IFRS 23 requires borrowing costs to be capitalized if they meet certain criteria. Borrowing costs must be capitalized if they are related to the acquisition, construction, or production of a qualifying asset. A qualifying asset is one that takes a substantial period of time to get ready for its intended use. Qualifying assets include inventory; plant, property, and equipment; intangible assets; or investment property. Borrowing costs that do not meet the rules for capitalization are expensed in the current period. Note that finance costs (interest expense) must be disclosed separately in the income statement.

G. Bonds

Similar to U.S. accounting standards, IAS 39 provides that financial liabilities are measured initially at fair value and measured subsequently at amortized cost using the effective interest method. An option can be made to value financial liabilities at fair value. Financial instruments with characteristics of both debt and equity are referred to as compound instruments. Accounting for compound instruments is another area where IFRS differs from U.S. GAAP. Convertible bonds, bonds with detachable warrants, and other compound instruments must be separated into their components of debt and equity. The liability component is recorded initially at fair value, and the residual value is assigned to the equity component. Each component is presented in the appropriate section of the balance sheet.

IFRS refers to the fair value option as "fair value through profit or loss" (FVTPL). If the fair value option is elected for a financial liability, then the liability is revalued at the end of the reporting period, and the resulting gain or loss is recognized in profit or loss for the period.

H. Pensions

The area of employee benefits and, more specifically, pensions is where there are many similarities between U.S. GAAP and IFRS.

In a defined contribution pension plan, the accounting is similar to U.S. GAAP. The employer recognizes an expense for the period equal to the required contribution. If payment is made to the plan, then cash is credited. If the contribution is not made by the end of the accounting period, then the entity would recognize a liability for the accrued contributions.

With respect to defined benefit plans, some vocabulary is different. In U.S. GAAP, the benefits-years-of-service method is used to calculate the projected benefit obligation (PBO). Under IFRS, the projected unit credit method is used to calculate the present value of the defined benefit obligation (PV-DBO). The concept is the same, but the terms are different. In addition, rather than the term "accumulated benefit obligation," IFRS uses the term "accrued benefit obligation."

In a defined benefit pension plan, the calculation of pension cost for the period is also similar to U.S. GAAP. Under IFRS, net periodic pension cost is comprised of six components:

1. Current service cost
2. Interest cost for the current period on the accrued benefit obligation
3. Expected return on plan assets
4. Actuarial gains and losses
5. Past service costs
6. Effects of curtailments and settlements

Under U.S. GAAP, the discount rate used is the "settlement rate" (the rate at which the plan's obligations could be settled). With IFRS, the discount rate is determined by the market yields at the end of the reporting period for high-quality corporate bonds having a similar term or maturity. Another difference in accounting for pensions is that under IFRS, an entity may recognize a portion of the net accumulated actuarial gains or losses, or it may elect to recognize all of the actuarial gains and losses. If the entity wishes to recognize a portion, then the amount recognized is the excess of a "corridor" amount. The corridor amount is the greater of 10% of the present value of the defined benefit obligation or 10% of the fair value of any plan assets. This excess gain or loss above the corridor amount is then amortized over the expected remaining working lives of the employees. Although the corridor rule is similar in U.S. GAAP, the other option for recognizing all actuarial gains and losses is allowed only under IFRS.

Finally, IFRS has specific rules for netting the balances of pension plan assets and pension liabilities. Netting of plan assets and liability balances is permissible only when there is a legally enforceable right to use the assets of one plan to settle the obligations of another plan.

Termination benefits. When an entity provides voluntary termination benefits, a liability and expense are reported when the entity is demonstrably committed to a detailed formal plan that it cannot withdraw. The plan should include information such as location, function, number of employees, benefits provided, and when the plan will be implemented.

I. Leases

Leasing is a topic where the IASB rules focus on substance over form. Unlike U.S. GAAP, which uses certain thresholds to determine whether a lease should be classified as a capital lease, IAS 17 classifies leases based on whether substantially all the risks or benefits of ownership have been transferred. Leasing is also a topic where subtle terminology differences exist, for example, capital lease (U.S. GAAP) versus finance lease (IFRS).

1. Criteria for Treatment of Leases Under U.S. GAAP, a lessee classifies a lease as either an operating lease or a capital lease. For the lessor, the lease is classified as an operating lease, a direct-financing lease, or a sales-type lease. However, under IAS 17, the lease is classified as either an operating lease or a finance lease for the lessee and the lessor. Of course, with a finance lease, the lessor is usually financing the item; if the lessor is a manufacturer or dealer, the lessor is selling the item through the leasing process.

Lease payments under an operating lease are recognized as expense on a straight-line basis over the lease term. The lessee must disclose in the footnotes the total future minimum payments for the next 12 months, payments due in Years 2 to 5, and payments due after five years as well as a general description of the lease terms and restrictions imposed by the lease.

IFRS provides that a lease is a finance lease if substantially all of the risks or benefits of ownership have been transferred to the lessee. If any one of the four criteria is met, the lease is considered a finance lease.

1. The lease transfers ownership to the lessee by the end of the lease term or the lease contains a bargain purchase option, and it is reasonably certain that the option will be exercised.
2. The lease term is for the major part of the economic life of the asset (title may or may not pass to the lessee).
3. The present value of the minimum lease payments at the inception of the lease is at least equal to substantially all of the fair value of the leased asset.
4. The leased assets are of a specialized nature such that only the lessee can use them without modifications.

Although these four criteria are similar to the rules under U.S. GAAP, notice that these rules do not carry specific thresholds, such as a 75% of the economic life or 90% of the fair value of the leased asset. Therefore, the proper classification is determined based on judgments about the substance of the transaction.

In addition, these three other circumstances may indicate that the lease should be treated as a finance lease:

1. If the lessee can cancel the lease, and the lessor's losses are borne by the lessee.
2. Gains or losses resulting from the fluctuations in fair value will accrue to the lessee.
3. The lessee has the ability to continue the lease for a supplemental term at a rent substantially lower than market value.

Under IFRS, a lease is classified as either an operating or finance lease at the inception of the lease. The inception of the lease is the earlier of the date of the lease agreement or the date of commitment to the lease agreement. The commencement date of the lease term is the date in which the lessee in entitled to use the leased asset. Although the lease must be classified as either an operating or finance lease on the date of inception, the lease is not recognized in the financial statements until the commencement date when the lessee is entitled to use the asset.

Another significant difference in classifying leases arises when land and buildings are leased together. Because land has an indefinite life, if title does not pass by the end of the lease term, the substantial risks and rewards of ownership do not transfer. Thus, in such cases the land lease cannot be classified as a finance lease. Under IFRS, the land and building would be treated as separate components; the land lease would be classified as an operating lease, and the building lease would be classified as a finance lease (assuming substantially all risks and rewards of ownership are transferred). The minimum lease payments would be allocated between the land and the buildings elements in proportion to the relative fair values of the leasehold interests of each element. If both elements of the lease are expected to pass to the lessee at the end of the lease term, then the entire lease is classified as a finance lease.

2. Accounting by Lessees Under IFRS, the finance lease is recorded as an asset and as a liability by the lessee at the fair value of the leased property at the inception of the lease or the present value of the minimum lease payments. For the lessee, the minimum lease payments include the payments over the lease term that are required to be made, the bargain purchase option, and amounts guaranteed by the lessee. For the lessor, the minimum lease payments also include any residual value guaranteed by a third party not related to the lessor.

The interest rate used to calculate the present value of the minimum lease payments is the implicit rate. However, if the implicit rate cannot be determined, then the lessee's incremental borrowing rate is used. Any indirect costs incurred by the lessee in connection with negotiating and arranging the lease are added to the cost of the asset.

Each period the minimum lease payments are apportioned between the finance charge and the reduction of the principal outstanding. Any contingent rents are charged to expense as they are incurred. In addition, depreciation expense should be recognized for the leased asset. If ownership transfers at the end of the lease term, then the asset is depreciated over its useful life. If ownership does not transfer, then the finance lease is depreciated over the shorter of the lease term or the asset's useful life.

Disclosures required for leases include the net carrying amount at the end of the reporting period; the future minimum lease payments at the end of the reporting period; and the present value of the lease payment due within one year, due after one year and less than five years, and due after five years. Disclosures should also indicate the contingent rents recognized as expense during the period, a description of the lease, and its terms and restrictions.

3. Accounting by Lessors   In a finance lease, the asset is removed from the lessor's balance sheet, and the net investment in the lease is recorded as an asset. The net investment in the lease is calculated as gross lease receivables less the unearned finance income (interest income).

Similar to U.S. GAAP, a manufacturer or dealer will recognize the sale, cost of goods sold, lease receivable, and unearned finance income.

4. Sales and Leaseback   A sale and leaseback transaction may be classified as either an operating lease or a finance lease. The same criteria (risk and benefits of ownership, substance over form) determine whether the sale and leaseback is an operating or a finance lease. If it is classified as a finance lease, the gain is deferred and amortized over the lease term. If it is classified as an operating lease, the profit or loss is recognized immediately. If it is an operating lease and the fair value at the time of the sale and leaseback transaction is less than the carrying amount of the asset, then a loss is recognized immediately.

J. Deferred Taxes

IFRS requires the use of the "liability method" to account for income taxes. Similar to U.S. GAAP, IFRS primary purpose is to focus on the statement of financial position and report deferred tax assets and deferred tax liabilities. IAS 12 prohibits deferred tax assets or deferred tax liabilities from being classified as current. Therefore, deferred taxes are classified as noncurrent items in the statement of financial position.

Current tax is the amount of income taxes payable or recoverable on the taxable profit or loss for the period. Deferred tax assets and liabilities arise due to temporary differences. Temporary differences are either taxable temporary differences or deductible temporary differences. A taxable temporary difference will result in an increase in taxable amounts in a future period. A deductible temporary difference will result in amounts that can be deducted in future periods.

A deferred tax asset arises when there is a deductible temporary difference. A deferred tax asset also arises when an entity has unused tax losses that can be deducted in the future or tax credits that can be used in the future. An entity can recognize a deferred tax asset if it is probable (more likely than not) that the tax benefit can be used. Deferred tax assets and liabilities are measured using the enacted rate or substantially enacted rate (unlike U.S. GAAP, which requires the use of the enacted tax rate).

The liability method requires an entity to identify all temporary differences. The differences are then classified as those giving rise to deferred tax liabilities, and those giving rise to deferred tax assets. This distinction is important because all deferred tax liabilities are reported, whereas deferred tax assets can be recognized only if it is probable (more likely than not) that the asset will be realized. Similar to U.S. GAAP, tax expense is the sum of current tax expense and the deferred tax expense.

One of the significant differences in accounting for income taxes between U.S. GAAP and IFRS is the classification of deferred taxes on the balance sheet. Recall that for U.S. GAAP, the netting procedures involve netting current deferred tax assets (DTA) with current deferred tax liabilities (DTL) to present one amount and netting noncurrent DTA with noncurrent DTL to present another amount. Under IFRS, deferred tax assets and liabilities may not be classified as current. The netting rules are also different. Netting of the components of deferred taxes is permissible only in certain situations. The rules for presentation and disclosure require that a current tax payable and a current tax recoverable (receivable) can be offset only if it relates to the same taxing authority. Likewise, the netting of deferred tax assets and deferred tax liabilities must relate to the same taxing authority. Therefore, in order to net these amounts, the entity must have a legal right to offset the amounts, and the amounts must relate to the same taxing authority.

K. Stockholders' Equity

Accounting for shareholders' equity may be influenced by the laws of a particular jurisdiction or country. Therefore, IFRS does not contain a comprehensive set of requirements for reporting shareholders' equity. Instead, IFRS provides some rules as to the minimum required disclosures. Note that in this area, there may be vocabulary differences when describing certain components of shareholders' equity.

IFRS requires disclosure of the issued share capital, retained earnings, and other components of equity. The par value and the number of authorized, issued, and outstanding shares must be disclosed. If shares were issued but not fully paid (referred to as subscribed stock in the United States and calls in other countries), the amount not collected is shown as a contra account in the equity section. A schedule must be presented that reconciles the number of shares of stock at the beginning and end of each period.

Additional items that are disclosed in the shareholders' equity section are the capital contributions in excess of par (also called additional paid-in capital, or "share premium"), the revaluation reserve, reserves for other items, and retained earnings. Mandatorily redeemable shares or puttable shares may not be treated as equity and should be classified as liabilities. Compound financial instruments that have the features of both debt and equity must be separated into a liability component and an equity component and recognized in the appropriate section of the balance sheet. Noncontrolling interest is included in the shareholders' equity section of the balance sheet.

Preferred shares that are convertible into ordinary shares are recorded in the preferred share account. Later, if the shares are converted, the book value method is used to account for the conversion of preferred stock into common stock.

Shares issued for services or property should be recorded at the fair value of the property or services. If the fair value of the property or services is not available, then the shares should be recorded at the fair value of the shares. However, if convertible debt is issued, the instrument is viewed as having a debt feature and an equity feature and should be allocated accordingly. The amount allocated to liabilities is the fair value of the liability component, and the residual amount is allocated to equity.

Notes to the financial statements should describe the rights, preferences, and restrictions with respect to dividends for each class of stock, cumulative dividends in arrears, reacquired shares, and shares reserved for future issuances under options and sales contracts.

Cash dividends are recorded in the same way as U.S. GAAP. Although IFRS does not address share (stock) dividends, guidance is based on national accounting rules. If dividends have been proposed but not declared or formally approved, such dividends must be reported in the notes to the financial statements. In addition, information regarding dividends declared after the end of the period but prior to issuance of the financial statements should be disclosed in the notes to the financial statements.

If ordinary and preferred shares are issued to investors as a unit (referred to as share units), the proceeds are allocated in proportion to the relative market values of the securities issued. If only one security is publicly traded, that security is valued at market value, and the residual is allocated to the other security. If the market value of neither security is known, then an appraisal value may be used.

For share subscriptions, the accounting relies on the laws of the particular jurisdiction. In some instances, the subscription receivable is shown as either a current or noncurrent asset based on the payment due date. However, in other instances, the subscription receivable is a contra account and reduces shareholders' equity.

For U.S. GAAP, donated assets are recognized at fair value and as revenue when the contribution is received. IFRS does not currently address donated assets.

Treasury shares are the entity's shares that have been reacquired. There are three methods for accounting for treasury shares: cost method, par value method, and constructive retirement method. The cost method and par method entries are the same as U.S. GAAP. The constructive retirement method is similar to the par value method except that the par value of the reacquired shares is charged to the share account instead of the treasury stock account. The constructive retirement method is used when management does not intend to reissue the shares or the jurisdiction of incorporation requires that reacquired shares be retired.

L. Share-Based Payments

IFRS accounting for share-based payments and U.S. GAAP are similar due to the convergence project. However, some vocabulary differences exist. IFRS has three categories for share-based payments: equity settled, cash settled, or a choice to settle in either cash or equity. Equity-settled share-based payments to nonemployees are valued at fair value of goods or services received if it can be measured reliably. If the fair value of goods or services cannot be measured, then the fair value of the equity instrument is used. Equity-settled payments to employees are valued at the fair value of the security. A debit is made to either an expense or an asset, and a credit is made to equity. For cash-settled, share-based payments, such as stock appreciation rights or options, a liability is measured at the fair value at the measurement date. The liability is then remeasured at every reporting date, and additional income or expense is recognized in profit or loss.

M. Investments

As discussed earlier in fixed assets, the term "investment" is used in the area of investment property as well as investments in financial instruments of other entities. The accounting rules for investment property were covered under the section on fixed assets.

The term "investments" refers to investments that are held for trading (HFT), available for sale (AFS), and held to maturity (HTM) as well as investments accounted for using the equity method and investments that require consolidated financial statements. The accounting for investments is covered by various IAS, depending on the type of investment.

A financial instrument should be classified as fair value through profit or loss (FVTPL), held to maturity (HTM), available for sale (AFS), or loans and receivables. The FVTPL category includes financial assets in the held-for-trading (HFT) category. HTM instruments have fixed and determinable payments and fixed maturity dates. HFT securities are securities in which the entity has the intent to sell in the near term. Available-for-sale financial assets are those that are not classified as FVTPL, HTM, or loans and receivables.

If an asset is classified as FVTPL, it is remeasured to fair value at the end of each accounting period, and any profit or loss is recorded in that period. An election can be made to use the FVTPL method for accounting purposes for an asset normally classified as AFS or HTM. However, if an equity security has no active market in which to determine fair value, then the equity security may not be classified as FVTPL. Once the item is classified as FVTPL, it may not be subsequently reclassified. Any equity instrument that does not have a quoted market price or a determinable fair value should be accounted for using the cost method.

If FVTPL is not elected, different rules apply. If the investment is classified as HTM, the investment is recorded at cost and is subsequently measured at amortized cost using the effective interest method. Similarly, if a financial asset is classified as loans or receivables, it is accounted for by using amortized cost and the effective interest method. If the investment is classified as AFS, the asset is measured at fair value, and any income or loss is recognized in other comprehensive income for the period. Note that if a debt security is classified as AFS, any premium or discount must be amortized using the effective interest method on the income statement, with the increase or decrease in fair value reported in other comprehensive income.

Investments in associates (affiliates) may also be accounted for using either the equity method or the FVTPL method. To qualify for the equity method, the entity must have significant influence over the investee. Significant influence is presumed when the investor owns between 20% and 50% of the voting power of another entity. Consistent with U.S. GAAP, the equity method requires the investment to be recorded at cost, with the investor's share of profit or loss recognized at year-end in the investment account and the investor's share of dividend distributions recognized as a reduction in the investment account. If the cost of the investment is greater than its share of the fair value of net assets, it is not recorded as goodwill. However, this portion of the cost of the investment over the carrying amount is amortized as the assets are realized. If the cost is less than the fair value of net assets (goodwill is negative), this difference is recognized as income in the year of acquisition. An impairment of an investment is recognized if the carrying amount of the investment is greater than its recoverable amount.

N. Business Combinations

IFRS requires business combinations to be accounted for using the acquisition method. Although the accounting for business combinations is similar for U.S. GAAP and IFRS, it is different in several respects.

Under U.S. GAAP noncontrolling interest is recorded at its fair value. IFRS, however, allows noncontrolling interest to be valued either at fair value or the proportionate share of the value of the identifiable assets and liabilities of the acquiree. If the noncontrolling interest is valued at fair value, the noncontrolling interest is calculated by determining the market price for equity shares not held by the acquirer. If the market value is not available, other valuation techniques may be used to measure the fair value. The second method for valuing noncontrolling interest is to calculate the fair value of net assets acquired and multiply that amount times the percentage of shares owned by the noncontrolling interest. Note that these two methods may result in a different amount of goodwill being recognized by the acquirer.

The calculation of goodwill is

Consideration transferred
+ Noncontrolling interest in acquiree (valued at % of FV or % share of net assets)
+ Fair value of previously held interests in acquiree
− Fair value of net assets acquired
_____
Goodwill

If goodwill is negative, a gain from bargain purchase should be recognized in the current period on the income statement.

Consolidated financial statements are required for all parent and subsidiaries wherein the parent has control. Similar to U.S. GAAP, control is presumed if the entity has more than 50% of the voting shares of another entity. However, under IFRS, a parent may exclude a subsidiary only if three conditions are met: (1) it is wholly or partially owned and its other owners do not object to nonconsolidation; (2) it does not have any debt or equity instruments publicly traded; and (3) its parent prepares consolidated financial statements that comply with IFRS.

O. Derivatives and Hedging Instruments

A derivative is a financial instrument that (1) requires little or no initial investment, (2) changes in value in response to a change in the value of another instrument or index (called an underlying), and (3) is settled in the future. Examples of derivatives include options, futures, forward contracts, and swaps. Derivatives are recognized in the financial statements using the fair value through profit and loss method (FVTPL). Derivatives are remeasured at fair value, with gains and losses recorded in profit or loss for the period.

A hedging instrument is a type of derivative that is classified as a fair value hedge, a cash flow hedge, or a hedge of a net investment in operations. Hedge accounting allows the optional treatment to offset profits and losses on hedged items. If a company elects to use hedge accounting, the accounting treatment differs depending on the type of hedge. A fair value hedge is accounted for by recognizing the gains and losses in profit and loss of the period. A cash flow hedge and a hedge of a net investment are accounted for by reporting gains and losses in other comprehensive income for the period.

P. Interim Reporting

IFRS does not mandate interim reporting. However, when interim reports are required, four financial statements are required: (1) statement of financial position, (2) statement of comprehensive income, (3) statement of changes in equity, and (4) statement of cash flows. For consistency purposes, the entity must use the same accounting policies as used in year-end financial statements.

Q. Segment Reporting

IFRS 8 on segment reporting includes guidance very similar to U.S. GAAP. It requires a management approach to identifying operating segments. An operating segment is a reportable segment if it meets one of these defined quantitative thresholds:

1. The segment's revenue (including internal and external sales) is 10% or more of combined revenue of all segments.
2. The absolute value of the profit or loss is 10% or more than the greater (in absolute value) of the (a) combined reported profit of all segments that did not report a loss or (b) the combined reported loss of all segments that reported a loss.
3. The assets are 10% or more of the combined assets of all segments.

In addition, the total external revenue by reportable segments must be at least 75% of the entity's revenue; otherwise additional segments must be identified and reported. Note that these thresholds are the same as for U.S. GAAP.

R. Foreign Currency Transactions and Translations

Currencies are defined as foreign, functional, or presentation currency. The functional currency is the currency of the primary economic environment in which the entity operates. A foreign currency is a currency other than the functional currency. The presentation currency is the currency in which financial statements are presented. Similar to U.S. GAAP, the three-step process for translating financial statements is:

1. Determine the functional currency.
2. Translate items into the functional currency.
3. Translate items into the presentation currency.

When translating financial statement items, the items are classified into two categories: monetary and nonmonetary items. Monetary items are translated at the year-end spot rate. Nonmonetary items measured at historical cost are translated at the historical exchange rate. Nonmonetary items measured at fair value are translated at the rate in effect when fair value was determined. If the functional currency is the same as the presentation currency, any gains and losses on translation are recognized in profit or loss in the period. However, there are several exceptions to this rule. Currency gains or losses on nonmonetary items for which gains and losses are recorded in other comprehensive income also should be reported in other comprehensive income.

If the functional currency is not the same as the presentation currency, then any translation gains and losses are recorded in other comprehensive income. In this case, assets and liabilities are recorded at the closing exchange rate, and income and expenses are recorded at the rate when the transaction occurred.

S. First-Time Adoption of IFRS

There are a number of options available upon first-time adoption of IFRS, as described below. Generally the adoption involves restating assets, liabilities, and equity using IFRS principles. The "date of transition to IFRS" is defined as the beginning of the earliest period for which an entity presents full comparative information under IFRSs in its first IFRS financial statements. The "first IFRS reporting period" is defined as the latest reporting period covered by an entity's first IFRS financial statements.

Business combinations. With respect to business combinations, the first-time adopter has the option of retrospectively adopting IFRS 3 for all periods presented or adjusting the assets and liabilities through retained earnings in the period of adoption.

Plant, property, and equipment. Unless an entity decides to use a fair value election, it will need to recalculate the life-to-date depreciation or amortization of any PPE or intangible assets under IFRS. This can be quite time consuming. Alternatively, the entity may use various methods to determine the fair value of the assets and use those amounts as the deemed cost at the time of adoption. IFRS would then be used going forward. The fair value election may be applied on an individual item basis.

SEC Reporting Requirements

Unless exempt by regulation, companies with assets of more than $10 million and 500 or more shareholders and securities that trade on a national securities exchange or an over-the-counter market must have the securities registered. Companies with registered securities (termed issuers) must file these reports with the SEC:

1. Annual report (Form 10-K) provides a comprehensive picture of a company's performance, including audited financial statements. The 10-K includes these sections:
   a. Business
   b. Risk factors
   c. Properties
   d. Legal proceedings
   e. Submission of matters to a vote of security holders
   f. Market
   g. Consolidated financial data
   h. Management's discussion and analysis
   i. Financial statements (three years of balance sheets and two years of income statements, statements of cash flows, and statements of comprehensive income).
2. The deadline for filing the Form 10-K is within 75 days after the close of the company's fiscal year for accelerated filers (companies with a market value of at least $75 million in equity held by nonaffiliates). Large accelerated filers (companies with a market value of at least $700 million in equity held by nonaffiliates) must file within 60 days. Small reporting companies (less than $75 million in market value of equity) must file within 90 days.
3. The quarterly report (Form 10-Q) provides quarterly information similar to that in the 10-K but in less detail. It includes quarterly financial statements that are reviewed (not audited) by public accountants. The company files three Form 10-Qs every year; the Form 10-K contains the quarterly results for the fourth quarter. The Form 10-Q must include these financial statements.
   a. An interim balance sheet as of the end of the most recent fiscal quarter and a balance sheet as of the end of the preceding fiscal year. An interim balance sheet as of the end of the corresponding fiscal quarter of the preceding fiscal year need not be provided unless necessary for an understanding of the impact of seasonal fluctuation on the company's financial condition.

b. Interim statements of income for the most recent fiscal quarter, for the period between the end of the preceding fiscal year and the end of the most recent fiscal quarter, and for the corresponding periods of the preceding fiscal year.

c. Interim statements of cash flows for the period between the end of the preceding fiscal year and the end of the most recent fiscal quarter, and for the corresponding period of the preceding fiscal year. Form 10-Qs are due 45 days after the end of the fiscal quarter for small reporting companies and 40 days after the end of the fiscal quarter for accelerated and large accelerated filers.

4. Information statements (Form 8-K) provide information about material events that affect the company, such as mergers and acquisitions, changes in directors or chief executive officers, other major changes in operations or status, changes in auditors, and so on. The Form 8-K must be filed within four business days of the occurrence of the event.

5. Regulation S-X describes the form and content of financial statements filed with the SEC.

Financial Statements of Trusts

Trusts are entities that formed to hold assets for the benefit of the beneficiaries. They are administered by trustees. Trusts generally present these three financial statements:

1. A statement of assets and liabilities
2. A statement of operations
3. A statement of changes in net assets

The financial statements of a trust generally are presented on the accrual basis, and the assets generally are presented at their fair values.

QUESTIONS ON THE NEW FINANCIAL ACCOUNTING AND REPORTING MATERIAL

1. Which of the following organizations is responsible for setting International Financial Reporting Standards?
    a. Financial Accounting Standards Board.
    b. International Accounting Standards Committee.
    c. Financial Accounting Committee.
    d. International Accounting Standards Board.

2. According to the IASB *Framework for the Preparation and Presentation of Financial Statements*, the qualitative characteristic of relevance includes:
    a. Timeliness, predictive value, and feedback value.
    b. Verifiability, neutrality, and representational faithfulness.
    c. Predictive value, confirmatory value, and materiality.
    d. Comparability and consistency.

3. According to the IASB *Framework*, the financial statement element that is defined as increases in economic benefits during the accounting period in the form of inflows or enhancements of assets or decreases of liabilities that result in increases in equity, other than those relating to contributions from equity participants, is:
    a. Revenue.
    b. Income.
    c. Profits.
    d. Gains.

4. According to the IASB *Framework*, the two criteria required for incorporating items into the income statement or statement of financial position are that:
    a. It meets the definition of relevance and reliability.
    b. It meets the definition of an element and can be measured reliably.
    c. It satisfies the criterion of capital maintenance.
    d. It meets the requirements of comparability and consistency.

5. If the outcome of rendering services cannot be estimated reliably, IFRS requires the use of which revenue recognition method?
    a. Percentage-of-completion method.
    b. Completed-contract method.
    c. Cost recovery method.
    d. Installment method.

6. IFRS requires changes in accounting principles to be reported:
    a. On a prospective basis.
    b. On a retrospective basis.
    c. By restating the financial statements.
    d. By a cumulative adjustment on the income statement.

7. Galaxy Corporation prepares its financial statements in accordance with IFRS. Galaxy intends to refinance a $10,000 note payable due

on February 20, 2011. The company expects the note to be refinanced for a period of five years. Under what circumstances can Galaxy report the note payable as a noncurrent liability on its December 31, 2010, statement of financial position?

a. If Galaxy has the intent and ability to refinance before December 31, 2010.

b. If Galaxy has executed an agreement to refinance by December 31, 2010.

c. If Galaxy has executed an agreement to refinance prior to the issuance of the financial statements in March 2011.

d. If Galaxy has the intent and ability to refinance before the issuance of the financial statements in March 2011.

8. Largo Corporation prepares its financial statements in accordance with IFRS. Which of the following items is required disclosure on the income statement?

a. Revenues, cost of goods sold, and advertising expense.

b. Finance costs, tax expense, and income.

c. Operating expenses, nonoperating expenses, and extraordinary items.

d. Gross profit, operating profits, and net profits.

9. Which of the following may **not** be disclosed on the income statement for a company that prepares its financial statements in accordance with IFRS?

a. Gain or loss.

b. Tax expense.

c. Gain or loss from extraordinary items.

d. Gain or loss from discontinued operations.

10. Glenda Corporation prepares its financial statements in accordance with IFRS. Glenda must report finance costs on the statement of cash flows:

a. In operating activities.

b. Either in operating activities or financing activities.

c. In financing activities.

d. In investing activities or financing activities.

11. Larimer Corporation prepares its financial statements in accordance with IFRS. Larimer acquired equipment by issuing 5,000 shares of its common stock. How should this transaction be reported on the statement of cash flows?

a. As an outflow of cash from investing activities and an inflow of cash from financing activities.

b. As an inflow of cash from financing activities and an outflow of cash from operating activities.

c. At the bottom of the statement of cash flows as a significant noncash transaction.

d. In the notes to the financial statements as a significant noncash transaction.

12. For IFRS purposes, cash advances and loans from bank overdrafts should be reported on the statement of cash flows as:

a. Operating activities.

b. Investing activities.

c. Financing activities.

d. Other significant noncash activities.

13. Which of the following are acceptable methods for reporting comprehensive income under IFRS?

  I. One comprehensive income statement.

  II. Two statements: an income statement and a comprehensive income statement.

  III. In the statement of owners' equity.

    a. I only.

    b. I and II only.

    c. I, II, and III.

    d. I and III only.

14. Brady Corporation values its inventory at the lower of cost or net realizable value as required by IFRS. Brady has the following information regarding its inventory:

Historical cost	$1,000
Estimated selling price	900
Estimated costs to complete and sell	50
Replacement cost	800

What is the amount for inventory that Brady should report on the balance sheet under the lower of cost or net realizable value method?

a. $1,000

b. $900

c. $850

d. $750

15. For companies that prepare financial statements in accordance with IFRS, plant, property, and equipment should be valued using which models?

a. The cost model or the revaluation model.

b. The cost model or the fair value model.

c. The cost model or the fair value through profit or loss model.

d. The revaluation model or the fair value model.

16. Which is true about the revaluation model for valuing plant, property, and equipment?

a. Revaluation of assets must be made on the last day of the fiscal year.

b. Revaluation of assets must be made on the same date each year.

c. There is no rule for the frequency or date of revaluation.

d. Revaluation of assets must be made every two years.

17. When the revaluation model is used for reporting plant, property, and equipment, the gain or loss should be included in:

a. Income for the period.

b. Gain from revaluation on the income statement.

c. A revaluation surplus account in other comprehensive income.

d. An extraordinary gain or loss on the income statement.

18. Linden Corporation has investment property that is held to earn rental income. Linden prepares its financial statements in accordance with IFRS. Linden uses the fair value model for reporting the investment property. Which of the following is true?

a. Changes in fair value are reported as profit or loss in the current period.

b. Changes in fair value are reported as other comprehensive income for the period.

c. Changes in fair value are reported as an extraordinary gain on the income statement.

d. Changes in fair value are reported as deferred revenue for the period.

19. Under IFRS, what valuation methods are used for intangible assets?

a. The cost model or the fair value model.

b. The cost model or the revaluation model.

c. The cost model or the fair value through profit or loss model.

d. The revaluation model or the fair value model.

20. Pinkerton Corp. uses the cost model for intangible assets. On April 10, 2009, Pinkerton acquired assets for $100,000. On December 31, 2009, it was determined that the recoverable amount for these intangible assets was $80,000. On December 31, 2010, it was determined that the intangible assets had a recoverable amount of $84,000. What is the impairment gain or loss recognized in 2009 and 2010 on the income statement?

	2009	2010
a.	$20,000 loss	$16,000 loss
b.	$20,000 loss	$0
c.	$20,000 loss	$4,000 gain
d.	$0	$0

21. On March 22, 2010, Cole Corporation received notification of legal action against the firm. Cole's attorneys determine that it is probable the company will lose the suit, and the loss is estimated at $2,000,000. Cole's accountants believe this amount is material and should be disclosed. Cole prepares its financial statements in accordance with IFRS. How should the estimated loss be disclosed in Cole's financial statements at December 31, 2010?

a. As a loss recorded in other comprehensive income.

b. As a contingent liability reported in the balance sheet and a loss on the income statement.

c. As a provision for loss reported in the balance sheet and a loss on the income statement.

d. In the footnotes to the financial statements as a contingency.

22. Roland Corp. signed an agreement with Linx, which requires that if Linx does not meet certain contractual obligations, Linx must forfeit land worth $40,000 to Roland. Roland's accountants believe that Linx will not meet its contractual obligations, and it is probable Roland that will receive the land by the end of 2011. Roland uses IFRS for reporting purposes. How should Roland report the land?

a. As investment property in the asset section of the balance sheet.

b. As a contingent asset in the current asset section of the balance sheet.

c. In a footnote disclosure if the economic benefits are probable.

d. As a contingent asset and other comprehensive income for the period.

23. On February 1, 2010, Blake Corporation issued bonds with a fair value of $1,000,000. Blake prepares its financial statements in accordance with IFRS. What methods may Blake use to report the bonds on its December 31, 2010 statement of financial position?

I.   Amortized cost.

II. Fair value method.

III. Fair value through profit or loss.

a. I only.

b. II only.

c. I and III only.

d. III only.

24. Which of the following methods is used in IFRS to account for defined benefit pension plans?

a. Projected-unit-credit method.

b. Benefit-years-of-service method.

c. Accumulated benefits method.
d. Vested years of service method.

25. Morgan Corp. signs a lease to rent equipment for 10 years. The lease payments of $10,000 per year are due on January 2 each year. At the end of the lease term, Morgan may purchase the equipment for $50. The equipment is estimated to have a useful life of 12 years. Morgan prepares its financial statements in accordance with IFRS. Morgan should classify this lease as a(n):
a. Operating lease.
b. Capital lease.
c. Finance lease.
d. Sales-type lease.

26. Santiago Corp. signs an agreement to lease land and a building for 20 years. At the end of the lease, the property will not transfer to Santiago. The life of the building is estimated to be 20 years. Santiago prepares its financial statements in accordance with IFRS. How should Santiago account for the lease?
a. The lease is recorded as a finance lease.
b. The lease is recorded as an operating lease.
c. The land is recorded as an operating lease and the building is recorded as a finance lease.
d. The land is recorded as a finance lease, and the building is recorded as an operating lease.

27. Klaus Corporation prepares its financial statements in accordance with IFRS. Klaus locates its business in two jurisdictions, France and Germany. Assume that each country has the legal right to offset the taxes receivable and payable. Klaus prepares its taxes based on taxing authority and has the following information related to its deferred tax assets and liabilities:

Classification	Amount	Taxing Jurisdiction
Deferred tax asset	$4,000	France
Deferred tax liability	$2,500	Germany
Deferred tax liability	$3,000	France

How should Klaus present its deferred taxes on its December 31, 2010, statement of financial position?

	Deferred tax asset	Deferred tax liability
a.	$4,000	$5,500
b.	$1,000	$2,500
c.	$0	$1,500
d.	$1,500	$3,000

28. Which of the following is true regarding reporting deferred taxes in financial statements prepared in accordance with IFRS?
a. Deferred tax assets and liabilities are classified as current and noncurrent based on their expiration dates.
b. Deferred tax assets and liabilities may be classified only as noncurrent.
c. Deferred tax assets are netted with deferred tax liabilities to arrive at one amount presented on the balance sheet.
d. Deferred taxes of one jurisdiction are offset against another jurisdiction in the netting process.

29. Logan Corporation issues convertible bonds for $500,000. At the date of issuance, it is determined that the fair value of the bonds is $480,000. Logan prepares its financial statements in accordance with IFRS. How should the issuance of the bonds be recognized?
a. As a bond liability for $500,000.
b. As a bond liability for $480,000 and other comprehensive income of $20,000.
c. As a bond liability for $480,000 and an equity component of $20,000.
d. As a bond liability for $500,000 and a contra liability of $20,000.

30. On March 1, 2010, Acadia purchased 1,000 shares of common stock of Marston Corp. for $50,000 and classified the investment as available-for-sale securities. On December 31, 2010, the Marston stock had a fair value of $53,000. Acadia Corp. prepares its financial statements in accordance with IFRS. Acadia elects to use the fair value through profit or loss to record its investments in available-for-sale securities. How is the gain on the investment in Marston stock reported in Acadia's 2010 financial statements?
a. As a $3,000 gain in other comprehensive income.
b. No gain or loss is reported in 2010.
c. As a $3,000 prior period adjustment to retained earnings.
d. As a $3,000 gain in current earnings of the period.

31. Which of the following is the SEC form used by issuer companies to file as an annual report with the SEC?
a. Form 10-Q.
b. Form 8-K.
c. Form 10-K.
d. Form S-1.

32. Which of the following best describes the content of the SEC Form 10-Q?
    a. Quarterly audited financial information and other information about the company.
    b. Annual audited financial information and nonfinancial information about the company.
    c. Disclosure of material events that affect the company.
    d. Quarterly reviewed financial information and other information about the company.

33. Under IFRS, changes in accounting policies are:
    a. Permitted if the change will result in a more reliable and more relevant presentation of the financial statements.
    b. Permitted if the entity encounters new transactions, events, or conditions that are substantively different from existing or previous transactions.
    c. Required on material transactions, if the entity had previously accounted for similar, though immaterial, transactions under an unacceptable accounting method.
    d. Required if an alternate accounting policy gives rise to a material change in assets, liabilities, or the current year net income.

34. Under IFRS, an entity that acquires an intangible asset may use the revaluation model for subsequent measurement only if:
    a. The useful life of the intangible asset can be reliably determined.
    b. An active market exists for the intangible asset.
    c. The cost of the intangible asset can be measured reliably.
    d. The intangible asset is a monetary asset.

35. Under IFRS, which of the following is a criterion that must be met in order for an item to be recognized as an intangible asset other than goodwill?
    a. The item's fair value can be measured reliably.
    b. The item is part of the entity's activities aimed at gaining new scientific or technical knowledge.
    c. The item is expected to be used in the production or supply of goods or services.
    d. The item is identifiable and lacks physical substance.

36. An entity purchases a trademark and incurs the following costs in connection with the trademark:

One-time trademark purchase price	$100,000
Nonrefundable VAT taxes	5,000
Training sales personnel on use of the new trademark	7,000
Research expenditures associated with purchase of new trademark	24,000
Legal costs incurred to register trademark	10,500
Salaries of administrative personnel	12,000

Applying IFRS and assuming that the trademark meets all of the applicable initial asset recognition criteria, the entity should recognize an asset in the amount of:
    a. $100,000.
    b. $115,500.
    c. $146,500.
    d. $158,500.

37. Under IFRS, when an entity chooses the revaluation model as its accounting policy for measuring property, plant, and equipment, which of the following statements is correct?
    a. When an asset is revalued, the entire class of property, plant, and equipment to which that asset belongs must be revalued.
    b. When an asset is revalued, individual assets within a class of property, plant, and equipment to which that asset belongs can be revalued.
    c. Revaluations of property, plant, and equipment must be made at least every three years.
    d. Increases in an asset's carrying value as a result of the first revaluation must be recognized as a component of profit or loss.

38. Upon first-time adoption of IFRS, an entity may elect to use fair value as deemed cost for:
    a. Biological assets related to agricultural activity for which there is **no** active market.
    b. Intangible assets for which there is **no** active market.
    c. Any individual item of property, plant, and equipment.
    d. Financial liabilities that are **not** held for trading.

39. Under IFRS, which of the following is the first step within the hierarchy of guidance to which management refers, and whose applicability it considers, when selecting accounting policies?
    a. Consider the most recent pronouncements of other standard-setting bodies to the extent they do not conflict with IFRS or the IASB *Framework*.

   b. Apply a standard from IFRS if it specifically relates to the transaction, other event, or condition.

   c. Consider the applicability of the definitions, recognition criteria, and measurement concepts in the IASB *Framework.*

   d. Apply the requirements in IFRS dealing with similar and related issues.

40. On January 1, Year 1, an entity acquires for $100,000 a new piece of machinery with an estimated useful life of 10 years. The machine has a drum that must be replaced every 5 years and costs $20,000 to replace. Continued operation of the machine requires an inspection every 4 years after purchase; the inspection cost is $8,000. The company uses the straight-line method of depreciation. Under IFRS, what is the depreciation expense for Year 1?

   a. $10,000.
   b. $10,800.
   c. $12,000.
   d. $13,200.

41. On July 1, Year 2, a company decided to adopt IFRS. The company's first IFRS reporting period is as of and for the year ended December 31, Year 2. The company will present one year of comparative information. What is the company's date of transition to IFRS?

   a. January 1, Year 1.
   b. January 1, Year 2.
   c. July 1, Year 2.
   d. December 31, Year 2.

42. A company determined the following values for its inventory as of the end of its fiscal year:

Historical cost	$100,000
Current replacement cost	70,000
Net realizable value	90,000
Net realizable value less a normal profit margin	85,000
Fair value	95,000

   Under IFRS, what amount should the company report as inventory on its balance sheet?

   a. $70,000.
   b. $85,000.
   c. $90,000.
   d. $95,000.

43. Which of the following is the minimum reporting requirement for a company that is preparing its first IFRS financial statements?

   a. Three statements of financial position.
   b. Two statements of financial position.
   c. One statement of comprehensive income.
   d. One statement of cash flows.

44. How should a first-time adopter of IFRS recognize the adjustments required to present its opening IFRS statement of financial position?

   a. All of the adjustments should be recognized in profit or loss.

   b. Adjustments that are capital in nature should be recognized in retained earnings, and adjustments that are revenue in nature should be recognized in profit or loss.

   c. Current adjustments should be recognized in profit or loss, and noncurrent adjustments should be recognized in retained earnings.

   d. All of the adjustments should be recognized directly in retained earnings or, if appropriate, in another category of equity.

45. A company is required to file quarterly financial statements with the U.S. Securities and Exchange Commission on Form 10-Q. The company operates in an industry that is not subject to seasonal fluctuations that could have a significant impact on its financial condition. In addition to the most recent quarter-end, for which of the following periods is the company required to present balance sheets on Form 10-Q?

   a. The end of the corresponding fiscal quarter of the preceding fiscal year.

   b. The end of the preceding fiscal year and the end of the corresponding fiscal quarter of the preceding fiscal year.

   c. The end of the preceding fiscal year.

   d. The end of the preceding fiscal year and the end of the prior two fiscal years.

46. A company is an accelerated filer that is required to file Form 10-K with the U.S. Securities and Exchange Commission (SEC). What is the maximum number of days after the company's fiscal year-end that the company has to file Form 10-K with the SEC?

   a. 60 days.
   b. 75 days.
   c. 90 days.
   d. 120 days.

ANSWER EXPLANATIONS FOR THE NEW FINANCIAL ACCOUNTING AND REPORTING MATERIAL

1. **(d)** The requirement is to identify the body that sets international accounting standards. Answer (d) is correct because the International Accounting Standards Board (IASB) issues International Financial Reporting Standards.

2. **(c)** The requirement is to identify the qualitative characteristics of relevance. Answer (c) is correct because the IASB *Framework* provides that relevance includes the qualities of predictive value, confirmatory value, and materiality. Answer (a) is incorrect because these are the characteristics of relevance in the FASB Concept Statements. Answer (b) is incorrect because these qualities are the characteristics of reliability in the FASB Concept Statements. Answer (d) is incorrect because comparability and consistency are a part of relevance in the IASB *Framework*.

3. **(b)** The requirement is to identify the element that is defined as increases in economic benefits in the form of inflows or enhancements of assets or decreases of liabilities that result in increases in equity other than those resulting from contributions from equity participants. Answer (b) is correct because the IASB *Framework* has five elements: asset, liability, equity, income, and expense. The definition given is that of income. Note that income includes both revenues and gains.

4. **(b)** The requirement is to identify the criteria under IFRS that must be met for an item to be included in financial statements. Answer (b) is correct because in order for an item to be recognized in the financial statements, IFRS requires that it meet the definition of an element and can be measured reliably.

5. **(c)** The requirement is to identify the revenue recognition method that must be used if the outcome of rendering services cannot be estimated reliably. Answer (c) is correct because if the outcome of rendering services cannot be measured reliably, IFRS requires use of the cost recovery method. Answer (a) is incorrect because the percentage-of-completion method is used when reliable estimates can be made. Answer (b) is incorrect because the completed contract method is not permissible under IFRS. Answer (d) is incorrect because the installment method is a revenue recognition method used under U.S. GAAP, not IFRS.

6. **(b)** The requirement is to identify the item that describes how changes in accounting principles are reported under IFRS. Answer (b) is correct because IFRS requires changes in accounting principles to be reported by giving retrospective application to the earliest period presented. Answer (a) is incorrect because a change in accounting estimate is accounted for on a prospective basis in the current and future periods. Answer (c) is incorrect because restatement is required for errors in the financial statements. Answer (d) is incorrect because cumulative adjustments on the income statement are not permitted.

7. **(b)** The requirement is to identify the circumstances in which Galaxy may present the note as a noncurrent liability. Answer (b) is correct because IFRS requires that Galaxy must have executed an agreement to refinance at the balance sheet date in order to classify the debt as a noncurrent liability. Inasmuch as no agreement existed at the balance sheet date, the note payable must be classified as a current liability. Therefore, answers (a), (c), and (d) are incorrect.

8. **(b)** The requirement is to identify the item required to be disclosed on the income statement. The correct answer is (b) because the income statement may be prepared by presenting expenses either by nature or by function. The minimum required disclosures on the income statement include income, finance costs, share of profits and losses using the equity method, tax expense, discontinued operations, profit or loss, noncontrolling interests in profits and losses, and the net profit (loss) attributable to equity holders of the parent. Therefore, answers (a), (c), and (d) are incorrect.

9. **(c)** The requirement is to identify the item that must be disclosed on the income statement under IFRS. Answer (c) is correct because gain or loss from extraordinary items is not allowed on an income statement prepared using IFRS. Answers (a), (b), and (d) are items that may be disclosed on the income statement.

10. **(b)** The requirement is to identify where finance costs are presented in the statement of cash flows. Answer (b) is correct because under IFRS finance costs (interest expense) may be reported in either the operating or financing section of the

statement of cash flows. However, once it is disclosed in a particular section, it must be reported on a consistent basis. Therefore, answers (a), (c), and (d), are incorrect.

11. **(d)** The requirement is to identify how the transaction should be reported on the statement of cash flows. Answer (d) is correct because this transaction did not involve an exchange of cash; therefore, it is not included on the statement of cash flows. IFRS requires that significant noncash transactions be reported in the notes to the financial statements. (Note that for U.S. GAAP, if there are only a few significant noncash transactions, they may be reported at the bottom of the statement of cash flows, or they may be reported in a separate schedule in the notes to the financial statements.)

12. **(a)** The requirement is to identify how cash advances and loans from bank overdrafts should be reported on the statement of cash flows. Answer (a) is correct because IFRS requires cash advances and loans from bank overdrafts to be classified as operating activities.

13. **(b)** The requirement is to identify the acceptable methods for presenting other comprehensive income. Answer (b) is correct because IFRS provides that comprehensive income may be presented either in one statement or in two statements. (U.S. GAAP allows the presentation in all three ways.)

14. **(c)** The requirement is to calculate the amount that should be presented for inventory. Answer (c) is correct because the lower of cost or net realizable value method requires net realizable value to be calculated as the estimated selling price less estimated costs of completion and estimated costs to sell. Therefore, the NRV is $850 ($900 – $50). The lower of cost or net realizable value is determined by comparing the cost of $1,000 to the NRV of $850, and using the lower amount. Inventory should be reported at $850.

15. **(a)** The requirement is to identify the models that may be used to value plant, property, and equipment. Answer (a) is correct because IFRS allows the use of the cost model or the revaluation model for reporting plant, property, and equipment.

16. **(c)** The requirement is to identify the true statement about the revaluation model. Answer

(c) is correct because IFRS does not provide requirements as to the frequency or date of revaluation of plant, property, and equipment.

17. **(c)** The requirement is to identify where the gain or loss should be presented. Answer (c) is correct because when the revaluation method is used for reporting plant, property, and equipment under IFRS, any gain or loss is recorded in a revaluation surplus account which is classified as other comprehensive income.

18. **(a)** The requirement is to identify the true statement regarding use of the fair value model. Answer (a) is correct because the fair value model requires that investment property be measured at fair value, and any changes in fair value are recognized in profit or loss of the period.

19. **(b)** The requirement is to identify the acceptable valuation methods for intangible assets. Answer (b) is correct because under IFRS, intangible assets can be measured using either the cost model or the revaluation model.

20. **(c)** The requirement is to determine the impairment gain or loss reported in the financial statements. Answer (c) is correct because if the cost model is used to record intangible assets, the impairment loss is recognized as a loss in the current period. If the cost model is used, a reversal of impairment losses may be recognized in the income statement up to the effects of the impairment loss previously recognized. Therefore, an impairment loss of $20,000 is recognized in 2009, and a gain is recognized in 2010 of $4,000.

21. **(c)** The requirement is to identify how the estimated loss should be disclosed in the financial statements. Answer (c) is correct because IFRS defines a provision as a liability that is uncertain in timing or amount. Provisions are made for estimated liabilities and recorded as a loss in earnings for the period if the outcome is probable and measurable. Answer (a) is incorrect because the loss should be recorded in the current period income statement. Answer (b) is incorrect because under IFRS, a contingency depends on some future uncertainty or event, is not probable that an outflow will be required to settle, or the amount cannot be measured with reliability. If an item qualifies as a contingency, it is disclosed in the notes to the financial statements. Answer (d) is incorrect because contingencies are disclosed in the footnotes.

22. **(c)** The requirement is to identify how Roland should report the land. Answer (c) is correct because IFRS provides that a contingent asset is a possible asset that arises from past events, and is confirmed only by the occurrence of uncertain future events that are not within the control of the reporting entity. A contingent asset is not recognized, but it is disclosed in the notes to the financial statements if the economic benefits are probable. Answer (a) is incorrect because it does not meet the definition of an asset. Answers (b) and (d) are incorrect because contingent assets are not recognized in the balance sheet.

23. **(c)** The requirement is to identify the method(s) that may be used to report the bonds. Answer (c) is correct because IFRS provides that financial liabilities may be reported at amortized cost or at the fair value through profit or loss (FVTPL). If FVTPL is elected, the resulting gain or loss is recognized in profit or loss for the period.

24. **(a)** The requirement is to identify the method that is used for defined benefit pension plans. Answer (a) is correct because IFRS requires the use of the projected-unit-credit method to calculate the present value of the defined benefit obligation. Answer (b) is incorrect because the benefit-years-of-service method is used in U.S. GAAP. Answers (c) and (d) are incorrect because these are not methods for reporting pension benefits.

25. **(c)** The requirement is to identify how the lease should be classified. Answer (c) is correct because IFRS requires a lease to be classified as a finance lease if substantially all the risks or benefits of ownership have been transferred to the lessee. Because the lease contains a bargain purchase option, it meets the criteria for a finance lease. Answer (a) is incorrect because the lease does not qualify as an operating lease since the risks and benefits of ownership have been transferred. Answer (b) is incorrect because U.S. GAAP uses the term "capital lease" whereas IFRS uses the term "finance lease." Answer (d) is incorrect because IFRS does not use the term "sales-type lease."

26. **(c)** The requirement is to identify how Santiago should account for the lease. Answer (c) is correct because IFRS provides that because land has an indefinite life, if title is not expected to pass by the end of the lease term, then the substantial risks and rewards of ownership do not

transfer. Thus, the lease should be separated into two components. The land should be recorded as an operating lease, and the building should be recorded as a finance lease.

27. **(b)** The requirement is to determine how deferred taxes should be presented. Answer (b) is correct because IFRS provides that the netting of deferred tax assets and liabilities may occur only if the accounts relate to the same taxing authority and the entity has a legal right to offset the taxes. Therefore, the deferred tax asset of $4,000 and the deferred tax liability of $3,000 related to France may be offset, which results in a $1,000 deferred tax asset. The deferred tax liability of $2,500 related to Germany may not be netted and is shown as a deferred tax liability of $2,500 on the balance sheet.

28. **(b)** The requirement is to identify the true statement about accounting for deferred taxes. Answer (b) is correct because IFRS does not permit deferred tax assets or liabilities to be classified as current. Therefore, deferred tax assets and liabilities are reported in the noncurrent section of the statement of financial position. Answer (a) is incorrect because deferred taxes may not be classified as current. Answers (c) and (d) are incorrect because deferred tax assets and liabilities may be netted only if there is a legal right to offset the amounts and they relate to the same taxing authority.

29. **(c)** The requirement is to identify how Logan should recognize the issuance of the bonds. Answer (c) is correct because IFRS provides that financial instruments with characteristics of both debt and equity are compound instruments and must be separated into their respective components. The liability is valued at the fair value at the date of issuance, and the residual value is assigned to the equity component. Therefore, the bond should be recorded at its fair value of $480,000, and an equity component should be recorded for 20,000. Answers (a), (b), and (d) are incorrect.

30. **(d)** The requirement is to identify how the gain is reported. Answer (d) is correct because IFRS requires that if an asset is classified as fair value through profit or loss, it is remeasured to fair value, and any profit or loss is recorded in the period. Therefore, Acadia should recognize a $3,000 gain in current earnings of the period. Answers (a), (b), and (c) are incorrect.

31. **(c)** The requirement is to identify the form used to file as an annual report with the SEC. Answer (c) is correct because the Form 10-K is the title of the annual report required to be filed annually by issuer companies. Answer (a) is incorrect because this is the title of the quarterly financial report. Answer (b) is incorrect because Form 8-K is the information report that may be filed any time during the year. Answer (d) is incorrect because a Form S-1 is an initial registration form for securities under the Securities Act of 1933.

32. **(d)** The requirement is to identify the content of the SEC Form 10-Q. Answer (d) is correct because the Form 10-Q presents reviewed quarterly information and other information about the company. Answer (a) is incorrect because the information is reviewed, not audited. Answer (b) is incorrect because this describes the Form 10-K. Answer (c) is incorrect because this describes the Form 8-K.

33. **(a)** The requirement is to select the item that describes when changes in accounting policies are permitted or required. Answer (a) is correct because changes are permitted if it will result in a more reliable and more relevant presentation of the financial statements.

34. **(b)** The requirement is to identify the circumstances that allow the entity to use the revaluation model. Answer (b) is correct because the revaluation method can be used only if there is an active market for the intangible asset.

35. **(d)** The requirement is to identify the criterion that must be met in order for an item to be recognized as an intangible asset other than goodwill. Answer (d) is correct because the asset must be identifiable and lack physical substance.

36. **(b)** The requirement is to determine the amount that should be recognized in the financial statements for the trademark. Answer (b) is correct because the trademark amount should include the purchase price ($100,000) plus the VAT taxes ($5,000) plus the legal cost incurred to register the trademark ($10,500), which is equal to $115,500. The research expenditures, training costs, and salaries should be expensed.

37. **(a)** The requirement is to identify the correct statement regarding the use of the revaluation model. Answer (a) is correct because when an asset is revalued, the entire class must be

revalued. Answer (b) is incorrect because the entire class must be revalued. Answer (c) is incorrect because there are no rules regarding the frequency of revaluation. Answer (d) is incorrect because the revaluation surplus is presented in other comprehensive income, not profit or loss.

38. **(c)** The requirement is to identify the assets for which the entity may use fair value as deemed cost upon adoption of IFRS. Answer (c) is correct because the entity may use fair value as deemed cost for any individual item of property, plant, and equipment.

39. **(b)** The requirement is to identify the first step within the hierarchy of guidance to which management refers when selecting accounting policies. Answer (b) is correct because the highest level in the hierarchy is an IFRS standard applicable to the transaction. Answers (a), (c), and (d) are incorrect because they all represent lower levels in the hierarchy.

40. **(d)** The requirement is to calculate depreciation for the asset. Answer (d) is correct because IFRS requires each major component to be depreciated over its respective useful life. The machinery cost $72,000 ($100,000 – $20,000 – $8,000) would be depreciated over 10 years. The drum would be depreciated over 5 years, and the inspection would be depreciated over 4 years. Therefore, depreciation would be calculated as $13,200 (($72,000/10) + ($20,000/5) + ($8,000/4)).

41. **(a)** The requirement is to identify the transition date. Answer (a) is correct because the "date of transition to IFRS" is defined as the beginning of the earliest period for which an entity presents full comparative information under IFRS.

42. **(c)** The requirement is to determine the amount that should be reported as inventory. Answer (c) is correct because under IFRS, inventory is reported at the lower of cost or net realizable value. Therefore, the amount is $90,000, which is the lower of $100,000 cost or $90,000 net realizable value.

43. **(a)** The requirement is to identify the minimum reporting requirement for a company that is preparing its first IFRS financial statements. Answer (a) is correct because IFRS requires three balance sheets, two income statements, two cash flow statements, and two statements of changes in equity for first-time adopters.

44. **(d)** The requirement is to identify how adjustments are reflected upon adoption of IFRS. Answer (d) is correct because upon first-time adoption of IFRS, any adjustments required to present the opening balances of the statement of financial position should be recognized directly in retained earnings or, if appropriate, in another category of equity.

45. **(c)** The requirement is to identify the balance sheet required in the Form 10-Q. Answer (c) is correct because the SEC requires that a Form 10-Q contain an interim balance sheet as of the end of the most recent fiscal quarter and a balance sheet as of the end of the preceding fiscal year. An interim balance sheet for the fiscal quarter of the preceding year does not need to be provided unless it is necessary for understanding the impact of seasonal fluctuations.

46. **(b)** The requirement is to identify the deadline for filing a Form 10-K for an accelerated filer. Answer (b) is correct because the maximum number of days for an accelerated filer to file a 10-K with the SEC is 75 days after the company's fiscal year-end. However, a large accelerated filer with $700 million of public float has a deadline of 60 days, and nonaccelerated filers have a deadline of 90 days.

EXAMPLES OF THE NEW TASK-BASED SIMULATIONS—FINANCIAL ACCOUNTING AND REPORTING

The simulations in the Financial Accounting and Reporting section of this manual also will help you review for the new smaller task-based simulations because many of the new task-based simulations are like single parts of the ones currently used.

Task-Based Simulation 1
(From Wiley Module 12)

Jasco Corporation is in its first year of operations. The company has pretax income of $400,000. The company has the following items recorded in its records. No estimated tax payments were made during 2009.

Premiums on life insurance of key officer	$10,000
Depreciation on tax return in excess of book depreciation	12,000
Interest on municipal bonds	5,300
Warranty expense	4,000
Actual warranty repairs	3,250
Bad debt expense	1,400
Beginning balance in allowance for uncollectible accounts	0
End balance for allowance for uncollectible accounts	800
Rent received in advance from clients that will be recognized evenly over the next three years	24,000
Tax rate for 2009 and future years	40%

Prepare the following schedule for the deferred tax amounts for the year. Choose items from this list:

Items	
Premium on life insurance	Warranties
Depreciation	Bad debts
Interest on municipal bonds	Rent received

Item	Difference between Taxable Amount and Income Statement Amount	Classification: Deferred Tax Asset Deferred Tax Liability	Current or Noncurrent	Deferred Tax Amount

Task-Based Simulation 2
(From Wiley Module 16)

Presented below are selected amounts from the separate unconsolidated financial statements of Poe Corp. and its 90%-owned subsidiary, Shaw Co., at December 31, 2010. Additional information follows.

	Poe	Shaw
Selected income statement amounts		
Sales	$710,000	$530,000
Cost of goods sold	490,000	370,000
Gain on sale of equipment	—	21,000
Earnings from investment in subsidiary	63,000	—
Interest expense	—	16,000
Depreciation	25,000	20,000
Selected balance sheet amounts		
Cash	$ 50,000	$ 15,000
Inventories	229,000	150,000
Equipment	440,000	360,000
Accumulated depreciation	(200,000)	(120,000)
Investment in Shaw	191,000	—
Investment in Shaw bonds	100,000	—
Discount on bonds	(9,000)	—
Bonds payable	—	(200,000)
Common stock	(100,000)	(10,000)
Additional paid-in capital	(250,000)	(40,000)
Retained earnings	(404,000)	(140,000)
Selected statement of retained earnings amounts		
Beginning balance, December 31, 2009	$272,000	$100,000
Net income	212,000	70,000
Dividends paid	80,000	30,000

Additional information

- On January 2, 2010, Poe, Inc. purchased 90% of Shaw Co.'s 100,000 outstanding common stock for cash of $155,000. On that date, the fair value of the noncontrolling interest was $1.70 per share. On that date, equity of Shaw's stockholders equaled $150,000, and the fair values of Shaw's identifiable assets and liabilities equaled their carrying amounts. Poe has accounted for the purchase as an acquisition.
- On January 3, 2010, Poe sold equipment with an original cost of $30,000 and a carrying value of $15,000 to Shaw for $36,000. The equipment had a remaining life of three years and was depreciated using the straight-line method by both companies.
- During 2010, Poe sold merchandise to Shaw for $60,000, which included a profit of $20,000. At December 31, 2010, half of this merchandise remained in Shaw's inventory.
- On December 31, 2010, Poe paid $91,000 to purchase 50% of the outstanding bonds issued by Shaw. The bonds mature on December 31, 2014, and were originally issued at par. The bonds pay interest annually on December 31 of each year, and the interest was paid to the prior investor immediately before Poe's purchase of the bonds.
- On September 4, 2010, Shaw paid cash dividends of $30,000.
- On December 31, 2010, Poe recorded its equity in Shaw's earnings.

1. On January 3, 2010, Poe sold equipment with an original cost of $30,000 and a carrying value of $15,000 to Shaw for $36,000. The equipment had a remaining life of three years and was depreciated using the straight-line method by both companies.
2. During 2010, Poe sold merchandise to Shaw for $60,000, which included a profit of $20,000. At December 31, 2010, half of this merchandise remained in Shaw's inventory.

3. On December 31, 2010, Poe paid $91,000 to purchase 50% of the outstanding bonds issued by Shaw. The bonds mature on December 31, 2014, and were originally issued at par. The bonds pay interest annually on December 31 of each year, and the interest was paid to the prior investor immediately before Poe's purchase of the bonds.

Task-Based Simulation 3
(From Wiley Module 12)

Using the authoritative literature from the accounting standards, identify the appropriate paragraph that provides the definition for deferred tax expense. Enter the exact section number and paragraphs and subparagraphs in the following fields.

FAS ACS | | | |

SOLUTIONS TO SIMULATIONS

Solution to Task-Based Simulation 1

Item	Difference between Taxable Amount and Income Statement Amount	Classification: Deferred Tax Asset Deferred Tax Liability	Current or Noncurrent	Deferred Tax Amount
Depreciation	12,000	Deferred tax liability	Noncurrent	4,800
Warranties	750	Deferred tax asset	Current	300
Bad debts	800	Deferred tax asset	Current	320
Rent received	8,000	Deferred tax asset	Current	3,200
Rent received	16,000	Deferred tax asset	Noncurrent	6,400

Explanation of Solutions

The adjustment to warranties is the difference between warranty expense deducted on the income statement and the actual warranty work performed during the period ($4,000 – $3,250 = $750). The adjustment to bad debt is the difference between bad debt expense subtracted on the balance sheet, and the actual bad debts written off during the period ($1,400 – $600 = $800). Note that rent received is taxable in the period received, and for deferred tax purposes, it must be fragmented into two components, current and noncurrent.

Solution to Task-Based Simulation 2
1.

Gain on equipment	21,000	
Accumulated depreciation		15,000
Equipment		6,000
Accumulated depreciation	7,000	
Depreciation expense		7,000

2.

Sales	60,000	
Cost of goods sold		50,000
Ending inventory		10,000

3.

Bonds payable	100,000	
Discount on bonds	9,000	
Gain on retirement of bonds		9,000
Investment in bonds		100,000

Explanation of Solutions

1. (**$14,000**) When preparing consolidated financial statements, the objective is to restate the accounts as if the intercompany transactions had not occurred. Therefore, the 2010 gain on sale of equipment of $21,000 ($36,000 – $15,000) must be eliminated, since the consolidated entity has not realized any gain. In addition, for consolidated statement purposes, 2010 depreciation is based on the original cost of the equipment to Poe. This elimination entry can be made in two separate entries. The first entry eliminated the gain, and restores the accumulated depreciation and equipment accounts as if the intercompany sale were never made. The second entry adjusts the current year depreciation expense to the amount that would have been recorded if the sale were never made. New depreciation is $36,000 ÷ 3 years = $12,000 for Shaw. Poe's depreciation was book value $15,000 ÷ 3 years = $5,000 per year. Therefore, depreciation expense must be adjusted by $12,000 – $5,000 = $7,000.

2. (**$10,000**) Unrealized profit in ending inventory arises when intercompany sales are made at prices above cost and the merchandise is not resold to third parties prior to year-end. The profit is unrealized because the inventory has not yet been sold outside the consolidated entity. In this case, one-half of the merchandise was left in Shaw's inventory at year-end. For the consolidated entity, one-half of the $20,000 profit has not been earned and must be eliminated.

3. (**$9,000**) When Poe purchased the bonds from an investor outside the consolidated entity, the bonds are viewed as retired from a consolidated viewpoint since there is no longer any obligation to an outside party. Therefore, the consolidated entity would recognize an ordinary gain of $9,000 ($100,000 carrying value of the bonds – $91,000 purchase price) on the retirement of the debt.

Solution to Task-Based Simulation 3

FAS ACS	740	10	30	4

4 REGULATION SECTION

The Content and Skills Specifications for the Regulation section of the CPA exam are the same as the current content specifications, with the following exceptions:

1. There is no significant new material on the Regulation section.
2. The topics of ethics and independence and responsibilities under the Sarbanes-Oxley Act have been moved from the Regulation section of the exam to the Auditing and Attestation section. Therefore, you do not need to study the first part of Module 21, Professional Responsibilities (dealing with ethics), and the section of Module 22, Securities Regulation, related to the Sarbanes-Oxley Act, and the related questions.
3. The section of Business Structures moved from BEC to REG. This includes Partnerships and Corporations.

EXAMPLES OF THE NEW TASK-BASED SIMULATIONS—REGULATION

The simulations in the Regulation section of this manual will also help you review for the new smaller task-based simulations because many of the new task-based simulations are like single parts of the ones currently used.

Task-Based Simulation 1
(From Wiley Module 33)

Frank and Dale Cumack are married and filing a joint 2009 income tax return. During 2009, Frank, 65, was retired from government service and Dale, 55, was employed as a university instructor. In 2009, the Cumacks contributed all of the support to Dale's father, Jacques, an unmarried French citizen and French resident who had no gross income.

For items 1 through 10, select the correct amount of income, loss, or adjustment to income that should be reported on page 1 of the Cumacks' 2009 Form 1040—Individual Income Tax Return to arrive at the adjusted gross income for each separate transaction. A tax treatment may be selected once, more than once, or not at all.

Any information contained in an item is unique to that item and is not to be incorporated in your calculations when answering other items.

Selections

A. $0	D. $3,000	G. $5,000	J. $25,000	M. $150,000
B. $1,000	E. $3,500	H. $9,000	K. $ 30,000	
C. $2,000	F. $4,000	I. $10,000	L. $125,000	

	(A)	(B)	(C)	(D)	(E)	(F)	(G)	(H)	(I)	(J)	(K)	(L)	(M)
1. During 2009, Dale received a $30,000 cash gift from her aunt.	○	○	○	○	○	○	○	○	○	○	○	○	○
2. Dale contributed $3,500 to her traditional Individual Retirement Account (IRA) on January 15, 2009. In 2009, she earned $60,000 as a university instructor. During 2009, the Cumacks were not active participants in an employer's qualified pension or annuity plan.	○	○	○	○	○	○	○	○	○	○	○	○	○

	(A)	(B)	(C)	(D)	(E)	(F)	(G)	(H)	(I)	(J)	(K)	(L)	(M)
3. In 2009, the Cumacks received a $1,000 federal income tax refund.	○	○	○	○	○	○	○	○	○	○	○	○	○
4. During 2009, Frank, a 50% partner in Diske General Partnership, received a $4,000 guaranteed payment from Diske for services that he rendered to the partnership that year.	○	○	○	○	○	○	○	○	○	○	○	○	○
5. In 2009, Frank received $10,000 as beneficiary of his deceased brother's life insurance policy.	○	○	○	○	○	○	○	○	○	○	○	○	○
6. Dale's employer pays 100% of the cost of all employees' group-term life insurance under a qualified plan. Policy cost is $5 per $1,000 of coverage. Dale's group-term life insurance coverage equals $450,000.	○	○	○	○	○	○	○	○	○	○	○	○	○
7. In 2009, Frank won $5,000 at a casino and had $2,000 in gambling losses.	○	○	○	○	○	○	○	○	○	○	○	○	○
8. During 2009, the Cumacks received $1,000 interest income associated with a refund of their prior years' federal income tax.	○	○	○	○	○	○	○	○	○	○	○	○	○
9. In 2009, the Cumacks sold their first and only residence for $400,000. They purchased their home in 1992 for $50,000 and have lived there since then. There were no other capital gains, losses, or capital loss carryovers. The Cumacks do not intend to buy another residence.	○	○	○	○	○	○	○	○	○	○	○	○	○
10. In 2009, Zeno Corp. declared a stock dividend and Dale received one additional share of Zeno common stock for three shares of Zeno common stock that she held. The stock that Dale received had a fair market value of $9,000. There was no provision to receive cash instead of stock.	○	○	○	○	○	○	○	○	○	○	○	○	○

Task-Based Simulation 2
(From Wiley Module 33)

Research

Assume that the Cumacks' automobile was stolen in 2010. The automobile was uninsured for theft and had a fair market value of $7,000, and an adjusted basis of $10,000. Which code section and subsection provide the limitations that apply to the deductibility of the Cumacks' uninsured theft loss? Indicate the reference to that citation in the shaded boxes below.

Section	Subsection
§ ▮	(▮)

Task-Based Simulation 3
(From Wiley Module 36)

Capital Corp., an accrual-basis calendar-year C corporation, began operations on January 2, 2007. Capital timely filed its 2009 federal income tax return on March 15, 2010.

The following items each require two responses:

- For each item below, determine the amount of Capital's 2009 Schedule M-1 adjustment necessary to reconcile book income to taxable income. On the CPA exam, a list of numeric answers would be presented for the candidate to select from.
- In addition, determine if the Schedule M-1 adjustment necessary to reconcile book income to taxable income increases, decreases, or has no effect on Capital's 2009 taxable income. An answer may be selected once, more than once, or not at all.

Selections	
I.	Increases Capital's 2009 taxable income.
D.	Decreases Capital's 2009 taxable income.
N.	Has no effect on Capital's 2009 taxable income.

	Amount of Adjustment	(I)	(D)	(N)
1. At its corporate inception in 2007, Capital incurred and paid $40,100 in organizational costs for legal fees to draft the corporate charter. In 2007, Capital correctly elected, for book purposes, to expense the organizational costs and to amortize the organizational expenditures over the minimum allowable period on its federal income tax return. For 2009, no organizational costs were deducted on its books.	_____	○	○	○
2. Capital's 2009 disbursements included $10,000 for reimbursed employees' expenses for business meals and entertainment. The reimbursed expenses met the conditions of deductibility and were properly substantiated under an accountable plan. The reimbursement was not treated as employee compensation.	_____	○	○	○
3. Capital's 2009 disbursements included $15,000 for life insurance premium expense paid for its executives as part of their taxable compensation. Capital is neither the direct nor the indirect beneficiary of the policy, and the amount of the compensation is reasonable.	_____	○	○	○
4. In 2009, Capital increased its allowance for uncollectible accounts by $10,000. No bad debt was written off in 2009.	_____	○	○	○

SOLUTIONS TO SIMULATIONS

Solution to Task-Based Simulation 1

	(A)	(B)	(C)	(D)	(E)	(F)	(G)	(H)	(I)	(J)	(K)	(L)	(M)
1. During 2009, Dale received a $30,000 cash gift from her aunt.	●	○	○	○	○	○	○	○	○	○	○	○	○
2. Dale contributed $3,500 to her traditional Individual Retirement Account (IRA) on January 15, 2009. In 2009, she earned $60,000 as a university instructor. During 2009, the Cumacks were not active participants in an employer's qualified pension or annuity plan.	○	○	○	○	●	○	○	○	○	○	○	○	○
3. In 2009, the Cumacks received a $1,000 federal income tax refund.	●	○	○	○	○	○	○	○	○	○	○	○	○

		(A)	(B)	(C)	(D)	(E)	(F)	(G)	(H)	(I)	(J)	(K)	(L)	(M)
4.	During 2009, Frank, a 50% partner in Diske General Partnership, received a $4,000 guaranteed payment from Diske for services that he rendered to the partnership that year.	○	○	○	○	○	●	○	○	○	○	○	○	○
5.	In 2009, Frank received $10,000 as beneficiary of his deceased brother's life insurance policy.	●	○	○	○	○	○	○	○	○	○	○	○	○
6.	Dale's employer pays 100% of the cost of all employees' group-term life insurance under a qualified plan. Policy cost is $5 per $1,000 of coverage. Dale's group-term life insurance coverage equals $450,000.	○	○	●	○	○	○	○	○	○	○	○	○	○
7.	In 2009, Frank won $5,000 at a casino and had $2,000 in gambling losses.	○	○	○	○	○	○	●	○	○	○	○	○	○
8.	During 2009, the Cumacks received $1,000 interest income associated with a refund of their prior years' federal income tax.	○	●	○	○	○	○	○	○	○	○	○	○	○
9.	In 2009, the Cumacks sold their first and only residence for $400,000. They purchased their home in 1992 for $50,000 and have lived there since then. There were no other capital gains, losses, or capital loss carryovers. The Cumacks do not intend to buy another residence.	●	○	○	○	○	○	○	○	○	○	○	○	○
10.	In 2009, Zeno Corp. declared a stock dividend and Dale received one additional share of Zeno common stock for three shares of Zeno common stock that she held. The stock that Dale received had a fair market value of $9,000. There was no provision to receive cash instead of stock.	●	○	○	○	○	○	○	○	○	○	○	○	○

Solution to Task-Based Simulation 2

Internal Revenue Code Section 165, subsection (h), provides that an individual's personal casualty loss is allowable to the extent that it exceeds $100, and that a net personal casualty loss is deductible to the extent that it exceeds 10% of adjusted gross income.

Section	Subsection
§ 165	(h)

Solution to Task-Based Simulation 3

		Amount of Adjustment	(I)	(D)	(N)
1.	At its corporate inception in 2007, Capital incurred and paid $40,100 in organizational costs for legal fees to draft the corporate charter. In 2007, Capital correctly elected, for book purposes, to expense the organizational costs and to amortize the organizational expenditures over the minimum allowable period on its federal income tax return. For 2009, no organizational costs were deducted on its books.	$ 2,340	○	●	○
2.	Capital's 2009 disbursements included $10,000 for reimbursed employees' expenses for business meals and entertainment. The reimbursed expenses met the conditions of deductibility and were properly substantiated under an accountable plan. The reimbursement was not treated as employee compensation.	$ 5,000	●	○	○

	Amount of Adjustment	(I)	(D)	(N)
3. Capital's 2009 disbursements included $15,000 for life insurance premium expense paid for its executives as part of their taxable compensation. Capital is neither the direct nor the indirect beneficiary of the policy, and the amount of the compensation is reasonable.	$0	○	○	●
4. In 2009, Capital increased its allowance for uncollectible accounts by $10,000. No bad debt was written off in 2009.	$10,000	●	○	○

Explanation of Solutions

1. **($2,340; D)** $5,000 of Capital's organizational costs of $40,100 would have been deducted in 2007 with remainder amortized over 180 months (15 years) for tax purposes. As a result, the tax amortization of organizational costs results in a tax deduction of $35,100 × 12/180 = $2,340 for 2009. Since no organizational costs were deducted per books for 2009, a Schedule M-1 decrease adjustment is necessary for the $2,340 difference.

2. **($5,000; I)** Only 50% of reimbursed employees' expenses for business meals and entertainment is deductible for tax purposes. As a result, an M-1 increase adjustment of $5,000 is necessary to reflect the fact that 50% of the $10,000 of reimbursed business meals and entertainment that was deducted for book purposes is not deductible for tax purposes.

3. **($0; N)** The $15,000 of life insurance premiums treated as reasonable compensation is fully deductible for both book and tax purposes and no M-1 adjustment is necessary.

4. **($10,000; I)** The reserve method of accounting for bad debts is not allowed for tax purposes. Instead, a bad debt deduction can be taken only when a specific debt is determined to be uncollectible. Since no bad debt was written off during 2009, an M-1 increase adjustment is necessary for the $10,000 addition to the allowance for uncollectible accounts for 2009.

RESHUFFLED MATERIAL—REGULATION SECTION

This represents material that was previously being tested on the Uniform CPA Exam but was covered in areas other than Regulation.

This section came from Wiley Module 38, Business Structures which was previously tested in the BEC Section.

Business Structure

Overview

A sole proprietorship has only one owner, which creates both advantages and disadvantages. A partnership is an association of two or more persons to carry on a business as co-owners for profit. The major areas tested on partnerships are: the characteristics of a partnership; comparisons with other structures; rights and liabilities of the partnership itself; the rights, duties, and liabilities of the partners among themselves and to third parties; the allocation of profits and losses; and the rights of various parties, including creditors, upon dissolution.

The law of joint ventures is similar to that of partnerships with some exceptions. Note that the joint venture is more limited in scope than the partnership form of business. The former is typically organized to carry out one single business undertaking or a series of related undertakings; the latter is formed to conduct ongoing business.

Subchapter S corporations are those corporations that elect to be taxed similar to partnerships under Subchapter S. Corporations that do not make this election are called Subchapter C corporations. In both cases, a corporation is an artificial person that is created by or under law and that operates under a common name through its elected management. It is a legal entity, separate and distinct from its shareholders. The corporation has the authority vested in it by statute and its corporate charter. The candidate should understand the characteristics and advantages of the corporate form over other forms of business organization.

Basic to preparation for questions on corporation law is an understanding of:

- The liabilities of a promoter who organizes a new corporation.
- The liability of shareholders.
- The liability of the corporation with respect to the preincorporation contracts made by the promoter.
- The fiduciary relationship of the promoter to the stockholders and to the corporation.
- The various circumstances under which a stockholder may be liable for the debts of the corporation.
- The rights of shareholders particularly concerning payment of dividends.

- The rights and duties of officers, directors, and other agents or employees of the corporation to the corporation, to stockholders, and to third persons.
- Subscriptions.
- The procedures necessary to merge, consolidate, or otherwise change the corporate structure.

State laws are now widely based on the Revised Business Corporation Act upon which changes to this module are based.

A. Nature of Sole Proprietorships

1. There is only one owner of business.
   a. Business is not a separate legal entity apart from owner.
   b. Owner does not share power or decision making with other owners.
2. Advantages over other business structures:
   a. Sole proprietorship is the simplest type of business structure.
      (1) Easy to form and to operate.
         (a) Federal or state governments do not require formal filing or approval to begin operation.
            1] If business is operating under name other than that of the sole proprietor, most states require that it file fictitious name statement with government.
   b. Business can be sold without need to obtain approval from others such as shareholders or partners.
   c. Owner has right to make all business decisions such as direction company should go, who to hire or fire, and so on.
   d. If the business generates profit, the sole owner need not share it with other owners or investors.
   e. The profits of the business are taxed on the personal tax return of the owner—profits are taxed only once.
3. Disadvantages over other business structures:
   a. If company has loss, the sole proprietor suffers all of it.
   b. Sole proprietorship cannot obtain capital from partners, shareholders, and so on.
      (1) Capital is limited by funds the owner has or can borrow.
   c. Sole proprietor has unlimited personal liability.

B. Nature of Partnerships

1. A partnership is an association of two or more persons to carry on a business as co-owners for profit.
   a. The phrase "to carry on a business" includes almost every trade, occupation, or profession.
      (1) It does not include passive co-ownership of property (e.g., joint tenants of a piece of land).
      (2) Partnerships do not include nonprofit unincorporated associations (e.g., labor unions, charitable organizations, clubs).
   b. Co-ownership of the "business" (and not merely of assets used in a business) is an important element in determining whether a partnership exists.
      (1) The most important and necessary element of co-ownership (and thereby partnership) is profit sharing.
         (a) Need not be equal but is treated equally unless otherwise stated.
         (b) Receipt of a share of profits is prima facie evidence (raises a presumption) of a partnership.
            1] Presumption rebutted by establishing that profit sharing was only for payment of debt, interest on loan, services performed, rent, and so on.
      (2) Another important element of co-ownership is joint control.
         (a) Each partner has an equal right to participate in management. Right to manage may be contracted away to a managing partner.
      (3) Under Revised Uniform Partnership Act, now adopted by majority of states, partner is no longer co-owner of partnership property.
2. A partnership relationship creates a fiduciary relationship between partners.
   a. A fiduciary relationship arises because each partner is an agent for partnership and for each other in partnership business.
3. A partnership relationship is based on contract but arrangements may be quite informal.
   a. Agreement can be inferred from conduct (e.g., allowing someone to share in management and profits may result in partnership even though actual intent to become partner is missing).

4. A partnership heavily on agency law because each partner is an agent as well as a principal of partnership.
   a. Most rules can be changed in individual cases by agreement between parties affected (e.g., rights and duties between partners).

      Example: A, B, and C form a partnership in which all three partners agree that A is liable for all of the product liability cases against the partnership. This agreement is enforceable between A, B, and C but not against other parties that never agreed to this. Therefore, as long as A is solvent, B and C can collect from A even though a third party recovers from all of them on a product liability problem.

5. Generally, any person (entity) who has the capacity to contract may become a partner:
   a. Corporations.
   b. Minors—but contract of partnership is voidable.
   c. Partnerships can become partners.
6. Common characteristics of partnerships:
   a. Limited duration.
   b. Transfer of ownership requires agreement.
   c. May sue and be sued as separate legal entities.
   d. Unlimited liability of partners for partnership debts.
   e. Ease of formation, can be very informal.
   f. Partnership does not pay federal income tax; partners must include their share of partnership operations on their tax returns.

C. Types of Partnerships and Partners

1. Limited partnership is a special statutory relationship consisting of one or more general partners and one or more limited partners.
   a. Limited partners contribute capital only and usually are liable only to that extent (analogous to shareholder of a corporation).
   b. Limited partners do not take part in management of partnership.
2. General partners are ones who share in management of business and have unlimited liability to creditors of partnership.
   a. Silent partner does not help manage partnership but still has unlimited liability.

D. Formation of Partnership

1. By agreement, express or implied.
   a. Agreement to share profits is prima facie evidence that partnership exists.
      (1) Need not agree to share losses because agreement to share profits assumes sharing of losses.
      (2) Sharing of gross receipts does not establish partnership.
   b. Partnership is not implied if profits received for some other purpose such as for payment of debt, wages, or lease.
2. Creation of a partnership may be very informal, either oral or written.
   a. Written partnership agreement not required unless within Statute of Frauds (e.g., partnership that cannot be completed within one year).

      Example: A, B, and C form a partnership that, although they expect it to last for several years, has no time period specified. This partnership agreement may be oral.

      Example: X, Y, and Z organize XYZ partnership that by agreement will last at least five years. This partnership agreement must be in writing.

      (1) Usually wise to have in writing even if not required by statute or contract law.
   b. Filing not required.
3. Articles of copartnership (partnership agreement)—not legally necessary but a good idea to have.
4. Fictitious name statutes require partners to register fictitious or assumed names.
   a. Failure to comply does not invalidate partnership but may result in fine.
   b. The purpose is to allow third parties to know who is in partnership.

E. Partner's Rights

1. Partnership agreement, whether oral or written, would be controlling.
   a. The following rules (2-8) are used unless partnership agreement states otherwise.

2. Partnership interest.
   a. Refers to partner's right to share in profits and return of contribution on dissolution.
   b. Is considered personal property.
      (1) Even if partnership property is real estate.
   c. Does not include specific partnership property, merely right to use it for partnership purposes.
   d. Is freely assignable without other partner's consent.
      (1) Assignee is not substituted as a partner without consent of all other partners.
      (2) Assignee does **not** receive right to manage partnership, to have an accounting, to inspect books, to possess or own any individual partnership property—merely receives rights in the assigning partner's share of profits and return of partner's capital contribution (unless partners agree otherwise).
         (a) Typically, assignments are made to secure a loan
            Example: C, a CPA, wishes to obtain a large loan. He is a member of a CPA firm and assigns rights in his partnership to the bank to secure the loan.
      (3) Assignor remains liable as a partner.
      (4) Does not cause dissolution unless assignor also withdraws.
3. Partnership property:
   a. Includes:
      (1) Property acquired with partnership funds unless different intent is shown.
      (2) Property is not acquired in partnership name is, however, partnership property if:
         (a) Partner acquires title to it in his/her capacity as a partner, or
         (b) Property acquired with partnership funds.
   b. Not assignable or subject to attachment individually, only by a claim on partnership.
      (1) Property may be assigned by agreement of all partners.
      (2) Any partner can assign or sell property if for the apparent purpose of carrying on the business of the partnership in the usual way.
   c. Upon partner's death, his/her estate is entitled to deceased partner's share of profits and capital but not to any specific partnership property.
      (1) Remaining partners have duty to account to the heirs of the deceased for value of interest.
      (2) Heirs are not automatically partners.
4. Participate in management:
   a. Right to participate equally in management.
      (1) Ordinary business decisions made by a majority vote.
      (2) Unanimous consent is needed to make fundamental changes.
   b. Power to act as an agent for partnership in partnership business.
   c. Also has right to inspect books and have full knowledge of partnership affairs.
   d. Silent partner is one who does not help manage.
      (1) Still has personal, unlimited liability.
5. Share in profits and losses:
   a. Profits and losses are shared equally unless agreement specifies otherwise.
      (1) Even if contributed capital is not equal.
      (2) For example, agreement may specify one partner to receive greater share of profits for doing more work, and so on, while losses still shared equally.
   b. If partners agree on unequal profit sharing but are silent on loss sharing, losses are shared per the profit-sharing proportions.
      (1) Partners may choose to share losses in a different proportion from profits.
         Example: A, B, and C form a partnership with capital contributions as follows: A, $100,000; B, $20,000; and C, $20,000. Their agreement is silent on how to split profits or losses. Therefore, profits and losses will be split equally.
         Example: Same as above except that they agree to give A 50% of the profits and B and C each get 25%. Profits as well as losses will be split based on these stated percentages.
         Example: Assume that A, B, and C agree to a 50%, 25%, 25% split if there is a profit but to a 20%, 40%, 40% split, respectively, for any annual losses. If there is a $100,000 annual loss, A will suffer $20,000 and B and C each will suffer $40,000 of the loss.
6. Other rights:
   a. Indemnification for expenses incurred on behalf of the partnership.

    b. General partners may be creditors, secured or unsecured, of the partnership.

        (1) May receive interest on loans.

        (2) No interest on capital contributions unless stated in partnership agreement.

    c. No right to salary for work performed because this is a duty unless they agree otherwise.

        (1) It is common for partners to agree to pay salaries, especially if only one or two do most of the work.

    d. May obtain formal accounting of partnership affairs.

        (1) Each partner partner has the right if used reasonably.

7. Every partner owes a fiduciary duty to every other partner (this is important).

    a. Each partner must act in best interest of others.

        (1) Each partner may pursue own self-interest as long as it is not competition and does not interfere with partner's duty to partnership.

        (2) Any wrongly derived profits must be held by partner for others.

        (3) Each partner must abide by partnership agreement.

        (4) Each party is liable to the other partners for liability caused by going beyond actual authority.

8. Incoming partners new to partnership have same rights as previous partners.

    a. Admitting a new partner requires consent of all partners unless otherwise stated in the partnership agreement.

    b. Profit sharing, loss sharing, and capital contributions are by agreement between all partners.

    c. A partnership may also be partner of separate partnership if all partners agree.

F. *Relationship to Third Parties*

1. Partners are agents of the partnership.

    a. Partners can bind partnership to contracts with third parties.

        (1) Even where no actual authority, partners can bind partnership where there is apparent (ostensible) authority, authority by estoppel, or implied authority.

           (a) Apparent (ostensible) or purported partnership is created when parties misrepresent to others that they are partners.

               1] Similar in concept to apparent (ostensible) agency.

               2] Partnership may make public recording of limitation on partner authority or statement of partnership authority to limit possible liability.

               3] Individuals are called apparent (ostensible) partners and are liable to third parties as if they were actual partners.

                   a] Individuals are usually liable even if this allows others to misrepresent him/her as partner

           (b) Partnership by estoppel is created when parties misrepresent to others that they are partners and others are hurt as they rely on this.

               1] Many courts treat partnership by estoppel and apparent partnership as essentially the same.

               2] Not actual partners but liable as if they were actual partners.

               3] Individuals are called partners by estoppel.

                 Example: A, B, and C form a partnership to sell widgets. Contrary to the wishes of B and C, A decides to buy in the partnership name some "super-widgets" from T. Even though A did not have actual authority to buy these, T can enforce the contract based on apparent authority. A, of course, breached his fiduciary duty to B and C.

    b. Partners normally have implied authority to buy and sell goods, receive money, and pay debts for partnership.

        (1) Each partner is agent of partnership to carry out typical business of firm or business of the kind carried on by partnership.

        (2) Third parties can rely on implied authority even though secret limitations may exist that were unknown to those third parties.

            Example: A and B have a partnership to sell furniture in a retail outlet. A and B agreed that neither would buy more than $10,000 of furniture from suppliers without the consent of the other. A, however, buys $20,000 of furniture from a regular supplier that was unaware of this limitation. When the supplier attempts to deliver, B refuses the furniture. Since A had implied authority, the supplier can enforce the contract for the full $20,000.

   c. Partnership is not liable for acts of partners outside of express, implied, or apparent authority.

      Example: A partner of a hardware store attempts to buy some real estate in the name of the partnership. Here apparent authority does not exist.

   d. Partnership is liable for partner's torts committed in course and scope of business and for partner's breach of trust (i.e., misapplication of third party's funds).

      Example: A partner takes a third party's money on behalf of the partnership to invest in government bonds. Instead he uses it himself to build an addition onto his home.

      Example: A partner, while driving on partnership business, injures a third party. If the partner is negligent, the partnership is also liable.

2. Unanimous consent of partners is needed unless otherwise stated in the partnership agreement (so no implied authority) for:

   a. Admission of a new partner.

   b. Amending the partnership agreement.

   c. Assignment of partnership property.

   d. Making partnership a surety or guarantor.

   e. Admitting to a claim against partnership in court.

   f. Submitting partnership claim to arbitrator.

   g. Any action outside the scope of the partnership business.

3. Partner's liability is personal, that is, extends to all his/her personal assets (not just investment in partnership) to cover all debts and liabilities of partnership.

   a. Partners are jointly and severally liable for all debts.

     (1) The Revised Uniform Partnership Act (RUPA) requires creditors to first attempt collection from partnership before partners unless partnership is bankrupt.

   b. Partners may split losses or liability between themselves according to any proportion agreed on; however, third parties can still hold each partner personally liable despite agreement.

     (1) If any partner pays more than his/her agreed share, he/she can get reimbursed from other partners.

       Example: X, Y, and Z as partners agreed to split losses 10%, 20%, and 70% respectively. A third party recovers $100,000 from X only based on a partnership tort. X can get $20,000 from Y and $70,000 from Z so that she ends up paying only her 10%.

       Example: Same as before except that Y is insolvent. X can recover the proportionate share from Z or $87,500 ($100,000 × 70%/80%).

       Example: A, B, and C are partners who agree to split losses 10%, 10%, and 80%, respectively. Y sues the partners for a tort based on the partnership business. C takes out bankruptcy. Y can recover from A and B and is not bound by the agreement between A, B, and C.

   c. New partners coming into a partnership are liable for existing debts only to the extent of their capital contributions:

     (1) Unless new partners assume personal liability for old debts.

   d. Partners withdrawing are liable for existing liabilities.

   e. Partners withdrawing are liable for subsequent liabilities unless notice of withdrawal or death is given to third parties.

     (1) Actual notice must be given to creditors who previously dealt with partnership.

     (2) Constructive (e.g., published) notice is sufficient for others who merely knew of partnership's existence.

   f. Estates of deceased partners are liable for partners' debts.

   g. Liability of withdrawing partner may be limited by agreement between partners but agreement is not binding on third parties (unless they join in on agreement).

   h. Partners are not criminally liable unless they personally participate in some way or unless statute prescribes liability to all members of management (e.g., environment regulation or sale of alcohol to a minor).

G. *Termination of a Partnership*

1. Termination happens when:

   a. Dissolution occurs (i.e., partners stop carrying on business together).

    b. Winding up takes place:

       (1) Collecting partnership assets and paying partnership debts.

2. Dissolution can occur by:

    a. Prior agreement (e.g., partnership agreement).

    b. Present agreement of partners.

    c. By decree of court in such cases as:

       (1) Partner continually or seriously breaches partnership agreement.

       (2) Partner guilty of conduct that harms business.

    d. Assignment, selling, or pledging of partnership interest does **not** cause dissolution even if there is no consent of other partners.

    e. Under RUPA, unlike previous law, partner's withdrawal, death, or bankruptcy does **not** automatically cause dissolution of partnership.

       (1) Partners that own majority of partnership may choose to continue general partnership within 90 days of partners' withdrawal, death, or bankruptcy.

       (2) Any partner has power to dissociate from partnership even if partner had agreed not to but is liable for breach of such a contract; dissociation can result from:

          (a) Notice to the partnership by the partner.

          (b) An event set forth in the agreement.

          (c) Expulsion of the partner under the terms of the agreement.

          (d) Expulsion of the partner by unanimous vote of the other partners because of issues with the partner (e.g., business cannot be legally conducted with the partner involved).

          (e) Court order.

          (f) Incapacity.

          (g) Death.

          (h) Insolvency.

          (i) Distribution of the entire interest by a trust or estate.

3. Winding up:

    a. Remaining partners may elect to wind up and terminate partnership or not wind up and continue business.

4. Order of distribution upon termination of general partnership:

    a. To creditors including partners as creditors.

    b. Capital contributions and profits or losses are calculated together.

       (1) Partners may receive money or even need to pay money at this stage.

5. Partners are personally liable to partnership for any deficits in their capital accounts and to creditors for insufficiency of partnership assets.

    a. Priority between partnership creditors and partner's personal creditors.

       (1) Partnership creditors have first priority to partnership assets; any excess goes to personal creditors.

       (2) Usually, personal creditors have first priority to personal assets; any excess goes to partnership creditors.

6. Partners can bind other partners and the partnership on contracts until third parties who have known of the partnership are given notice of dissolution.

    a. Actual notice must be given to third parties who have dealt with the partnership prior to dissolution.

    b. Constructive notice (e.g., notice in newspaper) is adequate for third parties who have only known of the partnership.

7. Dissolution of a general partnership does not require the filing of a dissolution document with the state.

H. *Limited Partnerships*

1. Revised Uniform Limited Partnership Act (RULPA) is designed to modernize law because today many limited partnerships are very large with many limited partners.

    a. RULPA has been adopted by majority of states.

2. Creation of limited partnership:

    a. Unlike general partnership that requires no formal procedures to create it, limited partnership requires compliance with state statute to create it.

    b. Certificate of limited partnership must be filed with secretary of state; if the partnership does not, it will be treated as a general partnership.

(1) The certificate be signed by all general partners and include names of all general partners:
   (a) Name and address of the limited partnership.
   (b) Name and address of its agent.
   (c) Latest date the partnership is to dissolve.
   (d) Names of limited partners not required.
   (e) The certificate of partnership must be amended to show any additions or deletions of general partners.
      1] The certificate must also be amended if any general partner becomes aware of false information in certificate

c. A limited partnership at least one general partner and at least one limited partner.
   (1) Sole general partner may be a corporation.
   (2) Liability of limited partner(s) is limited to amount of capital contributions (with some exceptions below).

d. General or limited partners' capital contributions may not be only in cash, services performed, or property but also now may be in promise to perform services, to give cash, or property in future.

e. Name of limited partner may not be used in name of limited partnership unless name is also name of a general partner.
   (1) If a limited partner **knowingly or negligently** allows his/her name to be part of limited partnership name, then the partner is liable to creditors who extend credit to business (unless creditors knew that limited partner was not a general partner).

f. "Limited partnership" words must be in firm's name.

g. Partnership interests may be purchased with cash, property, services rendered, promissory note.

h. Defective formation of limited partnership causes limited partners to be liable as general partners.
   (1) Under RULPA, partner who believes he or she is limited partner may avoid liability of general partner if upon learning of defective formation either:
      (a) Withdraws from partnership and renounces all future profits, or
      (b) Files amendment or new certificate that cures defect.
   (2) However, limited partner is liable for past transactions before withdrawal or amendment to any third party transacting business while believing partner was general partner.

i. A foreign limited partnership is one doing business in given state but was formed in another state.
   (1) Foreign limited partnership must register with secretary of state before doing business in state.

3. Rights of partners in limited partnership:
  a. General partners manage partnership.
  b. Limited partners invest.
   (1) Limited partner who substantially manages partnership like general partner obtains liability like general partner to third parties who believed he/she was general partner.
   (2) Limited partner is allowed to do following without risking loss of limited liability:
      (a) Acting as an agent or employee of limited
      (b) Consulting with and advising general. partner or limited partnership about partnership business.
      (c) Approving or disapproving amendments to limited partnership agreement.
      (d) Voting on dissolution or winding up of limited partnership.
      (e) Voting on loans of limited partnership.
      (f) Voting on change in nature of business.
      (g) Voting on removal of a general partner.
      (h) Bringing derivative lawsuit on behalf of limited partnership.
      (i) Being surety for limited partnership.
  c. Profit or loss sharing:
   (1) Profits or losses are shared as agreed on in certificate agreement.
      (a) Losses and any liability are limited to capital contributions for limited partners.
      (b) If no agreement on profit and losses exists, then profits or losses shared based on percentages of capital contributions.
         1] Note how this differs from a general partnership in which losses and profits are shared equally unless agreed otherwise.
  d. Admission of new partner requires written agreement of all partners unless partnership agreement provides otherwise.

e. Limited partnership interests may be assigned in part or in whole.
   (1) If all interest is assigned, then ceases to be partner unless otherwise agreed.
   (2) Assignee becomes actual limited partner if all other partners consent or if assignor gives assignee that status pursuant to authority (if given in certificate of partnership).
      (a) In such case, former limited partner is generally not released from liability to limited partnership.
   (3) Assignment does not cause dissolution of partnership.
f. Limited partners have right to inspect partnership books and tax return information.
g. A partner can be a limited and general partner at same time.
   (1) Limited partner has rights, powers, and liability of a general partner.
   (2) Limited partner rights against other partners with respect to contribution as a limited partner and also as a general partner.
h. Limited partners may own competing interests.
i. Limited partner may be a secured or unsecured creditor of partnership.
j. Limited partner may not withdraw capital contribution if it impairs creditors.

4. Duties of partners:
a. General partners owe fiduciary duties to general and limited partners. Limited partners in general do not owe fiduciary duties since they do not engage in the management of the business.

5. Dissolution of limited partnership takes place upon the following events:
a. Completion of time period specified in certificate.
b. Event specified in partnership agreement.
c. Unanimous written consent of all partners.
d. Dissolution of court decree when not practical to continue partnership.
e. Event that causes partnership business to be illegal.
f. Withdrawal of general partner by retirement, removal, bankruptcy (but not mere insolvency), fraud against other partners, insanity, death:
   (1) Unless all partners agree in writing to continue business.
   (2) Unless partnership agreement allows partners to continue business.
   (3) Withdrawal of limited partner does not cause dissolution.
   (4) Death of limited partner does not cause dissolution.

6. If partnership is not continued, winding up takes place with the following distribution of assets of partnership in order of priority:
a. To creditors including partners who are creditors.
b. To partners and ex-partners to pay off unpaid distributions.
c. To partners to return capital contributions.
d. To partners for partnership interests in proportions they share in distributions.
e. Note that in these priorities general and limited partners share equally.
f. Also, note that partners can vary their rights by agreement of all parties affected.

7. Upon dissolution, remaining partners typically complete winding-up process.
8. Dissolution of a limited partnership requires the filing of a dissolution document with the state.

I. Joint Ventures

1. Joint venture—An association of two or more persons (or entities) organized to carry out a single business undertaking (or series of related undertakings) for profit.
a. Generally, corporations may engage in joint ventures.
   Example: X Corporation, O Corporation, and N Corporation decide to form a joint venture to bring oil from the north to the south of Alaska.

2. Law of joint ventures is similar to that of partnerships with some exceptions:
a. Each joint venturer is not necessarily an agent of other joint venturers—limited power to bind others.
b. Death of joint venturer does not automatically dissolve joint venture.
c. Joint venture is interpreted as special form of partnership.
   (1) Fiduciary duties of partners in partnership law apply.
   (2) Each member has right to participate in management.
   (3) Liability is unlimited, and each joint venturer is personally liable for debts of joint venture.

3. Generally, a joint venture is not required to file a document or certificate with the state.

J. Limited Liability Companies (LLC)

1. Laws for this relatively new form of business have been developing in the majority of states and have come to be fairly uniform.
   a. This material will cover the laws passed by what is now a majority of states (and therefore testable on CPA exam).
   b. All states have passed some version (often with minor changes) of an LLC statute.
2. LLC is not considered a corporation, but a majority of states provide:
   a. All owners (often called members) have limited liability and therefore no personal liability.
      (1) Liability of owners is limited to their capital contributions plus any equity in LLC.
         (a) Typically, limited liability is retained even if members fail to follow usual formalities in conducting business.
            Example: Members of LLC fail to keep minutes of the LLC's meetings. This failure does **not** expose them to personal liability for the debts of the LLC.
            1] Note that if a **corporation** does not follow the corporate formalities, such as corporate meetings with relevant minutes, the corporate veil can be pierced; thus, the corporate entity is disregarded and then shareholders of company obtain personal liability for corporation's debts.
               a] This is another important advantage of LLC
      (2) Compare with limited partnership, in which only limited partners can have limited liability.
      (3) Some states allow sole proprietorship to be formed into LLC to obtain its advantages.
   b. LLC must be formed according to limited liability company statute of the state in which it is formed.
      (1) Some general partnerships or limited partnerships convert over to an LLC, in which case partners retain liability they had in former partnership; they obtain benefits as new members of LLC only for transactions that take place after conversion date to LLC.
      (2) LLC is foreign LLC in other states in which it does business, and laws of state where it was formed typically govern LLC in those other states.
   c. LLC is a separate legal entity so it can sue or be sued in its own name.
      (1) Foreign LLC must register with secretary of state before doing business in another state or cannot sue in state courts.
   d. Most states require that the name of the LLC include either phrase "limited liability company" or initials "LLC" to give notice to public.
      (1) Many states allow phrase "limited company" or just two initials "LC."
   e. To form an LLC, members must file articles of organization with secretary of state.
      (1) May be amended by filing articles of amendment with secretary of state.
3. Member of the LLC has no interest in any specific property in the LLC but has interest (personal property interest) in the LLC in general.
   a. Member has right to distributions according to profit and loss sharing agreed on in operating agreement.
      (1) Under Uniform Limited Liability Company Act, in absence of agreement otherwise, members divide profits and losses equally.
         (a) They may instead decide to share profits in proportion to their capital contributions.
         (b) They may agree to divide profits differently than losses based on different formulas.
            Example: The members agree that the various members each receive profits and losses on bases that are different for each member. Member Q, for example, receives 15% if there is a profit in a given year, but suffers a loss of 20% if the LLC were to suffer a loss. Member R, however, is allocated 12% whether there is a profit or a loss. This is enforceable since the members agree to this.
   b. Member has management interest.
      (1) Includes rights to manage affairs of firm, vote within firm, and get information about LLC.
      (2) Unless agreed otherwise, each member has equal voice in management.
   c. Member may assign financial interest in LLC unless operating agreement specifies otherwise.
      (1) Assignee does not become member, only receives assignor's share of profits assigned unless other members agree otherwise.
      (2) Member's interest is not freely transferable.
4. Authority and duties in LLCs:
   a. When an LLC designated as member-managed LLC, all members have authority to bind the LLC under agency law to contracts on behalf of the LLC.

    b. When an LLC is designated as manager-managed LLC, only managers have authority to bind the LLC to contracts for the LLC.

        a. An LLC is bound only to contracts that:

            1. Either the LLC has authorized under agency law, or

            2. Are made in the ordinary course of business.

    c. In either case:

        (1) Authority of both members and managers to bind an LLC to contracts can be restricted in articles of organization or in operating agreement.

        (2) Apparent authority of either members or managers to make contracts with third parties is not affected for those who have proper notice of restrictions on contract-making authority.

            (a) Restrictions in articles of organization are deemed proper notice to third parties if they are filed with secretary of state.

            (b) Restrictions in operating agreement are deemed to be proper notice to those third parties who actually receive direct notification of those restrictions.

5. Other compensation:

    a. Member who is not a manager has no right to compensation for services performed.

        (1) Exception is for services performed in winding up LLC.

    b. Managers of LLCs receive compensation according to agreed contract.

    c. An LLC must reimburse members and managers for payments they made in the name of the LLC.

    d. An LLC is required to indemnify managers and/or members.

6. Fiduciary duties owed by members and managers to LLC:

    a. Managers of a manager-managed LLC and members of a member-managed LLC owe the LLC fiduciary duties.

        (1) Both owe duty of due care to the LLC but is very limited.

            (a) Duty includes:

                1] To not be grossly negligent so that the LLC is injured.

                    a] Note that this duty of due care does not include ordinary negligence.

                2] To not intentionally, recklessly, or by breaking laws injure LLC.

        (2) Both owe duty of due care to not cause injury to third parties while acting within course and scope of LLC business.

            (a) This includes all duties listed above to not commit gross negligence and to not intentionally or recklessly or by breaking law injure third parties.

                1] Note that unlike duties owed to LLCs directly, this duty also makes LLCs liable for ordinary negligence of managers and members for conduct causing injury to third parties within course and scope of LLC business.

        (3) Both managers and members owe duty of loyalty to their LLC.

            (a) This includes duty to act honestly, to not usurp LLC's business opportunities for self, to not secretly compete with their LLC, to not make secret deals, to not receive kickbacks, and to not take position that harms their LLC.

                Example: Push, a member of a member-manager LLC, discovers a good deal on property that his LLC would want. Push wants this good deal for himself. Push must disclose the facts of the deal and let the LLC have the deal if the LLC chooses it.

7. Dissolution of LLC:

    a. Most state LLC statutes cause LLC to dissolve when:

        (1) All members agree in writing to dissolution.

        (2) A time period passes or event happens as specified in operating agreement.

        (3) A member withdraws, is voted out, dies, goes bankrupt, or becomes incompetent.

            (a) Most states allow remainder of members to continue the LLC if agreed on unanimously.

        (4) Court order dissolves it.

8. Distribution of assets upon dissolution are made in following priorities:

    a. To creditors including managers and members except for their shares in the distribution of profits.

    b. To members and past members for unpaid distributions unless agreed otherwise.

    c. To members to receive back capital contributions, unless agreed otherwise.

    d. To members for their distributions as agreed in operating agreement, or if not agreed on, in proportion to contributions they had made.

9. Dissolution of a LLC requires the filing of a dissolution document with the state.

K. Limited Liability Partnerships (LLP)

1. The majority of states now allow LLP.
2. Formation of LLP:
    a. Articles of LLP must be filed with secretary of state.
    b. Statutes of all jurisdictions require firm's name to include phrase "limited liability partnership" or "registered limited liability partnership" or initials "LLP" or "RLLP" to notify public.
    c. The majority of states require only majority, not unanimous, approval of partners to become LLP.
    d. Generally, laws of the state in which the LLP is formed govern affairs of the LLP in all other states.
    e. The LLP often works well for professionals who want to do business as professionals in a partnership but still pass through tax benefits while limiting personal liability of partners.
    f. Most states allow an easy transition from conventional partnership into limited liability partnership.
    g. Most common law and statutory law from partnership law applies to LLP.
3. Liability provisions of partners in LLP:
    a. Under traditional general partnerships and limited partnerships, big disadvantage is that general partners in both firms have unlimited personal liability for partnership obligations.
        (1) Most states allow LLP to be formed so there is no general partner who has unlimited personal liability.
            (a) In essence, each partner is limited partner with some exceptions.
                1] Regulations require specified amounts of liability malpractice insurance to, in theory, take the place of former unlimited liability of general partners.
                2] In general, partners in LLP under modern trend retain full unlimited liability for their own negligence and for wrongful acts of those in LLP they supervise or have control over.
                3] LLP statutes on partners' limits on liability vary somewhat by state but typically state statutes provide limits to partners' liability in important ways.
                    a] Some states limit liability for all debts of LLP.
                    b] When more than one partner is liable for negligence, liability is often proportioned.
    b. Under LLP, partners avoid some personal liability for mistakes or malpractice of other partners.
        (1) This is popular for professionals such as accounting firms and law firms.

L. Subchapter C Corporations

1. Under Federal Subchapter S Revision Act, all corporations are divided into two categories:
    a. Subchapter S corporations are discussed later in this module.
    b. Subchapter C corporations are all corporations that are not Subchapter S corporations.
        (1) The majority of this module covers "regular corporation," also referred to as Subchapter C corporation.
            (a) In general, most provisions for Subchapter C corporations and Subchapter S corporations are similar such as limited liability of shareholders and structure of corporate management.
                1] The main distinction is tax treatment.

M. Characteristics and Advantages of Corporate Form

1. Limited liability.
    a. Generally a shareholder in a corporation risks only his/her investment.
2. Transferability of interest.
    a. Shares in corporations are represented by stocks and can be freely bought, sold, or assigned unless shareholders have agreed to restrictions.
3. Continuous life.
    a. Unlike a partnership, a corporation is not terminated by death of a shareholder or his/her incapacity.
        (1) A corporation is regarded as perpetual and continues to exist until dissolved, merged, or otherwise terminated.
4. Separate entity.
    a. A corporation is a legal entity in itself and is treated separately from its stockholders.
        (1) Can take, hold, and convey property.
        (2) Can contract in own name with shareholders or third parties.
        (3) Can sue and be sued.
5. Financing.

a. Often easier to raise large amounts of capital than in other business organizations by issuance of stock or other securities (e.g., bonds).

b. More flexible because a corporation can issue different classes of stock and/or bonds to suit its needs and market demands.

6. Corporate management.

a. Persons who manage corporations are not necessarily shareholders and therefore may be more qualified.

b. Management of a corporation usually is vested in board of directors elected by shareholders.

c. Directors could be removed from office before their elected term is finished only for cause under common law.

(1) Increasingly states have been passing laws that allow directors to be removed at any time with shareholders' consent.

N. Disadvantages of Corporate Business Structure

1. Tax treatment.

a. Tax burdens may be more than on other business structures because of double taxation.

(1) This often happens when income is taxed at corporate level and then dividends paid from after-tax income are taxed again at shareholder level.

(a) Tax breaks may partially or completely avoid double taxation.

Example: Single, who owns an incorporated sole proprietorship, has no taxable income at the corporate level because, in part, he/she pays self a high salary rather than reporting taxable income at the corporate level and then paying self dividends. His/her salary, although high, "passes muster," and he/she thus avoids double taxation. He/she pays taxes once on his/her salary.

Corporation may alleviate double taxation as Subchapter S corporation by being taxed similar to partnership.

1] It may still retain advantages such as limited liability of shareholders.

2. Costs of incorporating, because must meet formal creation requirements.

3. Formal operating requirements must be met and there is a maximum number of shareholders allowed.

4. If the corporation goes public:

(1) There are substantial costs of compliance with federal securities laws.

(2) May be subject to hostile takeover.

O. Types of Corporations

1. A domestic corporation is one that operates and does business within the state in which it was incorporated.

2. A foreign corporation is one doing business in any state except the one in which it was incorporated.

a. Foreign corporations, if "doing business" in a given state, are not exempt from many requirements and details that domestic corporations must meet.

(1) Doing business in state is typically defined as maintaining an office or selling personal property in that state.

(a) These are not considered doing business in state:

1] Defending against a lawsuit.

2] Holding a bank account.

3] Using mail to solicit orders.

4] Collecting debts.

5] Using independent contactors to make sales.

(2) Foreign corporations can be required to qualify to do business in state; accomplished by obtaining certificate of authority from state.

(a) An agent must be appointed to receive service of process for suits against corporation.

(b) Specified fees must be paid.

(c) Information must be filed with secretary of state

b. If a foreign corporation does not qualify to do business in a state:

(1) It may be denied access to courts to sue.

(2) It is liable to the state for any fees, taxes, interest, and penalties as if it had qualified to do business.

(3) Is subject to fines.

3. Professional corporations are ones under state laws that allow professionals to incorporate (e.g., doctors, accountants, attorneys).
   a. All states allow professional corporations.
   b. Typically, shares may be owned only by licensed professionals.
   c. Individuals retain personal liability for their professional acts.
   d. Professional corporations other corporation benefits (e.g., limited liability for corporate debts, some tax benefits).
4. The Model Statutory Close Corporation Supplement was passed to allow corporations to choose to be close corporations.
   a. The Supplement often helps corporations made up of entrepreneurial individuals.
   b. Close corporations also can be called closely held corporations or closed corporations.
   c. Only corporations having 50 or fewer shareholders may choose status of statutory close corporations.
      (1) To choose such status, two-thirds of shares of each class of shares of corporation must approve it.
      (2) Articles of corporation must contain a statement that it is a statutory close corporation.
      (3) All share certificates must clearly state they are issued by statutory close corporation.
   d. Close corporations may function without some of the formalities of operating corporations.
      (1) If all shareholders approve, a close corporation may function without board of directors.
         (a) It is then managed by shareholders.
      (2) Close corporation need not hold shareholders' meetings unless at least one shareholder demands in writing that meetings be held.
      (3) Basically, shareholders may treat a close corporation as a partnership for purposes of governing.
         (a) Very importantly, statutory close corporation status allows shareholders to have limited liability.
5. A **de facto** corporation has been formed in fact but has not been formed properly under the law.
   a. Usually defective because of some small error.
   b. Now filing by secretary of state of articles of jncorporation is deemed conclusive proof that incorporators did all that was necessary to incorporate.
      (1) Third parties cannot now challenge that corporation exists.
      (2) Only state can challenge existence and dissolve or cancel corporation.
6. A **de jure** corporation has been formed correctly in compliance with the incorporation statute.

P. Formation of Corporation

1. Promoters are persons who form corporations and arrange capitalization to begin corporations.
   a. A promoter handles issuing of the prospectus, promoting stock subscriptions, and drawing up charter.
   b. A promoter has a fiduciary relationship with corporation and is not permitted to act against interests of corporation.
      (1) The fiduciary relationship does not prevent personal profit if fully disclosed.
   c. A promoter is not an agent of the corporation, because the corporation is still not in existence.
      (1) Any agreements (preincorporation contracts) made by a promoter are not binding on the future corporation until adopted after corporation comes into existence.
         (a) Requires actual resolution of board of directors.
         (b) Normally a promoter is personally liable on contract. Adoption by corporation does not relieve the promoter; **novation is required to relieve the promoter**. The other party must agree to substituting the corporation.
            1] A promoter has liability even if the promoter's name does not appear on contract.
            2] However, a promoter is not liable if third party clearly states that he/she would look only to corporation for performance.
         (c) Corporation is not liable to the promoter for his/her services unless adopted by corporation.
2. A corporation is formed only under state incorporation statutes ("creature of statute").
3. Incorporation.
   a. Articles of Incorporation (charter) are filed with the state and contain:
      (1) Proposed name of corporation and initial address.
      (2) Purpose of corporation.
      (3) Powers of corporation.

(4) Name of registered agent of corporation.

(5) Name and address of each incorporator.

    (a) Incorporators may be promoters.

(6) Number of authorized shares of stock and types of stock.

b. First shareholders' meeting:

(1) Stock certificates issued to shareholders.

(2) Resignation of temporary directors and election of new.

c. At same meeting or subsequent meeting, directors:

(1) Elect officers.

(2) Adopt or reject preincorporation contracts.

(3) Begin business of corporation.

(4) Adopt initial bylaws.

    (a) These need not be filed with any government agency.

    (b) The initial bylaws provide specific rules for management.

4. Articles of incorporation may be subsequently amended.

a. Approval of any adversely affected shareholders of amendment is needed.

(1) Often a majority vote or sometimes two-thirds vote required.

    (a) Dissenting minority shareholders may assert right of appraisal and therefore receive fair value for shares.

        1] Fair value is the value just before vote.

Q. Corporate Financial Structure

1. Definitions:

a. Uncertificated securities—securities not represented by written documents.

b. Authorized stock—amount permitted to be issued in articles of incorporation (e.g., amount and types).

c. Issued stock—authorized and delivered to shareholders.

d. Unissued stock—authorized but not yet issued.

e. Outstanding stock—issued and not repurchased by the corporation (i.e., it is still owned by shareholders).

f. Treasury stock—issued but not outstanding (i.e., corporation repurchased it).

(1) Shares of treasury stock are not votable and do not receive dividends.

(2) Corporation does not recognize gain or loss on transactions with its own stock.

(3) Must be purchased out of unreserved or unrestricted earned surplus as defined below and as permitted by state law.

    (a) If Articles of Incorporation so permit or if majority of voting shareholders permit, unrestricted capital surplus (see below) may also be used.

(4) May be distributed as part of stock dividend.

(5) May be resold without regard to par value.

(6) Can be resold without regard to preemptive rights.

(7) No purchase of treasury stock may be made if it renders the corporation insolvent.

g. Canceled stock—stock purchased or received by corporation that is canceled.

(1) No longer issued or outstanding.

(2) Makes room for more stock to be issued.

h. Par-value stock:

(1) Par value is amount set in articles of incorporation.

(2) Stock should be issued for this amount or more.

(3) Subsequently may be traded for any amount.

(4) Creditors may hold purchaser liable if stock was originally purchased at below par.

    (a) Purchaser is contingently liable for difference between amount paid and par value.

    (b) Subsequent purchaser also liable unless stock was purchased in good faith without notice that sale was below par.

i. No-par stock—stock issued without a set par value.

(1) May have a stated value.

j. Stated capital (legal capital)—number of shares issued times par value (or stated value).

(1) If no par or stated value, then includes total consideration received by corporation.

       (a) Under limited circumstances, portion may be allocated by board of directors to capital surplus as permitted by law.

    (2) Dividends normally may not be declared or paid out of it.

    (3) The following also increase stated capital by number of shares increased times par value (or stated value):

       (a) Exercise of stock option.

       (b) Small common stock dividend.

    (4) The following do not change stated capital:

       (a) Acquisition or reissuance of treasury stock under cost method.

       (b) Stock splits:

          1] Increase number of shares issued and decrease par or stated value (e.g., two-for-one stock split doubles the number of shares issued and cuts in half the par or stated value).

          2] Do not distribute assets or capital.

       (c) Payment of organization costs.

  k. Earned surplus (retained earnings)—cumulative amount of income (net of dividends) retained by the corporation during its existence or since a deficit was properly eliminated.

    (1) Note that under modern terminology, this is correctly referred to as retained earnings as indicated above; since laws written using old terms, CPA candidates should be familiar with old as well as new terms as learned in accounting.

  l. Net assets—excess of total assets over total debts.

  m. Surplus—excess of net assets over stated capital.

  n. Capital surplus —entire surplus of corporation less earned surplus.

    (1) Note that paid-in capital is considered capital surplus.

  o. Contributed capital—total consideration received by corporation upon issuance of stock.

2. Classes of stock

  a. Common stock usually gives each shareholder one vote per share and is entitled to dividends if declared by the directors.

    (1) Has no priority over other stock for dividends.

    (2) Shareholders are entitled to share in final distribution of assets.

    (3) Votes may be apportioned to shares in other ways (e.g., one vote per 10 shares).

    (4) Corporation may issue more than one class of common stock with varying terms (e.g., class may have no voting rights or different par value, etc.).

  b. Preferred stock is given preferred status as to liquidations and dividends, but dividends are still discretionary.

    (1) Is usually nonvoting stock.

    (2) The dividend rate is generally a fixed rate.

    (3) "Cumulative preferred" means that if a periodic dividend is not paid at the scheduled time, it accumulates and must be satisfied before common stock may receive a dividend

       (a) These arrearages are not liabilities of corporation until declared by board of directors.

          1] Disclosed in footnotes to financial statements.

       (b) "Noncumulative preferred" means that if the dividend is passed, it will never be paid.

       (c) Held to be implicitly cumulative unless different intent shown.

    (4) Participating preferred stock participates further in corporate earnings remaining after a fixed amount is paid to preferred shares.

       (a) Participation with common shares is generally on a fixed percentage basis.

  c. Callable (or redeemable) stock may be redeemed at a fixed price by the corporation.

    (1) Call price is fixed in articles of incorporation or may be subject to agreement among shareholders themselves.

  d. Convertible preferred gives shareholder option to convert preferred stock to common stock at a fixed exchange rate.

3. Marketing of stock:

  a. Stock subscriptions are contracts to purchase a given number of shares in an existing corporation or one to be organized.

    (1) Subscription to stock is a written offer to buy and is not binding until accepted by the corporation.

    (2) Under the Model Business Corporation Act, stock subscriptions are irrevocable for six months.

      (3) Once accepted, the subscriber becomes liable:

         (a) For the purchase, and

         (b) As a corporate shareholder.

      (4) An agreement to subscribe in the future is not a subscription.

  b. Watered stock:

      (1) Stock is said to be watered when the cash or property exchanged is less than par value or stated value.

      (2) Stock must be issued for consideration equal to or greater than the par or stated value under most state laws.

         (a) No-par stock may be issued for consideration that the directors determine to be reasonable.

      (3) Creditors of the corporation may recover from the stockholders the amount of water in their shares; that is, the amount the stockholders would have paid to the corporation had they paid the full amount required (i.e., par value less amount paid).

         (a) If the corporation becomes insolvent.

         (b) Subsequent purchaser of watered stock is not liable unless he/she had knowledge thereof.

  c. Valid consideration or value for shares can be any benefit to corporation:

      (1) Including cash, property, services performed, intangible property, promissory notes, other securities, or services contracted to be performed in future.

         (a) Directors have a duty to set value on property received.

            1] Directors' value set is conclusive unless fraud shown.

4. Debt securities (holders are not owners but creditors):

  a. A debenture is an instrument for long-term unsecured debt.

  b. A bond is an instrument for long-term secured debt.

R. *Powers and Liabilities of Corporation*

1. Corporations generally have the following powers:

  a. To acquire their own shares (treasury stock) or retire their own shares.

      (1) The shares are typically limited to the amount of surplus.

  b. To make charitable contributions.

  c. To guarantee obligations of others only if in reasonable furtherance of corporation's business.

  d. Loans to directors require shareholder approval.

  e. Loans to employees (even employees who are also directors) do not need shareholder approval and are appropriate if they benefit corporation.

  f. Generally, a corporation may also be a partner of a partnership.

2. Crimes:

  a. Corporations are liable for crimes they are capable of committing.

  b. Punishment generally consists of fines or forfeiture, although directors have been faced with prison sentences for crimes of the corporation.

3. Contracts:

  a. Rules under agency law apply in corporate dealings.

4. Torts:

  a. Corporations are liable for the damages resulting from torts committed by their officers, directors, agents, or employees within the course and scope of their corporate duties.

      Example: Fraudulent deceit against a customer.

      Example: Employee assaults a complaining customer.

5. **Ultra vires** acts:

  a. Illegal and ultra vires acts are not the same.

      (1) Illegal acts are acts in violation of statute or public policy.

         Example: False advertising.

      (2) Ultra vires acts are merely beyond the scope of the corporate powers (i.e., a legal act may be ultra vires).

         Example: Although legal to become a surety, the articles of incorporation may not allow it.

  b. The state's attorney general may dissolve corporation for ultra vires act.

  c. Stockholders have the right to object to ultra vires acts.

  d. Directors or officers may be sued by shareholders on behalf of the corporation or by the corporation itself if there are damages to the corporation for ultra vires acts.

S. Directors and Officers of Corporations

1. Directors are elected by shareholders.
2. Directors' duties and powers:
   a. A director as an individual has no power to bind the corporation—the director must act as a board member at a duly constituted meeting of the board.
      (1) A majority vote of those present is needed for most business decisions if quorum is present.
      (2) Action may be taken by board with no meeting:
         (a) Unless prohibited by articles of incorporation or by corporate bylaws, and
         (b) There must be unanimous written consent by board members for action to be taken.
   b. Powers and duties in general:
      (1) Declaration of dividends.
      (2) Selection of officers.
      (3) Directors must comply with articles of incorporation. The articles of incorporation can be amended only by voting shareholders.
      (4) Typically delegate some authority (e.g., day-to-day or routine matters to officers and agents).
      (5) Directors are not entitled to compensation unless so provided in articles, bylaws, or by a resolution of the board passed before the services are rendered.
         (a) May be reimbursed for expenses incurred on behalf of corporation.
3. Director's liability:
   a. General rule is that directors must exercise ordinary care and due diligence in performing the duties entrusted to them by virtue of their positions as directors, and act in a manner he/she believes to be in the best interests of the corporation.
      (1) Directors are liable for their own torts committed even if acting for corporation.
         (a) Corporation is **also** liable if torts are committed within the scope of corporate duties.
      (2) Business judgment rule—as long as director is acting in good faith, he/she will not be liable for errors of judgment unless he/she is negligent.
      (3) Directors are chargeable with knowledge of the affairs of the corporation.
         (a) If a director does not prevent (intentionally or negligently) the wrongs of other directors, the director may be held liable.
         (b) Normally a director may rely on reports of accountants, officers, and so on, if reasonable judgment is used.
      (4) If a corporation does not actually exist, then the director and others in business have personal liability.
   b. Directors liable for negligence if their action was the cause of the corporation's loss.
      (1) A corporation may indemnify directors (also officers, employees, agents) against suits based on their duties for the corporation if acted in good faith and in the best interests of the corporation.
         (a) Also applies to criminal actions if the director reasonably believed that actions were lawful.
      (2) Corporation may purchase liability insurance for officers and directors.
         (a) Corporation pays premiums.
         (b) Policies usually cover litigation costs as well as judgment or settlement costs.
   c. Directors owe a fiduciary duty to the corporation.
      (1) Directors owe fiduciary duties of loyalty and due care to the corporation.
      (2) Conflicts of interest:
         (a) Transactions of a corporation with director(s) or other corporation in which director(s) has interest are valid as long as at least one of the following can be established:
            1] Conflict of interest is disclosed or known to board and majority of disinterested members approve of transaction.
            2] Conflict of interest is disclosed or known to shareholders and those entitled to vote approve it by a majority.
            3] Transaction is fair and reasonable to corporation.
               Example: A plot of land already owned by a director is sold at the fair market value to the corporation. This contract is valid even without approval if the land is needed by the corporation.
   d. Directors are personally liable for **ultra vires** acts of the corporation unless they specifically dissented on the record.
      Example: Loans made to stockholders by a corporation.

    e. Directors are personally liable to corporation for approving and paying dividends that are illegal.

        (1) Directors who act in good faith may use the defense of business judgment rule.

4. Officers:

    a. Typically operate the day-to-day business.

        (1) Officers are delegated from directors.

    b. An officer of the corporation is an agent and can bind corporation by his/her individual acts if within the scope of his/her authority as set forth in the bylaws.

        (1) A corporation is not bound by acts of an agent beyond the scope of authority.

        (2) The president usually has authority for transactions that are part of usual and regular course of business.

            (a) The president has no authority for extraordinary transactions.

        (3) Acts of officers may be ratified by board.

    c. Officers and directors may be the same persons.

    d. Officers are selected by the directors for a fixed term under the bylaws.

        (1) If a term is not definite, it is governed by the directors.

    e. Officers have a fiduciary duty to corporation.

    f. Courts recognize a fiduciary duty owed by majority shareholders to minority shareholders when the majority shareholders have de facto control over the corporation.

5. Officers, like directors, are liable for own torts, even if committed while acting for corporation.

    a. Corporation is also liable if officer was acting within the scope of his/her authority.

6. Requirements of the Sarbanes-Oxley Act of 2002:

    a. All members of the audit committee of the board of directors must be independent and one must be a financial expert.

    b. The audit committee must appoint, compensate, and oversee the work of the firm's public accounting firm.

    c. The chief executive officer (CEO) and chief financial officer (CFO) must certify that the financial statements are fairly presented.

    d. Prohibits officer or director from exerting improper influence on the conduct of the audit.

    e. CEO and CFO must return compensation that was derived from misstated financial statements resulting from material noncompliance with the reporting requirements.

T. Stockholder's Rights

1. The right to transfer stock by endorsement and delivery or by separate assignment.

    a. Stock certificates are negotiable instruments.

    b. Limitations on transfer may be imposed, but they must be reasonable.

        (1) The Uniform Commercial Code requires that any restrictions must be plainly printed on the certificate to be effective against third party.

        (2) These limitations are most often imposed in closely held corporations.

            Example: Existing shareholders of the corporation may have first option to buy.

2. A stockholder has no right to manage corporation unless he/she is also officer or director.

    a. A stockholder retains limited liability, unlike limited partner, who participates in management.

3. The right to vote for election of directors, decision to dissolve the corporation, and any other fundamental corporate changes.

    a. Right is governed by the charter and class of stock owned.

    b. Annual meetings are required as specified in the bylaws.

    c. Stockholders may have voting agreements that are enforceable, which provide that they will vote a certain way on issues or vote for specified people for the board of directors.

    d. Cumulative voting may be required (i.e., a person gets as many votes as he/she has shares times the number of directors being elected).

        Example: 100 shares $\times$ 5 directors is 500 votes.

        (1) Cumulative voting gives minority shareholders an opportunity to get some representation by voting all shares for one or two directors.

    e. Stockholders can vote by proxy—an assignment of voting rights.

    f. Directors have the power to amend or repeal the bylaws unless reserved to the shareholders by the articles of incorporation.

g. Amendment of the articles of incorporation and approval of fundamental corporate changes such as a merger, consolidation, or sale of all assets generally require majority approval by shareholders.

4. Right to dividends:

a. Shareholders generally have no right to dividends unless they are declared by the board of directors.

   (1) Power to declare dividends is discretionary based on the board's assessment of business needs.

   (2) When there is a surplus together with available cash, the shareholders may be able to compel declaration of dividends if board's refusal to declare a dividend is in bad faith or its refusal is unreasonable, but this is difficult to establish.

b. Dividends become a liability of corporation only when declared.

   (1) True for all types of stock, such as common stock or even cumulative preferred stock.

   Example: Knave Corporation declares dividends of $10,000 to the 10,000 $1 cumulative preferred stockholders (there is no average on these shares) and $20,000 to the 500 common stockholders. The following year is so bad that Knave Corporation is liquidated. Furthermore, no dividends are declared, and general creditors are owed more than the corporation has. None of the shareholders gets any dividends in this following year.

c. Cash dividends may be paid out of unrestricted and unreserved earned surplus (retained earnings) unless corporation already is or will be insolvent because of dividend.

   (1) Some states have other regulations, sometimes allowing reductions in other accounts too.

   (2) Under Model Business Corporation Act, dividends are prohibited that cause total liabilities to exceed total assets after effect of the distribution is considered. Dividends may not be declared if payment of same will cause the corporation to become insolvent.

5. The right of stockholders to inspect books and records exists.

a. These books and records include minute books, stock certificate books, stock ledgers, and general account books.

b. Demand must be made in good faith and for a proper purpose.

   (1) A stockholder may get list of shareholders to help wage a proxy fight to attempt to control corporation.

   (2) A stockholder may not get list of shareholders or customers to use for business mailing list.

6. Preemptive right:

a. This is the right to subscribe to new issues of stock (at fair market value) so that a stockholder's ownership will not be diluted without the opportunity to maintain it.

   Example: A corporation has one class of common stock. Stockholder A owns 15%. A new issue of the same class of stock is to be made. Stockholder A has the right to buy 15% of it.

b. Usually applies only to common stock, not preferred.

c. Does not apply to treasury stock.

d. There is no preemptive right to purchase stock unless articles of incorporation so provide.

7. Stockholder's right to sue:

a. Stockholder can sue in his/her own behalf where his/her interests have been directly injured, for example:

   (1) Denial of right to inspect records.

   (2) Denial of preemptive right if provided for.

b. Stockholders can sue on behalf of the corporation (i.e., a derivative suit):

   (1) In cases where a duty to the corporation is violated and corporation does not enforce, for example:

      (a) Director violates his/her fiduciary duty to corporation.

      (b) Illegal declaration of dividends (e.g., rendering corporation insolvent).

      (c) Fraud by officer on corporation.

   (2) Unless demand would be futile, a stockholder must first demand that directors sue in name of corporation and then may proceed if they refuse.

      (a) The suit may be barred if directors make good-faith business judgment that the suit is not in corporation's best interests.

   (3) Damages go to the corporation.

8. Right to a pro rata share of distribution of assets on dissolution after creditors have been paid.

U. Stockholder's Liability

1. Generally stockholder's liability is limited to his/her price paid for stock.

2. A stockholder may be liable to creditors for:

    a. Original issue stock sold at below par value.

        (1) A stockholder is contingently liable for the difference between par value and original issuance price.

    b. Unpaid balance on no-par stock.

    c. Dividends paid that impair capital if the corporation is insolvent.

3. Piercing the corporate veil—courts disregard the corporate entity and hold stockholders personally liable.

    a. Rarely happens but may occur if:

        (1) Corporation is used to perpetrate fraud (e.g., forming an undercapitalized corporation).

        (2) Owners/officers do not treat corporation as separate entity.

        (3) Shareholders commingle assets, bank accounts, financial records with those of corporation.

        (4) Corporate formalities are not adhered to.

4. Majority shareholders owe fiduciary duty to minority shareholders and to corporation.

    a. Even shareholder who controls corporation (majority ownership not now needed) has fiduciary duty.

V. Substantial Change in Corporate Structure

1. Merger:

    a. Union of two corporations where one is absorbed by other.

        (1) Surviving corporation issues its own shares (common and/or preferred) to shareholders of original corporations.

2. Consolidation:

    a. Joining of two (or more) corporations into a single new corporation.

    b. All assets and liabilities are acquired by the new company.

    c. New corporation is liable for debts of old corporations.

3. Requirements to accomplish a merger or consolidation:

    a. Boards of both corporations must prepare and submit plan to shareholders of both corporations.

    b. Board of directors of both companies must approve.

    c. Shareholders of both corporations must be given copy or summary of merger plan.

    d. Majority vote of shareholders of each corporation.

    e. The surviving corporation gets all assets and liabilities of merging corporations.

    f. Dissatisfied shareholders of the subsidiary may dissent and assert appraisal rights, thereby receiving the fair value of their stock.

4. Dissolution:

    a. Once corporation is dissolved, it may do business only to wind up and liquidate business.

        (1) Liquidation is the winding up of affairs and distribution of assets.

            (a) Liquidation occurs in the following order:

                1] Expenses of liquidation and creditors.

                2] Preferred shareholders.

                3] Common shareholders.

        (2) Termination occurs when winding up and liquidation are completed.

    b. Dissolution may be done by voluntary dissolution or involuntary dissolution by state for cause.

        (1) Voluntary dissolution occurs when board of directors passes resolution to dissolve.

            (a) Resolution must be ratified by majority of stockholders entitled to vote.

    c. Shareholder may petition for judicial dissolution if directors or shareholders are deadlocked.

5. Dissolution of a corporation requires the filing of a dissolution document with the state.

W. Subchapter S Corporation

1. Herein are some basics.

2. When corporation elects to be Subchapter S corporation, it can avoid double taxation by not paying tax at the corporate level.

    a. Instead, the corporation income flows through to the income tax returns of the individual shareholders.

    b. Shareholders report the income or loss even when income not distributed to them.

    c. This flow-through may nevertheless be an advantage under some situations.

3. Rules involving the criteria needed to be met to be taxed as a Subchapter S corporation can change to one's detriment, creating another potential disadvantage of needing to stay abreast of rule changes.

    a. Some of the rules to watch out for involve:

(1) Corporation must be incorporated in the U.S. and have only one class of stock.
(2) The number of shareholders Subchapter S corporation can have is limited.
(3) Shareholders are limited to individuals, estates, qualified trusts, and similar entities.
(4) Nonresident aliens cannot own shares.
(5) A corporation cannot have excessive amounts of passive income.

MULTIPLE-CHOICE QUESTIONS

1. Which of the following statements is **not** true of a sole proprietorship?
   a. Federal and state governments typically require a formal filing with the appropriate government officials, whether the sole proprietorship uses a fictitious name or not.
   b. The sole proprietorship is not a separate legal entity apart from its owner.
   c. The capital to start the business is generally limited to the funds the sole proprietor either has or can borrow.
   d. It is generally considered to be the simplest type of business structure.

2. A general partnership must:
   a. Pay federal income tax.
   b. Have two or more partners.
   c. Have written articles of partnership.
   d. Provide for apportionment of liability for partnership debts.

3. Which of the following can be a partnership?
   a. Karen and Sharon form a charitable organization in which they received donations to give to their favorite charities.
   b. Frank and Pablo are members of a union at work that has 150 members.
   c. Janice and Stanley form a club to encourage business contacts for computer programmers.
   d. None of the above.

4. A silent partner in a general partnership:
   a. Helps manage the partnership without letting those outside the partnership know this.
   b. Retains unlimited liability for the debts of the partnership.
   c. Both of the above are correct.
   d. Neither of the above is correct.

5. Which of the following statements is correct with respect to a limited partnership?
   a. A limited partner may not be an unsecured creditor of the limited partnership.
   b. A general partner may not also be a limited partner at the same time.
   c. A general partner may be a secured creditor of the limited partnership.

   d. A limited partnership can be formed with limited liability for all partners.

6. A partnership agreement must be in writing if:
   a. Any partner contributes more than $500 in capital.
   b. The partners reside in different states.
   c. The partnership intends to own real estate.
   d. The partnership's purpose **cannot** be completed within one year of formation.

7. Sydney, Bailey, and Calle form a partnership under the Revised Uniform Partnership Act. During the first year of operation, the partners have fundamental questions regarding the rights and obligations of the partnership as well as the individual partners. Which of the following questions can be answered correctly in the affirmative?
   I.   Is the partnership allowed legally to own property in the partnership's name?
   II. Do the partners have joint and several liability for breaches of contract of the partnership?
   III. Do the partners have joint and several liability for tort actions against the partnership?
   a. I only.
   b. I and II only.
   c. II and III only.
   d. I, II, and III.

8. Which of the following is **not** true of a general partnership?
   a. Ownership by the partners may be unequal.
   b. It is a separate legal entity.
   c. An important characteristic is that the partners share in the profits equally.
   d. Each partner has an equal right to participate in management.

9. The partnership agreement for Owen Associates, a general partnership, provided that profits be paid to the partners in the ratio of their financial contribution to the partnership. Moore contributed $10,000, Noon contributed $30,000, and Kale contributed $50,000. For the year ended December 31, 2008, Owen had losses of $180,000. What amount of the losses should be allocated to Kale?

a. $40,000.
b. $60,000.
c. $90,000.
d. $100,000.

10. Lark, a partner in DSJ, a general partnership, wishes to withdraw from the partnership and sell Lark's interest to Ward. All of the other partners in DSJ have agreed to admit Ward as a partner and to hold Lark harmless for the past, present, and future liabilities of DSJ. As a result of Lark's withdrawal and Ward's admission to the partnership, Ward:
   a. Acquired only the right to receive Ward's share of DSJ profits.
   b. Has the right to participate in DSJ's management.
   c. Is personally liable for partnership liabilities arising before and after being admitted as a partner.
   d. Must contribute cash or property to DSJ to be admitted with the same rights as the other partners.

11. Cobb, Inc., a partner in TLC Partnership, assigns its partnership interest to Bean, who is not made a partner. After the assignment, Bean asserts the rights to:
   I. Participate in the management of TLC.
   II. Cobb's share of TLC's partnership profits.
   Bean is correct as to which of these rights?
      a. I only.
      b. II only.
      c. I and II.
      d. Neither I nor II.

12. The apparent authority of a partner to bind the partnership in dealing with third parties:
   a. Will be effectively limited by a formal resolution of the partners of which third parties are aware.
   b. Will be effectively limited by a formal resolution of the partners of which third parties are unaware.
   c. Would permit a partner to submit a claim against the partnership to arbitration.
   d. Must be derived from the express powers and purposes contained in the partnership agreement.

13. In a general partnership, which of the following acts must be approved by all the partners?
   a. Dissolution of the partnership.
   b. Admission of a partner.

   c. Authorization of a partnership capital expenditure.
   d. Conveyance of real property owned by the partnership.

14. Under the Revised Uniform Partnership Act, partners have joint and several liability for:
   a. Breaches of contract.
   b. Torts committed by one of the partners within the scope of the partnership.
   c. Both of the above.
   d. Neither of the above.

15. Which of the following actions require(s) unanimous consent of the partners under partnership law?
   I. Making partnership a surety.
   II. Admission of a new partner.
      a. I only.
      b. II only.
      c. Both I and II.
      d. Neither I nor II.

16. Which of the following statements best describes the effect of the assignment of an interest in a general partnership?
   a. The assignee becomes a partner.
   b. The assignee is responsible for a proportionate share of past and future partnership debts.
   c. The assignment automatically dissolves the partnership.
   d. The assignment transfers the assignor's interest in partnership profits and surplus.

17. Under the Revised Uniform Partnership Act, in which of the following cases will property be deemed to be partnership property?
   I. A partner acquires property in the partnership name.
   II. A partner acquires title to it in his/her own name using partnership funds.
   III. Property owned previously by a partner is used in the partnership business.
      a. I only.
      b. I and II only.
      c. II only.
      d. I, II, and III.

18. Wind, who has been a partner in the PLW general partnership for four years, decides to withdraw from the partnership despite a written partnership agreement that states "no partner may withdraw for a period of five years." Under the Uniform Partnership Act, what is the result of Wind's withdrawal?

a. Wind's withdrawal causes a dissolution of the partnership by operation of law.
b. Wind's withdrawal has no bearing on the continued operation of the partnership by the remaining partners.
c. Wind's withdrawal is not effective until Wind obtains a court-ordered decree of dissolution.
d. Wind's withdrawal causes a dissolution of the partnership despite being in violation of the partnership agreement.

19. Dowd, Elgar, Frost, and Grant formed a general partnership. Their written partnership agreement provided that the profits would be divided so that Dowd would receive 40%; Elgar, 30%; Frost, 20%; and Grant, 10%. There was no provision for allocating losses. At the end of its first year, the partnership had losses of $200,000. Before allocating losses, the partners' capital account balances were: Dowd, $120,000; Elgar, $100,000; Frost, $75,000; and Grant, $11,000. Grant refuses to make any further contributions to the partnership. Ignore the effects of federal partnership tax law.

    After losses were allocated to the partners' capital accounts and all liabilities were paid, the partnership's sole asset was $106,000 in cash. How much would Elgar receive on dissolution of the partnership?
    a. $37,000.
    b. $40,000.
    c. $47,500.
    d. $50,000.

20. Sharif, Hirsch, and Wolff formed a partnership with Sharif and Hirsch as general partners. Wolff was the limited partner. They failed to agree on a profit-sharing plan but put in capital contributions of $120,000, $140,000, and $150,000, respectively. At the end of the first year, how should they divide the profits?
    a. Sharif and Hirsch each receives half and Wolff receives none.
    b. Each of the three partners receives one-third.
    c. The profits are shared in proportion to their capital contribution.
    d. None of the above.

21. Which of the following is (are) true of a limited partnership?
    I. Limited partnerships must have at least one general partner.
    II. The death of a limited partner terminates the partnership.
      a. I only.
      b. II only.

c. Neither I nor II.
d. Both I and II.

22. Alchorn, Black, and Chan formed a limited partnership with Chan becoming the only limited partner. Capital contributions from these partners were $20,000, $40,000, and $50,000, respectively. Chan, however, helped in the management of the partnership, and Ham, who had several contracts with the partnership, thought Chan was a general partner. Ham won several breach-of-contract actions against the partnership, and the partnership does not have sufficient funds to pay these claims. What is the potential liability for Alchorn, Black, and Chan?
    a. Unlimited liability for all three partners.
    b. Unlimited liability for Alchorn and Black; $50,000 for Chan.
    c. Up to each partner's capital contribution.
    d. None of the above.

23. To create a limited partnership, a certificate of limited partnership must be filed with the secretary of state. Which of the following must be included in this certificate under the Revised Uniform Limited Partnership Act?
    I. Names of all of the general partners.
    II. Names of the majority of the general partners.
    III. Names of all of the limited partners.
    IV. Names of the majority of the limited partners.
      a. I only.
      b. II only.
      c. I and III only.
      d. I and IV only.

24. Mandy is a limited partner in a limited partnership in which Strasburg and Hua are the general partners. Which of the following may Mandy do without losing limited liability protection?
    I. Mandy acts as an agent of the limited partnership.
    II. Mandy votes to remove Strasburg as a general partner.
      a. I only.
      b. II only.
      c. Both I and II.
      d. Neither I nor II.

25. In a limited partnership, the limited partners' capital contribution may be in which of the following forms?
    a. A promise to perform services in the future for the partnership.
    b. An agreement to pay cash.

c. A promise to give property.

d. All of the above.

26. Hart and Grant formed Hart Limited Partnership. Hart put in a capital contribution of $20,000 and became a general partner. Grant put in a capital contribution of $10,000 and became a limited partner. During the second year of operation, a third party filed a tort action against the partnership and both partners. What is the potential liability of Hart and Grant respectively?

a. $20,000 and $0.

b. $20,000 and $10,000.

c. Unlimited liability and $0.

d. Unlimited liability and $10,000.

27. The admission of a new general partner to a limited partnership requires approval by:

I. A majority of the general partners.

II. All of the general partners.

III. A majority of the limited partners.

IV. All of the limited partners.

a. I only.

b. II only.

c. I and III only.

d. II and IV only.

28. The admission of a new limited partner to a limited partnership requires approval by:

I. A majority of the general partners.

II. All of the general partners.

III. A majority of the limited partners.

IV. All of the limited partners.

a. I only.

b. II only.

c. I and III only.

d. II and IV only.

29. Riewerts, Morgar, and Stonk form a limited partnership. Riewerts is the one general partner. Which of the following events will cause this limited partnership to be dissolved?

I. Riewerts dies and is survived by the other two partners.

II. Morgan dies leaving Riewerts and Stonk.

III. Riewerts takes out personal bankruptcy.

IV. Stonk takes out personal bankruptcy.

a. I only.

b. I and II only.

c. I and III only.

d. III and IV only.

30. Which of the following is **not** true of a joint venture?

a. Each joint venturer is personally liable for the debts of a joint venture.

b. Each joint venturer has the right to participate in the management of the joint venture.

c. The joint venturers owe each other fiduciary duties.

d. Death of a joint venturer dissolves the joint venture.

31. Which form(s) of a business organization can have characteristics common to both the corporation and the general partnership?

	Limited liability company	Subchapter S corporation
a.	Yes	Yes
b.	Yes	No
c.	No	Yes
d.	No	No

32. Which of the following is true of a limited liability company under the laws of the majority of states?

a. At least one of the owners must have personal liability.

b. The limited liability company is a separate legal entity apart from its owners.

c. Limited liability of the owners is lost if they fail to follow the usual formalities in conducting the business.

d. All of the above are true.

33. Which of the following is **not** characteristic of the typical limited liability company?

a. Death of a member (owner) causes it to dissolve unless the remaining members decide to continue the business.

b. All members (owners) are allowed by law to participate in the management of the firm.

c. The company has, legally, a perpetual existence.

d. All members (owners) have limited liability.

34. Owners and managers of a limited liability company (LLC) owe:

a. A duty of due care.

b. A duty of loyalty.

c. Both a duty of due care and a duty of loyalty.

d. None of the above.

35. Which of the following is true of the typical limited liability company?

a. It provides for limited liability for some of its members (owners), that is, those identified as limited members (owners).

b. The members' (owners') interests are not freely transferable.

c. Voting members (owners) but not all members can help choose the managers of the company.

d. No formalities are required for its formation.

36. In which of the following respects do general partnerships and limited liability partnerships **differ**?
    I.   In the level of liability of the partners for torts they themselves commit.
    II. In the level of liability of the partners for torts committed by other partners in the same firm.
    III. In the amount of liability of the partners for contracts signed by other partners on behalf of the partnership.
    IV. In the amount of liability of the partners for contracts they themselves signed on behalf of the firm.
        a. I only.
        b. II only.
        c. I and IV only.
        d. II and III only.

37. Under the federal Subchapter S Revision Act, all corporations are designated as:
    a. Subchapter S corporations only.
    b. Either a Subchapter S corporation or a Subchapter C corporation.
    c. One of seven different types of corporations.
    d. Both a Subchapter S corporation and a Subchapter C corporation at the same time.

38. Under the federal Subchapter S Revision Act, all corporations are:
    a. Now treated as Subchapter S corporations.
    b. Divided into either a Subchapter C corporation or a Subchapter S corporation.
    c. Divided into a Subchapter C corporation, a Subchapter E corporation, or a Subchapter S corporation.
    d. None of the above.

39. Which of the following statements is (are) true?
    a. Both Subchapter C corporations and Subchapter S corporations have limited liability for their shareholders.
    b. Both Subchapter C corporations and Subchapter S corporations are similar in their corporate management structure.
    c. All of the above are true.
    d. None of the above is true.

40. The main difference between Subchapter S corporations and Subchapter C corporations is:
    a. Their tax treatment.

b. That the federal Subchapter S Revision Act covers Subchapter S corporations but does not cover Subchapter C corporations.

c. Their limited liability of their shareholders.

d. Their structure of their corporate management.

41. Which of the following statements best describes an advantage of the corporate form of doing business?
    a. Day-to-day management is strictly the responsibility of the directors.
    b. Ownership is contractually restricted and is **not** transferable.
    c. The operation of the business may continue indefinitely.
    d. The business is free from state regulation.

42. Which of the following is **not** considered to be an advantage of the corporate form of doing business over the partnership form?
    a. A potential perpetual and continuous life.
    b. The interests in the corporation are typically easily transferable.
    c. The managers in the corporation and shareholders have limited liability.
    d. Persons who manage the corporation are not necessarily shareholders.

43. Which of the following is **not** a characteristic of a corporation?
    a. It has a continuous life.
    b. Shares in the corporation normally can be freely transferred.
    c. A corporation is treated as a legal entity separate from its shareholders.
    d. A corporation is automatically terminated upon the death of a majority of its shareholders.

44. A corporation as a separate legal entity can do which of the following?
    a. Contract in its own name with its own shareholders.
    b. Contract in its own name with its own shareholders only if a majority of its shareholders agree that such a contract can be made.
    c. Contract in its own name with third parties.
    d. Both a and c are correct.

45. Which of the following are characteristics of the corporate form of doing business?
    a. Persons who manage corporations need not be shareholders.

b. The corporation may convey or hold property in its own name.

c. The corporation can sue or be sued in its own name.

d. All of the above are true.

46. Which of the following is a disadvantage of a Subchapter C corporation?

a. It may face higher tax burdens than a Subchapter S corporation.

b. The shareholders lose their limited liability when they switch from a general partnership to a corporation.

c. A Subchapter C corporation is not well defined under the law.

d. A Subchapter C corporation does not protect its shareholders from liability as well as a Subchapter S corporation does.

47. Bond Company is incorporated in Florida but not in Georgia. Bond has branch offices in both states. Which of the following is correct?

I. Bond is a domestic corporation in Georgia.

II. Bond is a domestic corporation in Florida.

III. Bond needs to incorporate also in Georgia.

a. I and II only.

b. II only.

c. II and III only.

d. I, II, and III.

48. Colby formed a professional corporation along with two other attorneys. They took out loans in the name of the corporation. During the first year, Colby failed to file some papers on time for a client, causing the client to lose a very good case. For which does Colby have the corporate protection of limited liability?

I. The negligence for failure to file the papers on time.

II. The corporate loans.

a. I only.

b. II only.

c. Both I and II.

d. Neither I nor II.

49. Macro Corporation was incorporated and doing business in Illinois. It is doing business in various other states including Nevada. Which of the following statements is (are) true?

a. Macro must incorporate in Nevada.

b. Macro is a domestic corporation in Nevada.

c. Macro is a domestic corporation in Illinois.

d. All of the above are true.

50. Cleanit Corporation was incorporated in Colorado. Cleanit wishes to perform some transactions in other states but does not want to incorporate or obtain a certificate of authority to qualify to do business in those other states. Which of the following normally would require Cleanit to obtain a certificate of authority in other states?

a. Using the U.S. mail to solicit orders in those states.

b. Holding bank accounts in those states.

c. Collecting debts in those states.

d. None of the above.

51. Which of the following statements is true of professional corporations under the various state laws?

I. The professionals in the corporation have personal liability for their professional acts.

II. Normally under state laws, only licensed professionals are permitted to own shares in professional corporations.

a. I only is true.

b. II only is true.

c. Both I and II are true.

d. Neither I nor II is true.

52. Which of the following statements is correct with respect to the differences and similarities between a corporation and a limited partnership?

a. Stockholders may be entitled to vote on corporate matters, but limited partners are prohibited from voting on any partnership matters.

b. Stock of a corporation may be subject to the registration requirements of the federal securities laws, but limited partnership interests are automatically exempt from those requirements.

c. Directors owe fiduciary duties to the corporation, and limited partners owe such duties to the partnership.

d. A corporation and a limited partnership may be created only under a state statute, and each must file a copy of its organizational document with the proper governmental body.

53. Under the Revised Model Business Corporation Act, which of the following must be contained in a corporation's articles of incorporation?

a. Quorum voting requirements.

b. Names of stockholders.

c. Provisions for issuance of par and nonpar shares.

d. The number of shares the corporation is authorized to issue.

54. Which of the following facts is (are) generally included in a corporation's articles of incorporation?

	Name of registered agent	Number of authorized shares
a.	Yes	Yes
b.	Yes	No
c.	No	Yes
d.	No	No

55. Absent a specific provision in its articles of incorporation, a corporation's board of directors has the power to do all of the following **except**:
   a. Repeal the bylaws.
   b. Declare dividends.
   c. Fix compensation of directors.
   d. Amend the articles of incorporation.

56. Which of the following statements is correct concerning the similarities between a limited partnership and a corporation?
   a. Each is created under a statute and must file a copy of its certificate with the proper state authorities.
   b. All corporate stockholders and all partners in a limited partnership have limited liability.
   c. Both are recognized for federal income tax purposes as taxable entities.
   d. Both are allowed statutorily to have perpetual existence.

57. Promoters of a corporation that is not yet in existence:
   a. Are persons that form the corporation and arrange for capitalization to help begin the corporation.
   b. Are agents of the corporation.
   c. Can bind the future corporation to currently made contracts they make for the future corporation.
   d. Are shielded from personal liability on contracts they make with third parties on behalf of the future corporation.

58. Johns owns 400 shares of Abco Corp. cumulative preferred stock. In the absence of any specific contrary provisions in Abco's articles of incorporation, which of the following statements is correct?
   a. Johns is entitled to convert the 400 shares of preferred stock to a like number of shares of common stock.
   b. If Abco declares a cash dividend on its preferred stock, Johns becomes an unsecured creditor of Abco.

   c. If Abco declares a dividend on its common stock, Johns will be entitled to participate with the common stock shareholders in any dividend distribution made after preferred dividends are paid.
   d. Johns will be entitled to vote if dividend payments are in arrears.

59. Gallagher Corporation issued 100,000 shares of $40 par value stock for $50 per share to various investors. Subsequently, Gallagher purchased back 10,000 of those shares for $30 per share and held them as treasury stock. When the price of the stock recovered somewhat, Gallagher sold this treasury stock to Thomas for $35 per share. Which of the following statements is correct?
   I. Gallagher's purchase of the stock at below par value is illegal.
   II. Gallagher's purchase of the stock at below par value is void as an ultra vires act.
   III. Gallagher's resale of the treasury stock at below par value is valid.
      a. I only.
      b. II only.
      c. III only.
      d. I and II only.

60. An owner of common stock will **not** have any liability beyond actual investment if the owner
   a. Paid less than par value for stock purchased in connection with an original issue of shares.
   b. Agreed to perform future services for the corporation in exchange for original issue par value shares.
   c. Purchased treasury shares for less than par value.
   d. Failed to pay the full amount owed on a subscription contract for no-par shares.

61. Which of the following securities are corporate debt securities?

	Convertible bonds	Debenture bonds	Warrants
a.	Yes	Yes	Yes
b.	Yes	No	Yes
c.	Yes	Yes	No
d.	No	Yes	Yes

62. All of the following distributions to stockholders are considered asset or capital distributions **except**:
   a. Liquidating dividends.
   b. Stock splits.
   c. Property distributions.
   d. Cash dividends.

63. Which of the following constitute(s) valid consideration or value to purchase shares of stock?
   a. Services performed.
   b. Intangible property.
   c. Services contracted to be performed in the future.
   d. All of the above.

64. Brawn subscribed to 1,000 shares of $1 par value stock of Caldo Corporation at the agreed amount of $20 per share. She paid $5,000 on April 1 and then paid $9,000 on August 1. Caldo Corporation filed for bankruptcy on December 1, and the creditors of the corporation sought to hold Brawn liable under her subscription agreement. Which of the following is true?
   a. Brawn has no liability to the creditors because subscription contract was with the corporation, not the creditors.
   b. Brawn has no liability to the creditors because she has paid more than $1,000 to the corporation, which is the par value of the 1,000 shares.
   c. Brawn is liable for $6,000 to the creditors for the amount unpaid on the subscription price.
   d. Brawn is liable for $6,000 to the creditors based on the doctrine of ultra vires.

65. Pearl Corporation has some treasury stock on hand. Which of the following is (are) true?
   a. Pearl may not vote these shares of treasury stock.
   b. Pearl's treasury stock does not receive any dividends.
   c. Both of the above statements are true.
   d. Neither of the above statements is true.

66. Treasury stock of a corporation is stock that:
   a. Has been issued by that corporation but is not outstanding.
   b. Was purchased from another corporation and is retained for a specified purpose.
   c. Has been canceled.
   d. None of the above is true.

67. By law, a corporation:
   a. Must issue both common stock and preferred stock.
   b. May issue more than one class of common stock as well as more than one class of preferred stock.
   c. Must issue dividends if it has earned a profit.
   d. Must issue at least some cumulative preferred stock.

68. Mesa Corporation is planning on issuing some debt securities. Which of the following statements is true?
   a. The holders of debt securities are owners of the corporation.
   b. A bond is an instrument for long-term secured debt.
   c. A debenture is an instrument for long-term secured debt.
   d. None of the above is true.

69. Stock of a corporation is called watered stock when the cash or property exchanged to acquire the stock is:
   a. Less than the market value of the stock.
   b. More than the market value of the stock.
   c. Less than the par value or stated value of the stock.
   d. More than the par value or stated value of the stock.

70. Corporations generally have which of the following powers without shareholder approval?
   I. Power to acquire their own shares.
   II. Power to make charitable contributions.
   III. Power to make loans to directors.
      a. I only.
      b. I and II only.
      c. II and III only.
      d. I, II, and III.

71. Murphy is an employee of Landtry Corporation. Which of the following acts would make the corporation liable for Murphy's actions?
   I. Murphy deceived a customer to convince him to purchase one of Landtry's products.
   II. Murphy hit a customer with his fist, breaking his jaw. The management had warned Murphy that he and not the corporation would be responsible for any aggression against customers.
      a. I only.
      b. II only.
      c. Both I and II.
      d. Neither I nor II.

72. Which of the following statements is (are) true?
   I. Corporations can be found liable for crimes.
   II. Directors can face prison sentences for crimes committed by their corporations.
   III. Employees can be found guilty of crimes they commit while working for their corporation.
      a. I only.
      b. I and II only.
      c. III only.
      d. I, II, and III.

73. Norwood was a promoter of Parker Corporation. On March 15, Norwood purchased some real estate from Burrows in Parker's name and signed the contract "Norwood, as agent of Parker Corporation." Parker Corporation, however, did not legally come into existence until June 10. Norwood never informed Burrows on or before March 15 that Parker Corporation was not yet formed. After the corporation was formed, the board of directors refused to adopt the preincorporation contract made by Norwood concerning the real estate deal with Burrows. Burrows sued Parker, Norwood, and the board of directors. Which of the following is correct?
    a. None of these parties can be held liable.
    b. Norwood only is liable.
    c. Norwood and Parker are liable but not the board of directors.
    d. Norwood, Parker, and the board of directors are all liable.

74. Under the Revised Model Business Corporation Act, which of the following statements is correct regarding corporate officers of a public corporation?
    a. An officer may not simultaneously serve as a director.
    b. A corporation may be authorized to indemnify its officers for liability incurred in a suit by stockholders.
    c. Stockholders always have the right to elect a corporation's officers.
    d. An officer of a corporation is required to own at least one share of the corporation's stock.

75. The officers of West Corporation wish to buy some used equipment for West Corporation. The used equipment is actually owned by Parks, a director of West Corporation. For this transaction to **not** be a conflict of interest for Parks, which of the following is (are) required to be true?
    I. Parks sells the used equipment to West Corporation in a contract that is fair and reasonable to the corporation.
    II. Parks's ownership of the used equipment is disclosed to the shareholders of West who approve it by majority vote.
    III. Parks's ownership of the used equipment is disclosed to the board of directors, who approve it by a majority vote of the disinterested directors.
    a. Any one of I, II, or III.
    b. I and II are both required.
    c. I and III are both required.
    d. All three of I, II, and III are required.

76. The following are two statements concerning a fiduciary duty in a corporation.
    I. Officers and directors of a corporation owe a fiduciary duty to that corporation.
    II. Majority shareholders of a corporation can owe a fiduciary duty to the minority shareholders.
    Which of the statements is (are) correct?
    a. I only.
    b. II only.
    c. Both I and II.
    d. Neither I nor II.

77. Hogan is a director of a large corporation. Hogan owns a piece of land that the corporation wishes to purchase, and Hogan desires to sell this land at the fair market price. If Hogan sells the land to the corporation, has he breached any fiduciary duty?
    a. No, a director does not owe a fiduciary duty to his corporation.
    b. No, since Hogan is selling the land to his corporation in a fair and reasonable contract.
    c. Yes, unless he discloses his conflict of interest to the shareholders who must then approve the sale of by a simple majority.
    d. Yes, unless he discloses his conflict of interest to the shareholders, who must then approve the sale by a two-thirds vote.

78. Which of the following is **not** a power of the board of directors?
    a. May select the officers of the corporation.
    b. May declare the dividends to be paid to the shareholders.
    c. May amend the Articles of Incorporation.
    d. All of the above are powers of the board of directors.

79. Which of the following statements is (are) true under the law affecting corporations?
    I. A corporation may indemnify directors against lawsuits based on their good-faith actions for the corporation.
    II. A corporation may indemnify officers against lawsuits based on their good-faith actions for the corporation.
    III. A corporation is allowed to purchase liability insurance for its directors.
    a. I only.
    b. I and II only.
    c. I and III only.
    d. I, II, and III.

80. Which of the following is (are) true concerning corporations?

a. Directors owe a fiduciary duty to the corporation.
b. Officers owe a fiduciary duty to the corporation.
c. Both of the above are true.
d. None of the above are true.

81. McGarry is an officer of Norton Corporation. McGarry has committed a tort while acting for Norton Corporation within the scope of her authority. Which of the following is (are) true?
a. McGarry is liable for the tort committed.
b. Norton Corporation is liable for the tort committed.
c. Both McGarry and Norton are liable for the tort committed.
d. Neither McGarry nor Norton is liable for the tort committed.

82. Acorn Corp. wants to acquire the entire business of Trend Corp. Which of the following methods of business combination will best satisfy Acorn's objectives without requiring the approval of the shareholders of either corporation?
a. A merger of Trend into Acorn, whereby Trend shareholders receive cash or Acorn shares.
b. A sale of all the assets of Trend, outside the regular course of business, to Acorn for cash.
c. An acquisition of all the shares of Trend through a compulsory share exchange for Acorn shares.
d. A cash tender offer, whereby Acorn acquires at least 90% of Trend's shares, followed by a short-form merger of Trend into Acorn.

83. Price owns 2,000 shares of Universal Corp.'s $10 cumulative preferred stock. During its first year of operations, cash dividends of $5 per share were declared on the preferred stock but were never paid. In the second year, dividends on the preferred stock were neither declared nor paid. If Universal is dissolved, which of the following statements is correct?
a. Universal will be liable to Price as an unsecured creditor for $10,000.
b. Universal will be liable to Price as a secured creditor for $20,000.
c. Price will have priority over the claims of Universal's bond owners.
d. Price will have priority over the claims of Universal's unsecured judgment creditors.

84. Under the Revised Model Business Corporation Act, when a corporation's articles of incorporation grant stockholders preemptive rights, which of the following rights is (are) included in that grant?

	Right to purchase a proportionate share of a newly issued stock	Right to a proportionate share of corporate assets remaining on corporate dissolution
a.	Yes	Yes
b.	Yes	No
c.	No	Yes
d.	No	No]

85. Under the Revised Model Business Corporation Act, which of the following actions by a corporation would entitle a stockholder to dissent from the action and obtain payment of the fair value of his/her shares?
I. An amendment to the articles of incorporation that materially and adversely affects rights in respect of a dissenter's shares because it alters or abolishes a preferential right of the shares.
II. Consummation of a plan of share exchange to which the corporation is a party as the corporation whose shares will be acquired, if the stockholder is entitled to vote on the plan.
a. I only.
b. II only.
c. Both I and II.
d. Neither I nor II.

86. To which of the following rights is a stockholder of a public corporation entitled?
a. The right to have annual dividends declared and paid.
b. The right to vote for the election of officers.
c. The right to a reasonable inspection of corporate records.
d. The right to have the corporation issue a new class of stock.

87. Which of the following is correct pertaining to the rights of stockholders in a corporation?
a. Stockholders have no right to manage their corporation unless they are also directors or officers.
b. Stockholders have a right to receive dividends.
c. Stockholders have no right to inspect the books and records of their corporation.
d. Stockholders have a right to get a list of their corporation's customers to use for a business mailing list.

88. The limited liability of a stockholder in a closely held corporation may be challenged successfully if the stockholder:

a. Undercapitalized the corporation when it was formed.

b. Formed the corporation solely to have limited personal liability.

c. Sold property to the corporation.

d. Was a corporate officer, director, or employee.

89. The corporate veil is most likely to be pierced and the shareholders held personally liable if:

a. The corporation has elected S corporation status under the Internal Revenue Code.

b. The shareholders have commingled their personal funds with those of the corporation.

c. An ultra vires act has been committed.

d. A partnership incorporates its business solely to limit the liability of its partners.

90. Which of the following is correct about the law of corporations?

a. Each shareholder owes a fiduciary duty to his/her corporation.

b. Majority shareholders owe a fiduciary duty to their corporation.

c. Majority shareholders do not owe a fiduciary duty to minority shareholders.

d. All of the above are correct.

91. A parent corporation owned more than 90% of each class of the outstanding stock issued by a subsidiary corporation and decided to merge that subsidiary into itself. Under the Revised Model Business Corporation Act, which of the following actions must be taken?

a. The subsidiary corporation's board of directors must pass a merger resolution.

b. The subsidiary corporation's dissenting stockholders must be given an appraisal remedy.

c. The parent corporation's stockholders must approve the merger.

d. The parent corporation's dissenting stockholders must be given an appraisal remedy.

92. Under the Revised Model Business Corporation Act, a merger of two public corporations usually requires all of the following **except**:

a. A formal plan of merger.

b. An affirmative vote by the holders of a majority of each corporation's voting shares.

c. Receipt of voting stock by all stockholders of the original corporations.

d. Approval by the board of directors of each corporation.

93. Which of the following statements is a general requirement for the merger of two corporations?

a. The merger plan must be approved unanimously by the stockholders of both corporations.

b. The merger plan must be approved unanimously by the boards of both corporations.

c. The absorbed corporation must amend its articles of incorporation.

d. The stockholders of both corporations must be given due notice of a special meeting, including a copy or summary of the merger plan.

94. Which of the following must take place for a corporation to be voluntarily dissolved?

a. Passage by the board of directors of a resolution to dissolve.

b. Approval by the officers of a resolution to dissolve.

c. Amendment of the certificate of incorporation.

d. Unanimous vote of the stockholders.

95. A corporate stockholder is entitled to which of the following rights?

a. Elect officers.

b. Receive annual dividends.

c. Approve dissolution.

d. Prevent corporate borrowing.

96. When a consolidation takes place under the law of corporations, which of the following is true?

a. Two or more corporations are joined into one new corporation.

b. All assets are acquired by the new corporation.

c. The new corporation is liable for the debts of each of the old corporations.

d. All of the above are true.

97. When a corporation elects to be a Subchapter S corporation, which of the following statements is (are) true regarding the federal tax treatment of the corporation's income or loss?

I. The corporation's income is taxed at the corporate level and not the shareholders' level.

II. The shareholders report the corporation's income on their tax returns when the income is distributed to them.

III. The shareholders report the corporation's income on their tax returns even if the income is not distributed to them.

IV. The shareholders generally report the
corporation's loss on their tax returns.
a. I only is true.

b. II only is true.
c. III only is true.
d. III and IV only are true.

ANSWER EXPLANATIONS

A. Nature of Sole Proprietorships

1. **(a)** Federal or state governments do not typically require any formal filing. If the business operates under a name different from that of the sole proprietor, most states require that a fictitious name statement be filed. Answer (b) is incorrect because the sole proprietorship and the sole proprietor are not separate legal entities. Answer (c) is incorrect because a sole proprietor does not have partners or shareholders from whom to obtain capital. Answer (d) is incorrect because the simplicity of this business structure is one of its advantages in its formation and operation.

B. Nature of Partnerships

2. **(b)** A general partnership is an association of two or more persons to carry on a business as co-owners for profit. There must be at least two partners involved in order for a partnership to exist. Answer (a) is incorrect because a general partnership is normally not recognized as a taxable entity under federal income tax laws. Answer (c) is incorrect because execution of written articles of partnership is not required to create a general partnership. A partnership agreement may be oral or in writing. Answer (d) is incorrect because a partnership does not have to provide for apportionment of liability for partnership debt. Note that even if the partners agreed to split partnership liability in a specified proportion, third parties still can hold each partner personally liable despite the agreement.

3. **(d)** A partnership involves two or more persons to carry on a business as co-owners for a profit. Partnerships do not include nonprofit associations such as charitable organizations, labor unions or clubs.]

4. **(b)** A silent partner does not help manage the partnership but still has unlimited liability.

C. Types of Partnerships and Partners

5. **(c)** A general partner has a voice in management and has unlimited personal liability. Anyone, including a secured creditor of the limited partnership, may be a general partner if he/she takes on these responsibilities. Answer (a) is incorrect because an unsecured creditor of the limited partnership may also be a limited partner. A limited partner is defined as having no voice in management and his/her liability is limited to the extent of his/her capital contribution. Answer (b) is incorrect because a general partner also may be a limited partner at the same time. This partner would have the rights, powers, and liability of a general partner, and the rights against other partners with respect to his/her contribution as both a limited and a general partner. Answer (d) is incorrect because every limited partnership must have at least one general partner who will be liable for the partnership obligations.

D. Formation of Partnership

6. **(d)** A partnership agreement may be expressed or implied based on the activities and conduct of the partners. The expressed agreement may be oral or in writing with, in general, one exception. A partnership agreement that cannot be completed within one year from the date on which it is entered into must be in writing. Answer (b) is incorrect because the partners may reside in different states without having to put the partnership agreement in writing. Answer (a) is incorrect because the $500 amount applies to the sale of goods that must be in writing, not partnerships. Answer (c) is incorrect because the purpose of the partnership is irrelevant. Agreements to buy and sell real estate must be in writing while an agreement to form a partnership whose principal activity will involve the buying and selling of real estate normally need not be in writing unless the stated duration exceeds one year.

7. **(d)** Under RUPA, the partnership is a legal entity that can own property in its own name. The partners also have joint and several liability for all debts whether they are based in contract or tort.

8. **(c)** The partners may agree to share profits as well as losses unequally. Answer (a) is incorrect because the partners may agree that ownership in the partnership is unequal. Answer (b) is

incorrect because under RUPA, the partnership is a separate legal entity. Answer (d) is incorrect because the partners may agree to unequal management rights.

E. Partner's Rights

9. **(d)** Profits and losses in a general partnership are shared equally unless otherwise specified in the partnership agreement. If partners agree on unequal profit sharing but are silent on loss sharing, then losses are shared per the profit-sharing proportions. The partnership agreement for Owen Associates provided that profits be paid to the partners in the ratio of their financial contribution to the partnership.
    The ratios are:
    Total contributed $10,000 + 30,000 + 50,000 = $90,000

Moore	$10,000 \div 90,000 = 1/9
Noon	$30,000 \div 90,000 = 1/3
Kale	$50,000 \div 90,000 = 5/9

    For the year ended December 31, 2008, Owen had losses of $180,000. Therefore, Kale would be allocated $100,000 of the losses ($180,000 \times 5/9).

10. **(b)** An incoming partner has the same rights as all of the existing partners. Thus, an incoming partner has the right to participate in the management of the partnership. Answer (c) is incorrect since a person admitted as a partner into an existing partnership is liable only for existing debts of the partnership to the extent of the incoming partner's capital contribution. Answer (d) is incorrect because a partner need not make a capital contribution to be admitted with the same rights as the other partners.

11. **(b)** A partner is free to assign his interest in any partnership to a third party. However, the assignee does not become a partner by virtue of this assignment but merely succeeds to the assignor's rights as to profits and return of partner's capital contribution. The assignee does not receive the right to manage, to have an accounting, to inspect the books, or to possess or use any individual partnership property. Since Bean was not made a partner, he is entitled to Cobb's share of TLC's profits but does not have the right to participate in the management of TLC.

F. Relationship to Third Parties

12. **(a)** A partner's apparent authority is derived from the reasonable perceptions of third parties due to

the manifestations or representations of the partnership concerning the authority each partner possesses to bind the partnership. However, if third parties are aware of a formal resolution that limits the partner's actual authority to bind the partnership, then that partner's apparent authority also wil be limited. Answer (b) is incorrect because if third parties are unaware of such a resolution that limits the partner's actual authority, then the partner retains apparent authority to bind the partnership. Answer (c) is incorrect because third parties should be aware that in order for a partner to submit a claim against the partnership to arbitration, unanimous consent of the partners is needed. Therefore, a partner has no apparent authority to take such an action. Answer (d) is incorrect because, as stated above, the apparent authority of a partner to bind the partnership is not derived from the express powers and purposes contained in the partnership agreement.

13. **(b)** In a general partnership, unanimous consent is required of all of the partners to admit a new partner. Answer (a) is incorrect because any one partner can cause a dissolution by actions such as withdrawing. Answer (c) is incorrect because each partner is an agent of the general partnership and thus may purchase items for the business of the firm. Answer (d) is incorrect; an individual partner may sell real property on behalf of the partnership because he/she is an agent of the partnership.

14. **(c)** Under the Revised Uniform Partnership Act, partners have joint and several liability not only for torts but also breaches of contract. This is a change from previous law.

15. **(c)** Although individual partners normally have implied authority to buy and sell goods for the partnership, they do not have implied authority to do such things as making the partnership a surety or admitting a new partner. These require the consent of all partners.

16. **(d)** A partner's interest in a partnership is freely assignable without the other partners' consent. A partner's interest refers to the partners' right to share in profits and return of contribution. Answer (a) is incorrect because the assignee does not become a partner without the consent of all the other partners. Answer (b) is incorrect because the assignor remains liable as a partner. The assignee has received only the partner's right to share in profits and capital return. Answer (c)

is incorrect because assignment of a partner's interest does not cause dissolution unless the assignor also withdraws.

G. Termination of a Partnership

17. **(b)** Under RUPA, partnership property not only includes property purchased in the partnership name but also includes property purchased by a partner, who is an agent of the partnership, with partnership funds. Note that a partner may use property in the partnership business without it becoming partnership property.

18. **(d)** Even if a partner has agreed not to withdraw before a certain period of time, he or she has the power to do so anyway. That partner's withdrawal is a break of contract and causes a dissolution of the partnership. Answer (a) is incorrect because this dissolution is caused by an act of a partner rather than by operation of law. Answer (b) is incorrect because Wind's withdrawal does have an effect on the remaining partners because they must decide on what new terms they will operate or else wind up and terminate the partnership. Answer (c) is incorrect because the dissolution is effective once Wind does withdraw from the partnership. A court decree is not necessary.

19. **(a)** The best approach to answer this question is to make a chart as follows:

	Dowd 40%	Elgar 30%	Frost 20%	Grant 10%
Capital balance	$120,000	$100,000	$75,000	$11,000
Allocation of loss $200,000	(80,000)	(60,000)	(40,000)	(20,000)
Remaining balance	40,000	40,000	35,000	(9,000)
Distribution of deficit of insolvent partner:				9,000
40/90 × 9,000	(4,000)			
30/90 × 9,000		(3,000)		
20/90 × 9,000			(2,000)	
Balance	36,000	37,000	33,000	0
Cash distribution $106,000	(36,000)	(37,000)	(33,000)	0
	0	0	0	0

A capital deficit may be corrected by the partner investing more cash or assets to eliminate the deficit or by distributing the deficit to the other partners in their resulting profit and loss sharing ratio. The latter was done in this case, as the facts in the question indicated that Grant refuses to make any further contributions to the partnership. The remaining cash is then used to pay the three partners' capital balances.

H. Limited Partnerships

20. **(c)** Under the Revised Uniform Limited Partnership Act, when the partners do not agree how to split profits, the split is made in proportion to their capital contributions. Note that this is different for general partners under the Revised Uniform Partnership Act.

21. **(a)** Limited partnerships must have at least one general partner who has the unlimited personal liability of the firm. Unlike a general partner, the death of a limited partner does not cause a dissolution or termination of a partner.

22. **(a)** Since Chan acted like a general partner and Ham thought he was a general partner, Chan has the liability of a general partner to Ham. Answers (b), (c), and (d) are incorrect because Ham believed Chan was a general partner based on Chan's actions. Therefore, Chan had the liability of a general partner, that is, unlimited liability.

23. **(a)** Under the Revised Uniform Limited Partnership Act, none of the names of the limited partners needs to be listed in the certificate of limited partnership that is filed with the secretary of state. However, all of the general partners must be listed.

24. **(c)** A limited partner is allowed, without losing the protection of limited liability, to act as an agent of the limited partnership. The limited partner also may vote on the removal of a general partner.

25. **(d)** Partners' capital may be not only in cash, property, or services already performed but also in the form of promises to give or perform these at a future date.

26. **(d)** If the liability is more than the partnership can pay, each partner loses its capital contribution and then the general partner has personal, unlimited liability for the debt.

27. **(d)** The admission of a new general partner to a limited partnership under the Revised Uniform Limited Partnership Act requires the approval of all partners.

28. **(d)** Unlike the admission of a new general partner, the admission of a new limited partner requires the written approval of not only all of the general partners but also all of the limited partners.

29. **(c)** Death or bankruptcy of a general partner in a limited partnership will cause dissolution of the limited partnership. However, this is not true if a limited partner dies or goes bankrupt.

I. Joint Ventures

30. **(d)** The law of joint ventures is similar to the law of partnerships with some exceptions. One of these exceptions is that the death of a joint venturer does not automatically dissolve the joint venture. Answers (a), (b), and (c) are all incorrect because these are all examples in which joint venture law and partnership law are similar, involving liability, right to participate in management, and fiduciary duties.

J. Limited Liability Companies (LLC)

31. **(a)** A limited liability company provides for limited liability of its members, similar to the limited liability of the shareholders of a corporation. However, it typically has a limited duration of existence, similar to that of a partnership in which the death or withdrawal of a member or partner causes the business to dissolve unless the remaining members or partners choose to continue the business. The limited liability company also can be taxed similar to a partnership if formed to do so. The Subchapter S corporation has the limited liability of the corporation but is taxed similar to a partnership.

32. **(b)** The limited liability company statutes provide that it is a separate legal entity apart from its owners. Thus, it may sue or be sued in its own name. Answer (a) is incorrect because all owners have limited rather than personal liability. Answer (c) is incorrect because limited liability normally is retained even if the owners fail to follow the formalities usual in conducting the business. Answer (d) is incorrect because (b) is correct.

33. **(c)** Limited liability companies typically have a limited life. Provisions often provide that they exist for 30 years at most and dissolve if a member dies. Therefore (a) is an incorrect response. Answer (b) is also not chosen because members (owners) are permitted to participate in the management of the LLC or can choose the management. Answer (d) is an incorrect response because one of the main benefits of an LLC is the limited liability of its members (owners).

34. **(c)** Owners and managers of an LLC owe a duty of due care to not be grossly negligent. They also owe a duty to be loyal to their LLC.

35. **(b)** In the typical limited liability company (LLC), unlike the common corporation, the interests of the members are not freely transferable. The other members have to agree to admit new members. Answer (a) is incorrect because it provides for limited liability of all of its members. Answer (c) is incorrect because all members have a voice in the management of the LLC. Answer (d) is incorrect because a limited liability company must be formed pursuant to the filing requirements of the relevant state statute.

K. Limited Liability Partnerships (LLP)

36. **(b)** In a limited liability partnership (LLP), where permitted by state statute, the basic difference between it and a general partnership is limited liability in some cases. In the LLP, partners have limited liability for the torts of the other partners. This is not true of a general partnership. Answer (a) is wrong because both in the LLP and the general partnership, the partners have unlimited liability for their own torts. Answers (c) and (d) are wrong because any contracts signed on behalf of the firm make all of the partners jointly liable in both the LLP and the general partnership.

L. Subchapter C Corporations

37. **(b)** The federal Subchapter S Revision Act specifies that all corporations that do not meet the criteria of a Subchapter S corporation are categorized as a Subchapter C corporation. Answers (a), (c), and (d) are incorrect because the act provides that a corporation is either a Subchapter S or Subchapter C corporation but not both at the same time.

38. **(b)** All corporations are divided under the federal Subchapter S Revision Act as being either a

Subchapter C corporation or a Subchapter S corporation. Answer (a) is incorrect because the federal Subchapter S Revision Act provides that there are two categories of corporations: Subchapter C and Subchapter S corporations. Answer (c) is incorrect because this federal law provides for only two categories of corporations. A Subchapter E corporation is not one of these. Answer (d) is incorrect because answer (c) is correct.

39. **(c)** Both Subchapter C corporations and Subchapter S corporations are similar in their provisions for the limited liability of their shareholders and also in their corporate management structures. Answer (a) is incorrect because it does not include the similarity of the corporate management structures. Answer (b) is incorrect because it does not mention the similarity of the shareholders' limited liability. Answer (d) is incorrect for the reason that answer (c) is correct.

40. **(a)** Tax treatment is the main reason why Subchapter S corporations are formed instead of Subchapter C corporations. Answer (b) is incorrect because this federal act covers both types of corporations. Answers (c) and (d) are incorrect because the provisions on the limited liability of shareholders and the provisions for the structure of corporate management are some of the ways that Subchapter C and Subchapter S corporations are generally similar.

M. Characteristics and Advantages of Corporate Form

41. **(c)** One advantage of the corporate form of business is that it has a continuous life and is not terminated by the death of a shareholder or manager. Answer (a) is incorrect because although the power to manage the corporation is vested in the board of directors, they usually delegate the day-to-day management responsibilities to various managers. Answer (b) is incorrect because in most corporations, ownership is not contractually restricted. In fact, free transferability of the shares of stock is a major advantage of the corporate form of business. Answer (d) is incorrect because corporations are not free from state regulation.

42. **(c)** A major advantage is that shareholders have limited liability, that is, typically limited to what they paid for the stock. However, managers do not have limited liability for their actions as managers. If a manager is also a shareholder, he/she has limited liability for the ownership in the stock but still can be sued for misdeeds as a manager. Answers (a), (b), and (d) are all considered to be advantages of a corporation. Note that since a person can manage a corporation without necessarily being an owner, this can encourage professional managers to get involved.

43. **(d)** The death of one or more of a corporation's shareholders does not automatically terminate it. Answer (a) is incorrect because a corporation continues to exist until it is dissolved, merged, or otherwise terminated. Answer (b) is incorrect because shares in a corporation, represented by stocks, can be freely bought, sold, or assigned unless the shareholders have agreed to restrict this. Answer (c) is incorrect because a corporation is legally a separate entity apart from its shareholders.

44. **(d)** A corporation may make contracts in its own name with both its shareholders and third parties. Answer (a) is incorrect because it also may make contracts with third parties. Answer (b) is incorrect because corporations do not generally need the consent of other shareholders to contract with one shareholder. Answer (c) is incorrect because it may also contract with its shareholders.

45. **(d)** Persons who manage a corporation may be, but need not be, shareholders of that corporation. Also, a corporation as a separate legal entity may convey or hold property. It may also sue or be sued in its own name. Answers (a), (b), and (c) are not comprehensive enough.

N. Disadvantages of Corporate Business Structure

46. **(a)** A Subchapter S corporation often is formed to help avoid the double taxation that a Subchapter C corporation may face. Answer (b) is incorrect because partners in a general partnership have unlimited personal liability. Shareholders of a corporation have limited liability with few exceptions. Answer (c) is incorrect because a Subchapter C corporation is any corporation that is not a Subchapter S corporation. Answer (d) is incorrect because both Subchapter C and Subchapter S corporations provide their shareholders with limited liability with few exceptions.

O. Types of Corporations

47. **(b)** Bond is a domestic corporation in Florida since it incorporated there. It is a foreign corporation in Georgia since it did not incorporate there. Bond does not need to incorporate in Georgia but must qualify to do business there because it has branch offices in Georgia. This qualifying normally entails filing required documents with the state.

48. **(b)** In a professional corporation, the professional has most of the benefits of a corporation, such as limited liability for corporate debts. However, the professional has personal liability for professional acts. Colby cannot avoid liability for the damage caused the client due to negligence in a professional act.

49. **(c)** A domestic corporation is one that operates and does business in the state in which it was incorporated. Answer (a) is incorrect because Macro, instead of incorporating in Nevada, may qualify to do business by obtaining a certificate of authority from Nevada. Answer (b) is incorrect because Macro is a foreign corporation in Nevada because it did not incorporate there. Answer (d) is incorrect because the statement in (c) is the only one that is true.

50. **(d)** None of the listed items is normally considered doing business in the other states such that Cleanit would be required to qualify to do business and thus have to obtain certificates of authority from those states. Therefore, answers (a), (b), and (c) are incorrect.

51. **(c)** Normally, under state laws, only licensed professionals may own shares in professional corporations. Furthermore, the licensed professionals retain personal liability for their professional acts in the professional corporation. Therefore, (a), (b), and (d) are incorrect.

P. Formation of Corporation

52. **(d)** Corporations and limited partnerships may be created only pursuant to state statutes. Normally, both the articles of incorporation and a certificate of limited partnership must be filed with the secretary of state. Answer (c) is incorrect since limited partners do not owe fiduciary duties to the partnership. Answer (a) is incorrect since limited partners have the right to vote on partnership matters such as the dissolution or winding up of

the partnership, loans of the partnership, a change in the nature of the business of a partnership, and the removal of a general partner without jeopardizing their limited partner status. Answer (b) is incorrect since sale of limited partnership interests is not automatically exempted from the registration requirements of the general securities laws.

53. **(d)** Under the Revised Model Business Corporation Act, a corporation's articles of incorporation generally must include the name of the corporation, the purpose of the corporation, the powers of the corporation, the name of the incorporators, the name of the registered agent of the corporation, and the number of shares of stock the corporation is authorized to issue.

54. **(a)** The articles of incorporation are filed with the state and contain the names of the corporation, registered agent, and incorporators. This document also contains the purpose and powers of the corporation as well as a description of the types of stock and number of authorized shares.

55. **(d)** Normally, the board of directors of a corporation has the power to adopt, amend, and repeal the bylaws. It also has the power to declare dividends and fix the compensation of the directors. However, it does not have the power to amend the articles of incorporation.

56. **(a)** Corporations and limited partnerships may be created only pursuant to state statutes. Normally, both the articles of incorporation and a certificate of limited partnership must be filed with the secretary of state. Answer (b) is incorrect because a limited partnership requires at least one general partner who retains unlimited personal liability. Answer (c) is incorrect because a limited partnership is treated the same as a general partnership for tax purposes in that it is not recognized as a separate taxable entity. Answer (d) is incorrect because a limited partnership is not statutorily allowed perpetual existence.

57. **(a)** The basic concept of a promoter is one who forms a corporation with the goal of the corporation eventually coming into existence. Answer (b) is incorrect because for there to be an agent, there must be a principal. There is no principal yet because the corporation is not yet formed. Answer (c) is incorrect because the promoters are not agents who can bind the future corporations to contracts. Answer (d) is incorrect

because the promoters are not agents and thus cannot use agency law to protect them.

Q. Corporate Financial Structure

58. **(b)** The articles of incorporation must include, among other things, the amount of capital stock authorized and the types of stock to be issued. Specific provisions applicable to stock also must be stated. Examples of stock provisions that must be authorized by the articles of incorporation include number of authorized shares, whether the stock is to be par value or no-par value, and classes of stock, including voting rights and dividend provisions. Preferred stock is given preferred status as to liquidations and dividends. This is part of the definition of preferred stock and need not be included specifically in the articles of incorporation in order to be enforceable. Therefore, Johns becomes an unsecured creditor upon Abco's declaration of preferred stock dividend. In order for Johns to be entitled to convert his/her preferred shares to common shares, to participate with common shareholders in any dividend distribution made after preferred dividends are paid, or to be entitled to vote if dividend payments are in arrears, it must be stated in the articles of incorporation.

59. **(c)** Gallagher originally sold the stock at above par value. It may buy back and resell the shares without regard to par value.

60. **(c)** A corporation may resell treasury shares without regard to par value. Therefore, an owner of common stock who purchased treasury shares for less than par value will not have any liability beyond actual investment. Answer (a) is incorrect because an owner of common stock who paid less than par value for stock purchased in connection with an original issue of shares is contingently liable in many states to creditors for the difference between the amount paid and par value. Answer (b) is incorrect because a promise to perform future services in exchange for original issue par value shares is an executory promise, which is not considered valid consideration for shares. An owner of common stock who agreed to perform future services for the corporation in exchange for original issue par value shares is liable to creditors for the difference between any valid consideration (i.e., cash, property, or services performed) given and par value. Answer (d) is incorrect because once the corporation accepts an offer to buy stock

subscriptions, the subscriber becomes liable for the purchase. Therefore, an owner of common stock who failed to pay the full amount owed on a subscription contract for no-par shares is liable for the difference between any amounts already paid and the full amount owed according to the contract.

61. **(c)** Corporate debt securities include: (1) registered bonds, (2) bearer bonds, (3) debenture bonds, (4) mortgage bonds, (5) redeemable bonds, and (6) convertible bonds. A warrant is not a corporate debt security but rather is written evidence of a stock option that grants its owner the option to purchase a specified amount of shares of stock at a stated price within a specified period of time.

62. **(b)** A stock split increases the number of shares outstanding and proportionately decreases the par value per share. However, the total outstanding par value does not change, and therefore no charge is made to retained earnings or capital. Liquidating dividends represent a return of the stockholders' capital and are considered a capital distribution. Both cash and property distributions are considered asset distributions. Property distributions are recorded at the fair market value of the asset at the date of transfer.

63. **(d)** Valid consideration or value to purchase shares of stock can be any benefit to the corporation, including any services contracted for that are yet to be performed in the future.

64. **(c)** Since Brawn had a contract to purchase 1,000 shares at $20 per share, this is binding. Therefore, the creditors can recover in bankruptcy the remainder of the price not paid. Answer (a) is incorrect because the creditors have the right to see that the bankruptcy estate includes this amount owed the corporation. Answer (b) is incorrect because the contract required that the full $20,000 be paid, not just the par value. Answer (d) is incorrect because ultra vires acts are acts that are beyond the scope of the powers of the corporation. These do not apply to this fact pattern.

65. **(c)** Treasury stock is not votable, nor does it receive dividends. Therefore, answers (a), (b) and (d) are incorrect.

66. **(a)** Treasury stock is stock that a corporation issued previously but is no longer outstanding because the corporation purchased it back.

Answer (b) is incorrect because treasury stock is a corporation's own stock that it has repurchased. Answer (c) is incorrect because canceled stock is no longer issued or outstanding. Answer (d) is incorrect because (a) is correct.

67. **(b)** A corporation by law may issue one or more classes of common stock. This is also true for preferred stock. Answer (a) is incorrect because a corporation is not required to issue preferred stock. Answer (c) is incorrect because it is at the discretion of the board of directors to declare a dividend. They may wish to keep the earnings in the corporation for expansion purposes and the like. Answer (d) is incorrect because if it issues preferred stock, it may be either cumulative preferred stock or noncumulative preferred stock.

68. **(b)** A bond represents long-term secured debt. Answer (a) is incorrect because holders of debt securities are creditors rather than owners of the corporation. Answer (c) is incorrect because a debenture represents long-term unsecured debt, not long-term secured debt. Answer (d) is incorrect because there was one correct answer.

69. **(c)** The definition of watered stock refers to when the stock is acquired by exchanging cash or property worth less than the par or stated value of the stock.

R. Powers and Liabilities of Corporation

70. **(b)** Corporations generally have the power to acquire or retire their own shares without shareholder approval. They also can make charitable contributions without such approval. Loans to directors require shareholder approval.

71. **(c)** A business is liable for the torts of its employees committed within the course and scope of employment. This is true even if management has warned the employee that he and not the corporation will be liable. The injured third party can hold both the employee and the corporation liable in either case.

(d) All three statements are true in the interest of punishing all parties who commit crimes.

S. Du... rs and Officers of Corporations

73. **(b)** S... e the corporation never adopted the contract by words or actions, it is not liable. The board of directors is not personally liable either because it never agreed to the contract. However, Norwood is personally liable on the contract because he signed the contract and agency law will not protect him. This is true because he was not an agent, even though he claimed to be, because there was no principal to authorize him when the contract was made on March 15.

74. **(b)** Under the Revised Model Business Corporation Act, a corporation is authorized to indemnify its officers for expenses, attorney fees, judgments, fines, and amounts paid in settlement incurred in a suit by stockholders when the liability is a result of the officer's good faith, nonnegligent actions on behalf of the best interest of the corporation. Answer (a) is incorrect because a corporate officer also may serve as a director. Answer (c) is incorrect because officers are appointed by the directors of a corporation who are in turn elected by the shareholders. Answer (d) is incorrect because there is no requirement that an officer must own any shares of the corporation's stock.

75. **(a)** The transaction the director wishes to have with the corporation is not a conflict of interest if any one of these choices is true: (1) The transaction is fair and reasonable for the corporation. (2) The shareholders are given the relevant facts and they approve it by a majority vote. (3) The board of directors is given the relevant facts, and its members approve it by a majority vote of the disinterested members of the board.

76. **(c)** Officers and directors are in important positions in a corporation. As such, they owe a fiduciary duty to the corporation to act in the best interests of the corporation. Courts also have recognized that because majority shareholders can exercise a lot of power in a corporation from their stockholdings and voting rights, they owe a fiduciary duty to the minority shareholders when these majority shareholders have de facto control over the corporation by virtue of their concentrated ownership.

77. **(b)** A contract between a director and his/her corporation is valid if it is reasonable to the corporation. Hogan has not breached his fiduciary duty with the corporation since he is selling the land at fair market value. Answer (a) is incorrect because a director does owe a fiduciary duty to his/her corporation to act in its best interests. Answers (c) and (d) are incorrect because since

the transaction is fair and reasonable to the corporation, the shareholders need not approve it.

78. **(c)** The articles of incorporation may be amended by the shareholders' vote, not by the board of directors. Answer (a) is incorrect because one of the important powers of the directors is to select the officers of the corporation. Answer (b) is incorrect because it is up to the board of directors to declare any dividends to the shareholders. Answer (d) is incorrect because answer (c) is correct.

79. **(d)** A corporation may indemnify both its directors and its officers against suits based on their duties for the corporation if they acted in good faith and in the best interests of the corporation. A corporation also may purchase insurance to cover the liability for lawsuits lost based on actions of its directors and of its officers.

80. **(c)** Both directors as well as officers owe a fiduciary duty to their corporation.

81. **(c)** McGarry is liable for the tort she committed. Because she was acting within the scope of her authority in the corporation, Norton Corporation is also liable. Note that McGarry is not relieved of liability even though Norton Corporation also is liable because McGarry is the one who committed the tort. Therefore, answers (a), (b), and (d) are incorrect.

T. Stockholder's Rights

82. **(d)** When Acorn pays cash and buys 90% or more of Trend's shares, it has control of the Trend stock. It then can accomplish a short-form merger of Trend Corp. into Acorn Corp. Answer (a) is incorrect because this can require the approval of Acorn shareholders. Answer (b) is incorrect because this is not a regular sale of Trend's assets and will require shareholder approval. Answer (c) is incorrect because the entire compulsory exchange for Acorn shares to accomplish the acquisition does require shareholder approval.

83. **(a)** Upon declaration, a cash dividend on preferred stock becomes a legal debt of the corporation, and the preferred shareholders become unsecured creditors of the corporation. However, any dividends not paid in any year concerning cumulative preferred stock are not a liability of the corporation until they are declared. Therefore, Universal will be liable to Price as an unsecured creditor for $10,000, which is the amount of the declared dividends. Answers (c) and (d) are incorrect because Price has become a general unsecured creditor for the declared dividends and will have the same priority as the debenture (unsecured) bond owners and the unsecured judgment creditors. Answer (b) is incorrect because the undeclared dividends did not become a legal liability to Universal.

84. **(b)** The preemptive right gives the shareholder the right to purchase newly issued stock so as to keep the same overall percentage of ownership of the corporation. The Revised Model Business Corporation Act provides this right only if it is set forth in the articles of incorporation.

85. **(c)** When the rights of individual shareholders may be adversely affected, the shareholder is given the right to dissent and receive payment of the fair value of his/her shares. This is true even if the dissenting shareholder has voting rights when he/she is being outvoted. In statement I, the shareholder has this right because his/her preference rights are being abolished. In statement II, the dissenting shareholder has this right because his/her shares being acquired by another corporation may affect the value and rights of the shares of stock.

86. **(c)** Shareholders have the right to inspect the corporate records if done in good faith for a proper purpose. Answer (a) is incorrect because shareholders do not have a right to dividends. It is the decision of the board of directors whether to declare dividends or not. Answer (b) is incorrect because although at least one class of stock must have voting rights to elect the board of directors, the officers may be selected by the board of directors. Answer (d) is incorrect because the shareholders cannot force an issuance of a new class of stock.

87. **(a)** Stockholders do not have the right to manage their corporation. However, stockholders who are also directors or officers do have the right to manage as part of their rights as directors and officers. Answer (b) is incorrect because stockholders generally have no right to receive dividends unless the board of directors declares such dividends. Answer (c) is incorrect because stockholders are given the right to inspect the books and records of their corporation. Answer (d) is incorrect because the stockholders demand a list of shareholders for a proper purpose, such as to help wage a proxy right;

however, they may not require the corporation to give them a list of its customers to use for a mailing list.

U. Stockholder's Liability

88. **(a)** Normally, the liability of shareholders of corporations is limited to their capital contribution. However, the court will "pierce the corporate veil" and hold the shareholders personally liable for the debts of the corporation if the corporate entity is being used to defraud people or to achieve other injustices. Thus, if the shareholders establish a corporation knowing that it would have less capital than required for it to pay its debts, then the court will pierce the corporate veil and hold the shareholders personally liable. Answer (c) is incorrect because a shareholder may sell property to the corporation without becoming personally liable for the debts of the corporation. Answer (d) is incorrect because shareholders also may be corporate officers, directors, or employees without jeopardizing their limited liability status. Answer (b) is incorrect because the formation of a corporation solely to limit personal liability is a valid purpose so long as it is done without intent to defraud.

89. **(b)** The court will disregard the corporate entity and hold the shareholders individually liable when the corporate form is used to perpetrate a fraud or is found to be merely an agent or instrument of its owners. An example of when the corporate veil is likely to be pierced is if the corporation and its shareholders commingle assets and financial records. In such a situation, the shareholders lose their limited liability and will be held personally liable for the corporation's legal obligations. Answer (a) is incorrect because the election of S corporation status is allowable under the law and is not, in itself, grounds for piercing the corporate veil. Answer (d) is incorrect because the desire of shareholders to limit their personal liability is a valid reason to form a corporation. Limited personal liability is one advantage of the corporate entity. Answer (c) is incorrect since the court will hold personally liable only those corporate officers responsible for the commission of an ultra vires act. The court will not pierce the corporate veil and hold the shareholders personally liable for such act.

90. **(b)** ...jority shareholders now owe a fiduciary duty t...heir corporation. Answer (a) is incorrect

because minority shareholders do not owe a fiduciary duty to their corporation. Their main purpose normally is to be investors. Answer (c) is incorrect because majority shareholders now owe a fiduciary duty not only to their corporation but also to the minority shareholders. Answer (d) is incorrect because answer (b) is correct.

V. Substantial Change in Corporate Structure

91. **(b)** Under the Revised Model Business Corporation Act, a corporation that owns at least 90% of the outstanding shares of each class of stock of the subsidiary may merge the subsidiary into itself without approval by the shareholders of the parent or subsidiary. The approval of the shareholders or the subsidiary's board of directors is unnecessary since the parent owns 90% of the subsidiary. This ownership assures that the plan of the merger would be approved. The only requirement is a merger resolution by the board of directors of the parent corporation. Furthermore, the dissenting shareholders of the subsidiary must be given an appraisal remedy, that is, the right to obtain payment from the parent for their shares. The shareholders of the parent do not have this appraisal remedy because the merger has not changed their rights materially.

92. **(c)** In order for a merger of two public corporations to be accomplished, it is required that a formal plan of merger be prepared and that the merger plan be approved by a majority of the board of directors and stockholders of both corporations.

93. **(d)** As one of the steps leading up to a merger of two corporations, the stockholders need to be given notice of the merger plan. This is true of the stockholders of both corporations, so a special meeting is called inviting both sets of stockholders. Answers (a) and (b) are incorrect because unanimous approval is not needed by either the stockholders or the boards of either corporation. Answer (c) is incorrect because the absorbed corporation will no longer exist after the merger plan is accomplished.

94. **(a)** A corporation voluntarily dissolves when its board of directors passes a resolution to dissolve and liquidate. Answer (d) is incorrect because this resolution must be ratified by a majority of stockholders who are entitled to vote. Following ratification, the corporation must file a certificate of dissolution with the proper state authority,

cease business, wind up its affairs, and publish notice of its dissolution. Answers (b) and (c) are incorrect because they are not requirements of a voluntary dissolution.

95. **(c)** Shareholders have the right to vote on the dissolution of the corporation. Stockholders also have the right to elect the directors of the corporation, who in turn elect the officers. Answer (b) is incorrect as shareholders do not have the right to receive dividends unless they are declared by the board of directors. Answer (d) is incorrect as shareholders are not necessarily involved in the management of the corporation and cannot prevent corporate borrowing.

96. **(d)** Under corporate law, when a consolidation takes place, one new corporation comes from the joining of two or more corporations. Also, the assets and liabilities of the old corporations are acquired by the new corporation and the new corporation is liable for the debts of the old corporations.

W. Subchapter S Corporation

97. **(d)** When a corporation elects to be a Subchapter S corporation, the corporate income and loss flow through to the income tax returns of the individual shareholders, even when the income is not distributed to them. Answer (a) is incorrect because the corporation's income is not taxed at the corporate level when the Subchapter S election is made. Answer (b) is incorrect because the income flows through to the stockholders' tax returns regardless of when the distribution takes place. Answer (c) is incorrect because statement IV as well as statement III are both correct as discussed above.

5 BUSINESS ENVIRONMENT AND CONCEPTS SECTION

Following is the new information that will now be tested on the Business Environment and Concepts (BEC) portion of the CPA exam. Some of the information is newly tested information, and other information is material that had previously been tested on the CPA exam but is now being moved from other sections to the BEC section.

The Content and Skills Specifications for the BEC section of the CPA exam are somewhat similar to the current content specifications. However, a number of topics have been added, including:

1. Corporate governance and internal controls.
2. Enterprise risk management.
3. Additional coverage of business process management and systems design.
4. Project management.
5. Additional coverage of valuation of assets and liabilities.
6. Additional coverage of economic globalization.

In addition, you should review "New Responsibilities and Provisions under Sarbanes-Oxley Act," which was in Wiley Module 21, section F, and is included at the end of this chapter.

As discussed previously, you should be prepared for the **written communication** questions. As with the current written communication questions, they will not be graded for technical accuracy, providing they are on topic. However, the topics of the questions will now be Business Environment and Concepts topics.

NEW MATERIAL—BUSINESS ENVIRONMENT AND CONCEPTS SECTION

Corporate Governance and Internal Controls

Effective corporate governance and appropriately designed internal controls are essential to the appropriate operation of an organization and reliable financial reporting.

A. Corporate Governance

In the corporate form of organization, owners (shareholders) are separated from operations (management) of the firm. This creates an agency problem in that management (the agents) may not act in the best interest of the shareholders (the principals). Managers may be tempted to engage in self-serving activities, such as shirking, taking too little or too much risk, or consuming excessive perks. Effective corporate governance involves establishing incentives (i.e., forms of compensation) and monitoring devices to prevent this inappropriate activity.

Forms of Executive Compensation

Various types of compensation are used to attempt to align management behavior with the objectives of the shareholders. A key objective in setting executive compensation is to align management's decisions and actions with the long-term interests of shareholders (e.g., long-term stock price). If managers are given too much fixed compensation, they may become too complacent and not take appropriate risks to increase share price. If managers are given too much incentive compensation based on operating profit or short-term stock price, they have incentives to manage profit or take excessive risks to maximize their compensation. Common types of management compensation are described next.

a. Base salary and bonuses. Using this system, managers are compensated based on performance, which typically is measured by accounting profit. Compensation systems based on accounting measures of profit are problematic because accounting profit can be manipulated or managed. For example, the timing of research and development and maintenance expenditures may be altered to manage profit and maximize bonuses. Managers may put too much focus on short-term profits instead of focusing on maximizing the long-term wealth of shareholders.

b. Stock options. The use of stock options as a form of compensation provides managers with an incentive to manage the corporation to increase the stock price, which is consistent with the goal of shareholders. A disadvantage of stock options is that managers may have an incentive to increase the stock price in the short-term at the expense of long-term stock value, even by manipulating accounting income to increase stock price. In addition, stock options may encourage management to take on risks that are that are in excess of shareholders' risk appetite. Finally, if the stock price falls substantially, the stock options may be so underwater that they no longer provide an incentive to management.

c. Stock grants. Stock grants involve issuing shares of stock as part of management's compensation. Two common types of stock grants are:

   (1) Restricted stock—The issuance of stock that cannot be sold by the manager for a specific period of time, usually about 10 years. This form of compensation is effective because it encourages managers to undertake operations that increase the long-term value of the corporation's stock price.

   (2) Performance shares—The issuance of stock to management if certain levels of performance are met. If the price of the corporation's stock increases, the value of the manager's compensation increases.

d. Executive perquisites (perks). Management also may get various perquisites, such as retirement benefits, use of corporate assets, golden parachutes, and corporate loans.

e. Best forms of executive compensation. It is generally believed that the best compensation systems include a combination of fixed compensation and incentive compensation that is related to long-term stock price. For example, the incentive compensation may be in the form of stock options or stock that can be exercised or sold only after being held for a long period of time (e.g., 5 to 10 years). Bonuses are effective if they are based on a composite of performance measures in addition to net profit, such as the amount of research and development expenditures, the corporation's market share, the number of new products developed, and/or the percentage of stock held by institutional investors (who tend to hold the stock for the long term). Such performance systems are often referred to as a balanced scorecard.

2. Monitoring Devices

   In the United States, various devices exist to monitor management behavior. Some of the devices are internal (e.g., the board of directors and internal auditors) while others are external (e.g., external auditors, analysts, credit agencies, attorneys, the Securities and Exchange Commission (SEC), and the Internal Revenue Service (IRS).

a. Boards of directors. The board of directors is charged with running the corporation on behalf of the shareholders and other stakeholders. It is responsible for providing strategic direction and guidance about the establishment of the key business objectives of the corporation. The board also provides governance oversight. To be effective, board members must be competent, and a majority of the board members should be independent. "Independence" means the board member is not part of management of the corporation and does not receive significant benefit from the corporation other than compensation as a board member. Board members also must be adequately trained and be provided with complete and accurate information to carry out the board's functions.

   Boards are responsible for representing the shareholders by (1) hiring and, in some cases, top management; (2) voting on major operating and financial proposals; (3) providing advice management; and (4) ensuring accurate financial reporting by the corporation. These

   Boards should have a set of governance guidelines that are reviewed and revised annual guidelines will set forth the board organization, which will include its various committee include subcommittees. Those that are particularly important to effective corporate governan

(1) the nominating/corporate governance committee, (2) the compensation committee, and (3) the audit committee.

(1) The nominating/corporate governance committee (a) oversees board organization, including committee assignments, (b) determines director qualifications and training, (c) develops corporate governance principles, and (d) oversees chief executive officer (CEO) succession.

(2) The audit committee plays a critical role in corporate governance. The Sarbanes-Oxley Act defines the audit committee as a "committee established by and amongst the board of directors of an issuer for the purpose of overseeing the accounting and financial reporting processes of the issuer; and audits of the financial statements of the issuer." A major responsibility of the audit committee is the appointment, compensation, and oversight of the corporation's external auditor, including the resolution of any disagreements between management and the external auditor. An independent audit committee is mandated by the Sarbanes-Oxley Act and regulations of the New York Stock Exchange (NYSE) and Nasdaq. Other important characteristics of an audit committee include:

    (a) The Sarbanes-Oxley Act provides that at least one member should be a "financial expert." The names of the financial experts must be disclosed. If the firm does not have a financial expert, it must provide an explanation.

    (b) The audit committee should appoint, determine compensation of, and oversee the work of the corporation's external auditor.

    (c) External auditors must report directly to the audit committee.

    (d) Internal auditors should have direct access to the audit committee.

    (e) The audit committee should establish procedures for the receipt and treatment of complaints regarding accounting or auditing matters, including submission of concerns by employees (whistle-blowers).

(3) The compensation committee: (a) reviews and approves CEO compensation based on meeting performance goals, (b) makes recommendations to the board with respect to incentive and equity-based compensation plans, and (c) attempts to align incentives with shareholder objectives and risk appetite.

b. New York Stock Exchange and Nasdaq rules related to corporate governance and director independence. Among other items, the NYSE and Nasdaq require listed corporations to:

(1) Have a majority of independent directors on their boards.

(2) Make determination of independence of members and provide information to investors about the determination. Specific NYSE and Nasdaq rules that make a director not independent include:

    (a) A director is not independent if he/she has been an employee of the corporation or an affiliate in the last five years (three years for Nasdaq).

    (b) A director is not independent if a family member has been an officer of the corporation or affiliate in the last five years (three years for Nasdaq).

    (c) A director is not independent if he/she was a former partner or employee of the corporation's external auditor in the last five years (three years for Nasdaq).

    (d) A director is not independent if he/she or a family member in the last three years received more than $120,000 (for a 12-month period) in payments from the corporation other than for director compensation.

    (e) A director is not independent if he/she is an executive of another entity that receives significant amounts of revenue from the corporation.

(3) Identify certain relationships that automatically preclude a board member from being independent.

(4) Have nonmanagement directors meet at regularly scheduled executive sessions.

(5) Adopt and make publicly available a code of conduct applicable to all directors, officers, and employees, and disclose any waivers of the code for directors or executive officers.

(6) Have an independent audit committee. In addition, nominating/corporate governance and compensation decisions must be made by independent committees (or a majority of independent directors for Nasdaq).

    It is important to remember that judgment must be used to determine whether a director is independent. For example, based on the facts and circumstances it may be concluded that a director is not independent even though he/she receives less than $120,000 in payments (other than director compensation).

c. Internal auditors. Internal auditors perform audits of the risk management activities, internal control, and other governance processes for the corporation. Such audits often are referred to as assurance services. The results of these audits should be communicated directly to the audit committee of the board of directors. To ensure the adequate performance of their activities, internal auditors should be independent and competent. For effective independence, the chief audit executive (CAE) ideally should report functionally to the audit committee and administratively to the CEO of the corporation. This helps to prevent internal auditors' work from being influenced by management of the corporation. The CAE should have direct communication with the audit committee to assist the committee in performance of its oversight activities. The internal auditors must be provided with access to all of the aspects of the corporation's operations. In addition, the internal auditors should not perform any functions that would impair their independence in auditing that function. For example, it would be improper for the internal auditors to perform routine internal control procedures for the corporation because they are responsible for auditing for compliance with control procedures. The NYSE requires its listed companies to maintain an internal audit function to provide management and the audit committee with ongoing assessments of the company's risk management processes and system of internal control.

The Institute of Internal Auditors is a professional organization that issues professional standards for internal auditors. This organization also administers the Certified Internal Auditor (CIA) program. To become a CIA, an individual must pass a multipart exam and have a minimum of two years of internal audit experience (or its equivalent). The CIA designation helps to demonstrate that the individual is competent to perform internal audits.

d. External auditors. The external auditor is responsible for performing an audit of the corporation's financial statements and internal control in accordance with standards of the Public Company Accounting Oversight Board (PCAOB). The external auditor is a major external corporate governance monitoring device for a corporation. The external audit helps assure that corporation financial reports are accurate and management is not engaging in fraudulent financial reporting.

External auditors are required to communicate to the audit committee information that will help the committee perform its oversight function, including these matters:

(1) Auditor responsibility to form and express an opinion.
(2) An audit does not relieve management or the audit committee with their responsibilities for governance.
(3) Planned scope and timing of the audit.
(4) Significant audit findings, including
  (a) Auditor views of qualitative aspects of significant accounting practices.
  (b) Significant difficulties encountered during the audit.
  (c) Disagreements with management.
  (d) Other findings or issues which the auditor believes are significant and relevant.
  (e) Uncorrected misstatements other than those that are trivial.
(5) Material corrected misstatements.
(6) Significant issues discussed with management.
(7) Auditor's views about significant matters on which management consulted with other accountants.
(8) Written representations the auditor is requesting.
(9) Significant deficiencies and material weaknesses in internal control.

e. Investment banks and securities analysts. Investment bankers help corporations issue equity and debt offerings. Therefore, they represent an external monitoring device because they must evaluate the company prior to becoming involved in selling the securities.

Securities analysts analyze companies to attempt to develop recommendations to "buy," "h or "sell" a particular corporation's stock. Therefore, securities analysts act as an external mon device because they use financial and nonfinancial information, including information about corporate management to make their recommendations. An issue with considering the recommendations of analysts is potential conflicts of interest. For example, analysts may employed by firms that also perform investment banking activities, and the analyst's recommendations may be influenced by the fees received from the corporation for investment banking services.

  f. Creditors. Creditors also act as an external monitoring device. Debt agreements contain covenants (requirements) that must be complied with to prevent the creditor from taking actions such as accelerating payment terms. Creditors monitor compliance by the corporation with the covenants of these agreements. One limitation of creditors as a monitoring device is that they monitor based largely on information provided by management. However, they often do engage external auditors to perform procedures to provide assurance about the corporation's compliance with certain covenants of the loan agreements.

  g. Credit rating agencies. Credit rating agencies rate the creditworthiness of corporate bonds. Credit rating agencies are an external corporate monitoring device much like securities analysts. The biggest criticism of credit rating agencies is that they may improperly set the initial rating and are slow to downgrade the rating once the corporation gets in financial difficulty.

  h. Attorneys. Corporate legal counsel provide another external monitoring device in that they review securities filings and provide management advice on legal matters.

  i. Securities and Exchange Commission. The SEC is responsible for protecting investors; maintaining fair, orderly, and efficient markets; and facilitating capital formation. In achieving these responsibilities, the SEC enforces the U.S. securities laws. The SEC consists of five presidentially appointed commissioners. The SEC's activities act as an important external monitoring device for corporate government. The divisions and offices of the SEC that are particularly relevant to corporate governance include:

    (1) Division of Corporate Finance. This division reviews documents of publicly held companies that are filed with the SEC. Through the review process, the division checks to see if companies are meeting disclosure requirements and seeks to improve the quality of the disclosures by companies.

    (2) Division of Enforcement. This division assists the SEC in executing its law enforcement function by recommending the commencement of investigations of securities law violations, recommending which cases to take to court, and prosecuting these cases on behalf of the SEC.

    (3) Office of the Chief Accountant. The chief accountant advises the SEC on accounting and auditing, oversees the development of accounting principles, and approves the auditing rules put forward by the Public Company Accounting Oversight Board.

Several provisions of the Sarbanes-Oxley Act improved the SEC's power as an external monitoring device, including

    (1) The Sarbanes-Oxley Act requires the CEO and the chief financial officer (CFO) to certify the accuracy and truthfulness of periodic financial reports filed with the SEC. If the certification of the reports is later found to be inaccurate, the CEO and CFO can be found criminally liable and face imprisonment of 10 to 20 years. Also, civil penalties can involve fines of up to $5 million.

    (2) Under Sarbanes-Oxley, any person who knowingly perpetrates or attempts a scheme to defraud any other person by misrepresenting or making false claims in connection with the purchase or sale of securities can be fined or imprisoned for up to 25 years, or both. While securities fraud has long been an offense under the other securities acts, Sarbanes-Oxley made prosecution much easier.

    (3) The destruction, mutilation, alteration, concealment, or falsification of documentation with the intent to obstruct or influence an investigation that is ongoing or being considered can result in fines or imprisonment of up to 20 years.

    (4) Sarbanes-Oxley prohibits any acts of retaliation against employees who alert the government to possible violations of securities laws (whistle-blowers). The punishment for a violation of this provision can include fines or imprisonment of up to 10 years or both.

Internal Revenue Service. The IRS acts as an external governance device by requiring certain accounting information on the corporation's income tax return. The IRS also audits corporations' tax returns and enforces penalties for filing false tax returns.

Corporate takeovers. Takeovers also act as a corporate governance device. If management is performing poorly, the corporation may be subject to takeover by a firm that believes it can utilize corporation's resources more efficiently. This provides an incentive for management to operate corporation consistent with the interests of the shareholders.

l. Shareholder activism. When management is not operating the corporation in the best interests of the shareholders, the shareholders may engage in activism. Large shareholders can be especially effective because they have the ability to elect board members.

B. Internal Controls

A number of internal control frameworks are used as benchmarks. The most commonly used framework in the United States is *Internal Control—Integrated Framework* developed by COSO. According to COSO, internal control is:

A process, effected by the entity's board of directors, management, and other personnel designed to provide reasonable assurance regarding the achievement of objectives in the categories of (1) reliability of financial reporting, (2) effectiveness and efficiency of operations, and (3) compliance with applicable laws and regulations.

Under COSO, internal control can be viewed as including five components: (1) control environment, (2) risk assessment process, (3) control activities, (4) information and communication, and (5) monitoring.

1. Control Environment

    The control environment sets the tone of an organization by influencing the control consciousness of people. It may be viewed as the foundation for the other components of internal control. Control environment factors include: integrity and ethical values; commitment to competence; board of directors or audit committee; management's philosophy and operating style; organizational structure; assignment of authority and responsibility; and human resource policies and practices.

    a. Integrity and ethical values. The effectiveness of internal control depends on the communication and enforcement of integrity and ethical values. Management should establish a tone at the top of the organization that encourages appropriate behavior. Top management should communicate these values through a code of conduct, official policies, and by example.

    b. Commitment to competence. Effective internal control depends on having employees who possess the skills and knowledge essential to performing their jobs, especially when they are responsible for performing important control functions.

    c. Board of directors or audit committee. The control environment is significantly influenced by the effectiveness of the board of directors and its audit committee. The characteristics and requirements for an effective board and audit committee were discussed in the section on corporate governance.

    d. Management's philosophy and operating style. The manner in which management runs the organization can have a significant effect on the control environment. Management that takes undue risks or stresses making profit goals by any means can create an environment where employees are motivated to engage in unethical or illegal activities.

    e. Organizational structure. An effective organizational structure provides a basis for planning, directing, and controlling operations.

    f. Assignment of authority and responsibility. Personnel need a clear understanding of their responsibilities and the rules and regulations that govern their actions. Authority and responsibility is communicated through documents such as job descriptions and organizational charts.

    g. Human resource policies and procedures. The control environment is enhanced by effective policies and practices for hiring, training, evaluating, counseling, promoting, and compensating employees.

2. Risk Assessment

    Effective internal control requires that management have a system of risk assessment. Risk assessment is management's process for identifying, analyzing, and responding to risks. This process is described more fully in the section on enterprise risk management.

3. Control Activities

    Control activities are policies and procedures that help ensure that management directives are carried out. These policies and procedures promote actions that address the risks that face the organization. Typical controls include performance reviews, information processing controls, physical controls, and segregation of duties, which encompass the routine controls over processes and transaction cycles.

4. Information and Communication

    To make effective decisions, managers must have access to timely, reliable, and relevant information. Information systems should be implemented to capture information and process, summarize, and report the information on an accurate and timely basis. Proper communication involves providing employees with an understanding of their roles and responsibilities. Open communication channels are essential to the proper functioning of internal control.

5. Monitoring

Monitoring of controls is a process used to assess the quality of internal control performance over time. Monitoring may be achieved by performing ongoing activities or by separate evaluations. Ongoing monitoring activities include regularly performed supervisory and management activities, such as continuous monitoring of customer complaints, or reviewing the reasonableness of management reports. Separate evaluations are monitoring activities that are performed on a nonroutine basis, such as periodic audits by the internal auditors.

Technology has enhanced an organization's ability to monitor internal controls and risk. Information systems can have embedded modules that look for unusual or suspicious transactions or relationships. This allows management to monitor controls and risks on a much more effective basis. Internal auditors often use technology to perform continuous auditing of transactions and processes for the same purpose.

C. Controls over Business Processes

Organizations use various approaches to executing and controlling financial transactions. Some are still very manual in nature. However, more and more transactions are being processed completely by technology through private links within and between companies or over the Internet. All transactions have risks that must be controlled.

A fundamental control over transactions is segregation of duties. For each transaction cycle, the functions of authorization, approval (for certain types of transactions), execution (custody of assets), and record keeping should be segregated. In a manual accounting system, segregation of duties is achieved by having different individuals physically performing the functions. In a technology-based system, the computer performs many of these processes, and segregation of duties is achieved by controlling access to terminals and through the use of passwords. Of course, in a technology-based system, control is achieved over processing and data by appropriate information technology controls as discussed in Wiley Module 39.

The next table presents two major processes (transaction cycles) including the risks and examples of controls that might be used to mitigate those risks.

Sales and Collections Business Process

Risk	Nature of the process	Example controls
Inaccurate or incomplete sales data and lack of security over sales order information	Sales orders inputted manually Sales over the Internet	Password control over terminals to ensure that sales are authorized by sales department; accuracy and completeness controls over inputs;* physical controls over terminals and files. Encryption of transmitted data; accuracy and completeness controls over inputs; password control over access to information to maintain a segregation of duties; data controls to ensure that sales prices are accurately inputted and updated.
Sales to customers that are not creditworthy	Outsource credit to credit card company Organization has credit department that extends credit	Protect credit card information with password control and physical security over terminals and files. Credit department should be independent of sales function and approve credit limits; effective practices for collecting credit information to make evaluations to grant credit.
Maintaining too much or too little inventory	Inventory control and management	Use of a perpetual inventory system; use of techniques such as just-in-time, economic order quantity, and reorder point as methods of managing inventory; heavy reliance on technology to determine when and how much to order.
Inaccurate filling of orders	Manual filling of orders Use technology to fill orders	Have an individual not involved in filling the order check it for accuracy. Input controls to ensure information is correct in computer fulfillment process; use technology such as bar code scanners to pack goods.

*Accuracy and completeness controls include controls such as validity checks, missing data checks, logic checks, limit tests, and the like.

Sales and Collections Business Process (*Continued*)

Risk	Nature of the process	Example controls
Inaccurate billing of customers	Manual billing process	Individuals doing billing match sales order to shipping document to ensure the accuracy of billing invoice; use of prenumbered documents and accounting for all documents; invoice checked for clerical accuracy by an individual not involved in preparation; billing department is independent of individuals maintaining receivables records; account for numerical sequence of documents.
	Technology used for billing	Accuracy and completeness input controls to ensure billing information is accurate and based on accurate shipping information input by shipping personnel; accuracy and completeness controls to ensure that pricing information is accurate and based on authorization from the sales department; password control over terminals to ensure segregation of duties.
Errors or fraud in processing and depositing cash receipts	Cash receipts received through the mail	Segregation of cash handling from accounts receivable records or use of a lockbox at a financial institution.
	Electronic funds transfer system	Control over access to the system through the use of a password system; use of accuracy and completeness controls over input of cash receipt information.
Accounts may be written off without authorization	Manual	Individual independent of sales and cash receipts should be authorized to write off accounts; use of prenumbered authorization forms; accounting for all forms.
	Technology-based system	Access to terminal for authorization by independent individual should be restricted by password system

Acquisitions and Payments Process

Risk	Nature of the Process	Example Controls
Ordering unneeded goods	Manual or technology-based system	Use of a perpetual inventory system; ordering based on inventory management techniques, such as just-in-time, economic order quantity, and reorder points.
Purchasing goods from unauthorized vendors	Manual or technology-based system	Establish preferred vendor relationships; establish criteria for authorized vendors. Creation of purchase orders; accuracy and completeness controls over inputting purchasing information into the computer; password control over terminals.
Receiving goods that were not ordered	Manual system	Matching of purchase order to goods received.
	Technology-based system	Computer comparison of purchase information input by the purchasing department with information on goods received inputted by the receiving department.
Receiving goods that are damaged or inferior	Manual or technology-based system	Inspect goods received.
Payment of goods not received	Manual system	Matching of purchase orders with receiving reports; accounting for all prenumbered documents; individual authorized to sign checks is independent of those maintaining records and receiving personnel; check signer cancels supporting documentation.
	Computer generation of payments based on purchase and receiving information	Accuracy and completeness input controls for purchase and receiving information; segregation of those maintaining records and processing payments from those authorized to make payments; password control to ensure segregation of duties.

(Continued)

Acquisitions and Payments Process (*Continued*)

Risk	Nature of the Process	Example Controls
Authorization of cash payments	Manual system	Segregation of duties of accounting and authorized check signers.
	Technology-based system	Passwords and controls over terminals prevent issuance of unauthorized payments.
Loss or theft of assets	Manual or technology-based system	Periodic reconciliations of physical assets to accounting records by individuals independent of individuals having custody of the assets and those maintaining the accounting records for the assets; examples include reconciliations of bank accounts, taking physical inventories, and inventories of supplies and equipment.

D. Change Control Processes

Management must effectively control the inevitable changes that occur in processes, policies and procedures, and systems. An effective change control process enables management to control (1) change requests; (2) change analyses; (3) change decisions; and (4) change planning, implementation, and tracking. When a change occurs in an organization, it often has an effect on other areas of the organization. It is important that the change control process considers these effects and incorporates them into the analysis, planning, and implementation phases of the change. Also, a system of documentation should be established to ensure that changes are authorized, communicated, and documented. Finally, changes should be thoroughly tested before being implemented. If employees are not adequately trained on new processes, control may break down.

Enterprise Risk Management

In addition to an internal control framework, COSO has also developed a framework for enterprise risk management (ERM). The framework defines ERM as follows:

> Enterprise risk management is a process, effected by an entity's board of directors, management and other personnel, applied in a strategy setting and across the enterprise, designed to identify potential events that may affect the entity, and manage risk to be within its risk appetite, to provide reasonable assurance regarding the achievement of entity objectives.

ERM helps align the risk appetite of the organization with its strategy, enhances risk response decisions, reduces operational surprises and losses, identifies and manages cross-enterprise risks, provides integrated responses to multiple risks, helps the organization seize opportunities, and improves the deployment of capital.

A key aspect of ERM is the identification and management of events that have a negative impact, positive impact, or both. Events with negative impact represent risks. Events with positive impact may offset negative impacts or represent opportunities.

Everyone in the organization has some responsibility for ERM. The best-run organizations have a culture of risk management that is understood by every employee. Many organizations assign a risk officer, financial officer, and/or internal auditor with key support responsibilities. The internal control of the organization is an integral part of the organization's ERM system.

A. Components of ERM

According to COSO, ERM consists of eight interrelated components, including: (1) internal environment, (2) objective setting, (3) event identification, (4) risk assessment, (5) risk response, (6) control activities, (7) information and communication, and (8) monitoring.

1. Internal Environment

    The internal environment is the basis for all other components of ERM, providing discipline and structure. It encompasses the tone of the organization and sets the basis for how risk is viewed and addressed by an organization's people, including risk management philosophy and risk appetite, and integrity and ethical values.

    The board of directors is a critical part of the internal environment. The board provides oversight over management's implementation of ERM, helping to make sure that it is effective.

    Integrity and ethical values help ensure that management and other individuals within the organization are not inclined to engage in unethical or illegal activities. Management sets an ethical tone by action and example, and communicates the tone through codes of conduct and established policies. Management also should avoid the use of incentives and temptations to engage in unethical behavior, unless effective controls are established to prevent such behavior.

Other factors that contribute to an effective internal environment include competent, well-trained employees, an appropriate organizational structure, properly assigned authority and responsibility, and effective human resource policies and procedures.

An important aspect of the organization's internal environment is its risk appetite. "Risk appetite" means the amount of risk an organization is willing to accept to achieve its goals. It reflects the organization's culture and operating style and is directly related to the organization's strategy. Some organizations consider risk appetite qualitatively (e.g., low, moderate, high) while others consider risk quantitatively (e.g., in percentages). The term "risk tolerance" relates to the organization's objectives. It is the acceptable variation with respect to a particular objective. For example, a company may have an objective of 97% customer satisfaction rating but may tolerate as low as a 94% customer satisfaction rating.

2. Objective Setting

Objectives must exist before management can identify potential events affecting their achievement. ERM ensures that management has in place a process to set objectives and that the chosen objectives support and align with the organization's mission and are consistent with its risk appetite. The organization's mission sets forth in broad terms what the organization aspires to achieve. Strategic objectives are high-level goals aligned with the organization's mission. These high-level objectives are linked and integrated with the specific objectives established for various activities. By setting objectives, the organization can identify critical risk factors, which are the key things that must go right for the objectives to be met.

Objectives may be divided into three categories:

a. Operations objectives, which relate to the effectiveness and efficiency of operations.

b. Reporting objectives, which relate to reliable reporting of internal and external, financial and nonfinancial information.

c. Compliance objectives, which relate to adherence to laws and regulations.

3. Event Identification

Potential internal and external events affecting achievement of an organization's objectives must be identified, distinguishing between risks and opportunities. An event is an incident that occurs or might occur that affects implementation of strategy or achievement of objectives. Events may be negative (risks), positive (opportunities) or both. Risks require a response while opportunities should be channeled back to management's strategy or objective-setting processes. Some events may be external in nature, such as those resulting from economic, natural environment, political, social, or technological factors. Other events result from internal factors, such as the organization's infrastructure, personnel, processes, or technology.

Event identification techniques include:

a. Event inventories. This involves developing a detailed listing of potential events.

b. Internal analysis. This may be done at regular staff meetings. It may involve using information from other stakeholders, such as customers, suppliers, and the like.

c. Escalation or threshold triggers. Management predetermines limits that cause an event to be further assessed. For example, a pricing problem may be triggered when competitor sales prices change by a predetermined percentage.

d. Facilitated workshops or interviews. This technique involves soliciting information about events from management and staff. For example, a facilitator may lead a discussion of events that might affect achieving an organization's objectives.

e. Process flow analysis. This involves breaking processes down into inputs, tasks, responsibilities, and outputs to identify events that might adversely affect the process.

f. Leading event indicators. This technique involves monitoring data correlated to events, to identify when the event is likely to occur.

g. Loss event data methodologies. By developing repositories of data on past loss events, management can identify event trends and the root causes of events. Management also can perform **black swan analysis,** which involves evaluating the occurrence of events that had negative effects and were unanticipated or viewed as highly unlikely.

4. Risk Assessment

Risks are analyzed, considering likelihood and impact, as a basis for determining how they should be managed. Management should assess both inherent risk and residual risk for an event. The term "inherent risk" refers to the risk to the organization if management does nothing to alter its likelihood or impact. "Residual risk" is the risk of the event after considering management's response. Risks are assessed in terms of their likelihood of occurring and their impact (e.g., financial effect). Management often uses qualitative techniques to assess risk when risks do not lend themselves to quantification or when sufficient reliable data are not available to use a quantitative model. Probabilistic or nonprobabilistic models may be used to quantify risk. Probabilistic models associate a range of events and the resulting impact with the likelihood of those events based on certain assumptions. Examples of probabilistic models include value at risk, cash flow at risk, earnings at risk, and development of credit and operational loss distributions. Nonprobabilistic models use subjective assumptions in estimating the impact of events without quantifying an associated likelihood. Examples of nonprobabilistic models include sensitivity measures, stress tests, and scenario analysis.

5. Risk Response

In this aspect of ERM, management selects risk responses that are consistent with the risk appetite of the organization, including:

a. Avoidance. This response involves exiting the activity that gives rise to the risk.

b. Reduction. This response involves taking action to reduce risk likelihood or impact, or both. For example, it might involve managing the risk or adding additional controls to processes.

c. Sharing. This response involves reducing risk likelihood or impact by transferring or sharing a portion of the risk. Techniques for sharing include insurance, hedging, and outsourcing.

d. Acceptance. No action is taken because the risk is consistent with the risk appetite of the organization.

All risk responses must be assessed in terms of their costs and benefits to select the responses that should be implemented.

6. Control Activities

Policies and procedures should be established and implemented to help ensure the risk responses are carried out effectively.

7. Information and Communication

Relevant information is identified, captured, and communicated to enable people to carry out their responsibilities. Information is needed at all levels of the organization to identify, assess, and respond to risks. Communication should effectively convey the importance and relevance of effective ERM, the organization's objectives, the organization's risk appetite and risk tolerances, a common risk language, and the roles and responsibilities of personnel in effecting and supporting the components of ERM.

8. Monitoring.

The entire ERM process should be monitored to make needed modifications. Monitoring is accomplished by ongoing management activities, and separate evaluations, such as those internal auditors.

B. *Limitations of ERM*

In considering the limitations of ERM, three distinct concepts must be recognized:

1. Risk relates to the future, which is uncertain,

2. ERM provides information about risks of achieving objectives, but it cannot provide even reasonable assurance that objectives will be achieved.

3. ERM cannot provide absolute assurance with respect to any of the objective categories. Specific limitations include:

a. The effectiveness of ERM is subject to the limitations of the ability of humans to make judgments about risk and impact.

b. Well-designed ERM can break down.

c. Collusion among two or more individuals can result in ERM failures.

d. ERM systems can never be perfect due to cost-benefit constraints.

e. ERM is subject to management override.

Business Process Management and Systems Design

A. Business Process Management

Business processes are the structured activities of an organization that produce a product or service. Business process management focuses on continuously improving processes to align all activities with the desires and needs of the customer. As a managerial approach, business process management views processes as strategic assets that must be understood, managed, and improved. To improve processes, management focuses on both the human and technological aspect of processes and the interaction of the two. Many organizations are finding it productive to improve processes by focusing on this human–technology interaction, as they try to develop technology that is designed for a task and the way the particular individual works.

The lifecycle of business process management includes design, modeling, execution, monitoring, and optimization.

1. Design

    The design phase involves identification of existing processes and design of process improvements. Good process design is critical to preventing problems over the life of the process.

2. Modeling

    In the modeling phase, management simulates the process in a test environment and performs what-if analysis to try to determine how it will work under varying conditions.

3. Execution

    Execution involves installing software, training personnel, and implementing the new processes. It also involves testing the new processes.

4. Monitoring

    The monitoring phase is continuous after the execution phase. It involves tracking the processes with performance statistics.

5. Optimization

    This phase of the life cycle involves retrieving performance statistics from modeling or monitoring and identifying potential bottlenecks or other problems for additional improvement of the process.

    As processes are analyzed for improvement, it is sometimes discovered that processes that once were performed by several departments should be centralized in one department. For example, employee training might become a centralized process to improve efficiency and effectiveness. Alternatively, management may decide to outsource a process to an external organization or even to an organization in another country (often referred to as off-shoring). There are a number of reasons why an organization may decide to outsource or off-shore, including cost saving, quality improvement, tax benefit, scalability, or to focus on core competencies. However, such strategy may present additional risks including

    - Quality risk. The company may have less control over the quality of outsourced or off-shored activities.
    - Language risk. Control over activities and customer service may be affected by language issues.
    - Information security risk. Control over confidential company or customer information may be put at risk.
    - Intellectual property risk. Information about the company's products and processes may be put at risk.
    - Public opinion risk. The company's reputation may be put at risk because it is off-shoring jobs.
    - Social responsibility risk. The company's reputation may be put at risk based on the practices of the organizations used in other countries.

Obviously, the company can implement policies and controls, including requiring effective operating agreements, to mitigate these risks.

B. Systems Design and Process Improvement

In the current environment, designing and implementing a new information and control system provides an opportunity to reexamine business processes, especially if the new system is an enterprise resource (ERP) system. Management can take advantage of the capabilities of the technology to redesign business processes making them more efficient and effective. The systems development life cycle includes seven steps: (1) planning, (2) analysis, (3) design, (4) development, (5) testing, (6) implementation, and (7) maintenance.

1. Planning Phase

    Major steps in the planning phase include:

    a. Define the system to be developed. This involves identifying and selecting the system to be developed based on the strategic goals of the organization.

    b. Determine the project scope. In this step, the high-level requirements are defined. A project scope document is used to describe the project scope. During the process of systems design, the scope of the project may be revisited and revised.

    c. Develop a project plan. The project plan defines the activities that will be performed and the individuals and resources that will be used. A project manager is the individual who develops the plan and tracks its progress. The plan establishes project milestones that set forth dates by which certain activities need to be performed.

2. Analysis Phase

    This phase involves teams including end users, information technology specialists, and process design specialists to understand the requirements for the proposed system. During this phase, a **needs assessment** may be performed. A needs assessment involves determining the requirements for the system in terms of processes, data capture, information, and reporting. Next, an analysis is performed on the existing system along the same dimensions. Then a gap analysis is performed to examine the differences (gaps) between the required system and the existing system. Finally, priorities will be established for the gaps (requirements) that will be documented in a requirements definition document, which will receive sign-off from the end users. It is during this phase that a company can take advantage of the processes inherent in the new system to improve existing processes.

3. Design Phase

    The primary goal of the design phase is to build a technical blueprint of how the proposed system will work.

4. Development Phase

    During the development phase, the documents from the design phase are transformed into the actual system. In the design phase, the platform on which the system is to operate is built and the programs and databases are developed.

5. Testing Phase

    The testing phase involves verifying that the system works and meets the business requirements as set forth in the analysis phase. The testing phase is obviously critical. These types of tests should be performed:

    a. Unit testing. Unit testing involves testing the units or pieces of code.

    b. System testing. System testing involves testing of the integration of the units or pieces of code into a system.

    c. Integration testing. Integration testing involves testing whether the separate systems can work together.

    d. User acceptance testing. User acceptance testing determines whether the system meets the business requirements and enables users to perform their jobs efficiently and effectively.

6. Implementation Phase

    The implementation phase involves putting the system in operation by the users. In order to implement the system effectively, detailed user documentation must be provided to the users, and the users must be adequately trained. An organization may choose from a number of implementation methods, including:

    a. Parallel implementation. This method uses both systems until it is determined that the new system is operating properly. This has the advantages of a full operational test of the new system with less risk of a system disaster. The disadvantage of this method is the additional work and cost during the period in which both systems are operating.

    b. Plunge implementation. Using this method, the organization ceases using the old system and begins using the new system immediately. This method is less costly than the parallel method, but it has higher risk of a system breakdown.

    c. Pilot implementation. This method involves having a small group of individuals using the new system until it is seen to be working properly. This has the advantage of providing a partial operational test of the new system at a lower cost than parallel implementation.

    d. Phased implementation. This method involves installing the system in a series of phases.

7. Maintenance Phase

    This phase involves monitoring and supporting the new system. In this phase, the organization provides ongoing training, help desk resources, and a system for making authorized and tested changes to the system.

Project Management

A project is a series of activities and tasks that:

- Have specific definable objectives.
- Have defined start and end dates.
- Are subject to funding constraints.
- Consume resources, people, equipment, and so on.
- Cut across various functional areas of the organization.

Projects usually are planned and executed by multidisciplinary teams consisting of individuals from different functional areas and led by a project manager. Team members must be knowledgeable and able to work together to plan and execute work in a team setting. Some projects are assigned a project oversight or steering group, which takes responsibility for the business issues related to the project. These committees are responsible for approving budgetary strategy; defining and realizing benefits; and monitoring risks, quality, and timeliness.

Effective project management involves efficiently achieving the project objectives within time and cost constraints. To achieve effective project management, the project leader must manage the four basic elements of a project:

1. Resources—people, equipment, materials, and so on.
2. Time—task durations, task interdependencies, the critical path, and so on.
3. Money—costs, contingencies, profit, and so on.
4. Scope—project size, goals, requirements, and so on.

The processes involved in project management include project initiation, project planning, project execution, project monitoring and control, and project closure.

1. Project initiation includes:
    a. Selection of the best project given resource constraints.
    b. Recognizing the benefits of the project.
    c. Authorizing the project. The project must have full support of the organization's management. Since projects often cross functional lines, a commitment by top management of the organization is critical to the success of any project.
    d. Assigning the project manager (leader). The project manager should be competent and have sufficient authority to get access to needed resources and people. The project manager should have these skills: planning, organizational, negotiating, administration, resource allocation, and entrepreneurial. A **project charter** authorizes the project and sets forth the project manager's authority and responsibility.
2. Project planning involves determining the activities that need to be performed, who should perform them, and when the activities need to be completed. Planning includes:
    a. Defining the work requirements.
    b. Defining the quality and quantity of the work.
    c. Indentifying the needed resources.
    d. Scheduling the activities and tasks.
    e. Indentifying and assessing risks.
        The planning process results in a number of documents. The scope of the work is often set forth in a **statement of work (SOW),** which is a narrative description of the work to be performed to complete the project, including the deliverables. One of the most common reasons for a scope change in a project is a poorly defined statement of work.
        The statement of work often includes the **project specifications,** which are detailed listings of the man-hour, equipment, and materials requirements. The **milestone schedule** sets forth the start date, the end date, and other major milestones involved in completing the project. Finally, the **work breakdown structure (WBS)** breaks the project into manageable, independent, and measurable elements that can be budgeted and for which responsibility can be assigned. The WBS provides a basis for costing, risk analysis, control, and scheduling the project.
        Many companies use a **life-cycle approach** in planning, in which project planning is divided into defined phases, such as conceptualization, feasibility study, and the like. At the end of each phase, an assessment is done to evaluate the success of the phase and determine whether the next phase should be undertaken.

Many different techniques are used to schedule and control a project, including:

a. Gantt chart—a type of bar chart that illustrates the scheduled start and finish of elements of a project over time.

b. Milestone chart—a type of chart that illustrates the milestones for a project over time.

c. Line of balance—a type of chart that illustrates the series of activities that are related. It is appropriate where a project has a series of repetitive activities.

d. Network diagram—illustrates the logical representation of activities that defines the sequence of the work of a project. It illustrates the path of a project. A network diagram has advantages over other forms of techniques because it (1) illustrates the interdependencies between activities, (2) identifies critical paths in a project, (3) facilitates risk analysis for the activities in the project, and (4) enables management to evaluate the effect of an activity delay on the project completion date.

e. Program Evaluation and Review Technique (PERT)—PERT is a network technique that formally focuses on the interdependency of activities and the time required to complete an activity to schedule and control the project. This technique focuses on the **critical path**, which is the shortest amount of time necessary to accomplish the project. Any slippage in the time of performing the activities along the critical path will result in a delay in completion of the project. Therefore, management knows which activities and events are most critical to timely completion of the project. PERT uses three time estimates (optimistic, most likely, and pessimistic) to derive expected time to complete a particular task. In PERT analysis, **slack time** is the difference between the expected time and the latest time the activity can be completed without delaying the project. PERT is probabilistic in nature, which allows the calculation of the risk in completing the project. PERT typically is used where there is a high variability of completion time, such as research and development projects.

f. PERT cost—allows the addition of resource cost considerations to the schedule produced by the PERT technique. This allows the inclusion of cost uncertainty into the analysis.

g. Critical path method (CPM)—CPM is similar to PERT, but it only uses one time estimate that represents the normal time to complete an activity. CPM is used for projects where there is less variability in time estimates. CPM includes a procedure for time/cost trade-off to minimize the sum of direct and indirect project costs.

h. Graphical Evaluation and Review Technique (GERT)—GERT is similar to PERT, but it has the advantage of allowing looping and branching based on the results of a particular activity. It is appropriate for projects that may be completed in number of ways.

i. "Project crashing" is a term used to describe the practice of adding resources to shorten selected activity time on the critical path of a project. In effect, the manager is trading off money for time. Therefore, each activity may be viewed as having two types—a normal (planned) time and the crash time (the shortest possible time).

j. Another technique that is often used in conjunction with any of these scheduling techniques is **ABC analysis**. ABC analysis involves the categorization of tasks into groups. These groups are often marked A, B, and C—hence the name. Activities are ranked on these general criteria:

> **A**—Tasks that are perceived as being urgent and important.
> **B**—Tasks that are important but not urgent.
> **C**—Tasks that are neither urgent nor important.

Then each group is rank-ordered in priority. This technique is particularly applicable to project management because it focuses attention on the critical activities or tasks.

Risk management is also applicable to project management. Project risks include those related to cost overruns, time slippage, inappropriately defined scope, and dissatisfaction with the deliverables. The steps in the risk management of a project include (1) identification of risks, (2) quantifying the risks, (3) prioritizing risks, and (4) developing a risk response. Like any type of risk management, the response may involve such activities as developing controls or shifting the risk to another party.

3. Project execution includes:

a. Negotiating for the team members.

b. Directing the work.

c. Managing team members to improve performance.

Management of a project requires much the same skills as managing any function. However, if the project crosses functional lines, the management process becomes complicated. Problems in project management typically arise from one of these issues:

- Organizational uncertainty. The working relationship between the project manager and the functional managers has not been adequately defined by senior management.
- Unusual decision pressures. Project managers must make quick decisions in uncertain situations and with incomplete information. Senior management must recognize these difficulties and support the project manager's decisions.
- Inadequate senior management support. Delays in approval, inability to resolve reporting conflicts, and delays in providing resources can significantly delay or derail projects.

4. Project monitoring and control includes:
   a. Tracking progress of the project.
   b. Comparing actual outcomes to predicted outcomes.
   c. Analyzing variances and their effects.
   d. Making adjustments.

   Many of the typical management techniques are used to control projects, including budgets, variance analysis, and status analysis. The scheduling techniques discussed above also facilitate control of the project by allowing management to focus its attention on critical activities.

5. Project closure includes:
   a. Determining that all work has been completed.
   b. Closure of the contract, financial charges, and paperwork.

Asset and Liability Valuation

An important part aspect of financial statements and finance is the valuation of assets and liabilities. Valuations are needed for a number of purposes including investment evaluation, capital budgeting, mergers and acquisitions, financial reporting, tax reporting, and litigation. The major types of valuation models include: market values obtained from active markets for identical assets; market values derived from active markets for similar but not identical assets; and valuation models.

A. Using Active Markets for Identical Assets

The most straightforward method of valuing a financial instrument is using prices for identical instruments in an active market. The use of such markets is appropriate if they have sufficient volume of transactions to ensure that the market price is reliable.

B. Using Active Markets for Similar Assets

Another method for valuing instruments involves deriving values from the market prices of similar but not identical instruments. The key to this method of valuation is accurate adjustment for differences that exist between the instrument being valued and the instrument that is traded in the market. For example, the price might need to be adjusted for such factors as restrictions on sales, or differences in maturity dates, exercise dates, block sizes, credit risk, and so on. Financial models often are used to adjust the value of the instrument for these differences.

C. Valuation Models

A method that can be used in the absence of an active market is determining estimated fair value based on a valuation model, such as discounted cash flows. Such valuations generally rely on assumptions about future events and conditions that affect income and cash flows. These assumptions could materially affect the fair value estimate. Accordingly, they must be examined to determine whether they are reasonable and consistent with existing market information, the economic environment, and past experience. For example, in determining the fair value of a rare asset for which market information is not available, consideration should be given to sales of similar assets, the general economic environment in which the asset is used, and past experiences with similar assets. As another example, discount rates for calculating discounted cash flows must reflect market expectations of future rates and be consistent with the level of risk inherent in the future cash flows.

In determining estimates of fair values, it is also important that the model being used is appropriate based on the nature of the asset and current economic conditions.

Economic Globalization

The term "economic globalization" refers to the increasing economic interdependence of national economies across the world through a rapid increase in cross-border movement of goods, services, technology, and capital. It has led to a single world market in which developed economies have integrated with less developed countries by means of foreign direct investment, the reduction of trade barriers, and the modernization of the developing countries. The comparative advantages of natural resources or low-cost labor attract businesses and capital to developing (emerging) economies. Companies in developed countries are able to compete with companies in developing countries in a number of ways, including:

- Use of sophisticated technology to reduce costs.
- Effective process management.
- Innovation in products or services.
- Product quality.
- Customer service.
- Adopting a global strategy.

In operating in a global economy, it is important that executives understand the cultural differences among countries. Differences in customs, values, and behavior result in problems that can be managed only by cross-cultural communication and interaction. These cultural differences affect negotiations, personnel management, and commerce.

Multinational companies generally pursue a global strategy in which they locate and consolidate operations in countries with the greatest strategic advantages. Organizations that pursue a global strategy can benefit in a number of ways.

- Pooling international production to one or a few locations can achieve increased economies of scale.
- Manufacturing costs can be cut by moving production to low-cost countries.
- A firm that can switch production among different countries has increased bargaining power over labor, suppliers, and host governments.
- Worldwide access to resources, labor, suppliers, and customers.

QUESTIONS ON NEW BUSINESS ENVIRONMENT AND CONCEPTS MATERIAL

1. Which of the following best identifies the reason that effective corporate governance is important?
   a. The separation of ownership from management.
   b. The goal of profit maximization.
   c. Excess management compensation.
   d. Lack of oversight by boards of directors.

2. Which of the following forms of compensation would most likely align management's behavior with the interests of the shareholders?
   a. A fixed salary.
   b. A salary plus a bonus based on current period net income.
   c. A salary plus stock options that cannot be exercised for 10 years.
   d. A salary plus stock.

3. Which of the following forms of compensation would encourage management to take on excess risk?
   a. A fixed salary.
   b. A salary and bonuses based on current period net income.
   c. A salary plus stock options that cannot be exercised for 10 years.
   d. A salary plus restricted stock.

4. Which of the following is **not** a requirement of the New York Stock Exchange regarding corporate governance of companies listed on the exchange?
   a. Have a majority of independent directors of the corporate board.
   b. Adopt and make publicly available a code of conduct.
   c. Prohibit the chief financial officer from serving on the board of directors.
   d. Have an independent audit committee.

5. Which of the following does not act as an external corporate governance mechanism?
   a. External auditors.
   b. The SEC.
   c. Credit analysts.
   d. Independent boards of directors.

6. The Sarbanes-Oxley Act provides that at least one member of the audit committee should be:
   a. Independent.
   b. The chief financial officer of the company.
   c. A financial expert.
   d. A CPA.

7. Which of the following is more effective as an external monitoring device for a publicly held corporation than the others?
   a. Internal auditors.
   b. External auditors.
   c. The SEC.
   d. Attorneys.

8. An important corporate governance mechanism is the internal audit function. For good corporate governance, the chief internal audit executive should have direct communication to the audit committee and report to the:
   a. Chief financial officer.
   b. Chief executive officer.
   c. Controller.
   d. External auditors.

9. Securities analysts act as one form of monitoring device from a corporate governance standpoint. What is a limitation that often is identified when considering the effectiveness of securities analysts in this regard?
   a. Conflicts of interest.
   b. Lack of competence.
   c. Use of only nonfinancial information for analyses.
   d. They are employees of the company.

10. Which of the following divisions of the SEC reviews corporate filings?
    a. Office of the Chief Accountant.
    b. Division of Enforcement.
    c. Division of Corporate Disclosure.
    d. Division of Corporate Finance.

11. Which of the following components is considered the foundation of the internal controls established by an organization?
    a. Control activities.
    b. Monitoring.
    c. The control environment.
    d. The audit committee.

12. Which of the following is **not** a control environment factor?
    a. Integrity and ethical values.
    b. Board of directors or audit committee.
    c. Human resources policies and procedures.
    d. Control monitoring.

13. Which of the following components of internal control would encompass the routine controls over business processes and transactions?
    a. The control environment.
    b. Information and communication.
    c. Control activities.
    d. Risk assessment.

14. Which of the following is **not** a component in the COSO framework for internal control?
    a. Control environment.
    b. Segregation of duties.
    c. Risk assessment.
    d. Monitoring.

15. Management of Johnson Company is considering implementing technology to improve the monitoring component of internal control. Which of the following best describes how technology may be effective at improving monitoring?
    a. Technology can identify conditions and circumstances that indicate that controls have failed or risks are present.
    b. Technology can ensure that items are processed accurately.
    c. Technology can provide information more quickly.
    d. Technology can control access to terminals and data.

16. Jarrett Corporation is considering establishing an enterprise risk management system. Which of the following is **not** a benefit of enterprise risk management?
    a. Helps the organization seize opportunities.
    b. Enhances risk response decisions.
    c. Improves the deployment of capital.
    d. Ensures that the organization shares all major risks.

17. In the COSO enterprise risk management framework, the term "risk tolerance" refers to
    a. The level of risk an organization is willing to accept.
    b. The acceptable variation with respect to a particular objective.
    c. The amount of risk of an event after considering management's response.
    d. Events that require no risk response.

18. Management of Warren Company has decided to respond to a particular risk by hedging the risk with futures contracts. This is an example of risk:
    a. Avoidance.
    b. Acceptance.
    c. Reduction.
    d. Sharing.

19. Which of the following is **not** a technique for identifying events in an enterprise risk management program?
    a. Process flow analysis.
    b. Facilitated workshops.
    c. Probabilistic models.
    d. Loss event data methodologies.

20. Devon Company is using an enterprise risk management system. Management of the company has set the company's objectives, identified events, and assessed risks. What is the

next step in the enterprise risk management process?

a. Establish control activities to manage the risks.
b. Monitor the risks.
c. Determine a response to the risks.
d. Identify opportunities.

21. Which of the following is **not** an advantage of establishing an enterprise risk management system within an organization?

a. Reduces operational surprises.
b. Provides integrated responses to multiple risks.
c. Eliminates all risks.
d. Identifies opportunities.

22. Kelly, Inc. is considering establishing an enterprise risk management system. Which of the following is **not** a limitation of such a system?

a. Business objectives usually are not articulated.
b. The system may break down.
c. Collusion between two or more individuals can result in system failure.
d. Enterprise risk management is subject to management override.

23. In an attempt to improve operations, companies often go through analyses and redesign of the way processes are performed. Which of the following is **not** considered to be an aspect of a business process that may be focused on to achieve improvement?

a. Technology.
b. Human performance.
c. The interaction between technology and human performance.
d. Strategic goals.

24. Management of organizations that engage in business process management view business processes as:

a. Requirements for good control over the organization.
b. Systems that provide information for good management.
c. Strategic assets that must be understood, managed, and improved.
d. Mechanisms that keep employees from shirking.

25. At which phase in the business process management life cycle does management simulate performance of the process in a test environment?

a. Design.
b. Modeling.
c. Execution.
d. Optimization.

26. Which of the following is **not** a risk that is generally enhanced by a decision to off-shore business processes to a developing nation?

a. Language risk.
b. Technology risk.
c. Public opinion risk.
d. Social responsibility risk.

27. Samco Inc. is in the process of designing a new customer relations system. In which phase of the development life cycle would a needs assessment most likely be performed?

a. Analysis.
b. Design.
c. Development.
d. Testing.

28. Which of the following system implementation models has the advantage of achieving a full operational test of the new system before it is implemented?

a. Parallel implementation.
b. Plunge implementation.
c. Pilot implementation.
d. Phased implementation.

29. Which of the following involves comparing measures of actual progress of a project to planned progress?

a. Project planning.
b. Project scheduling.
c. Project control.
d. Project closure.

30. Which of the following is a detailed listing of the man-hour, equipment, and materials requirements for a project?

a. Statement of work.
b. Work breakdown structure.
c. Project specifications.
d. Milestone schedule.

31. Which of the following is used to describe the practice of adding resources to shorten selected activity time on the critical path of a project?

a. Making adjustments.
b. Project crashing.
c. Slack time.
d. Reengineering.

32. When a project can be completed in a number of completely different ways that might involve branching after performing activities, the best schedule and control technique would be:
    a. Program Evaluation and Review Technique.
    b. Gantt chart.
    c. Critical path method.
    d. Graphical Evaluation and Review Technique.

33. A technique that often is used in project management to identify tasks where attention should be focused because they are the most critical is referred to as:
    a. ABC analysis.
    b. Milestone analysis.
    c. Work breakdown analysis.
    d. Tasking.

34. Which of the following methods of valuation provides the most reliable measure of fair value?
    a. Use of a discounted cash flow method.
    b. Market values obtained from active markets.
    c. Combination of valuation models and active markets.
    d. Sophisticated valuation models.

35. All of the following are ways that companies in developed countries generally may compete with companies in developing countries except:
    a. Technology.
    b. Customer service.
    c. Quality.
    d. Low-cost resources.

36. According to the Sarbanes-Oxley Act of 2002, which of the following statements is correct regarding an issuer's audit committee financial expert?
    a. The issuer's current outside CPA firm's audit partner must be the audit committee financial expert.
    b. If an issuer does **not** have an audit committee financial expert, the issuer must disclose the reason why the role is **not** filled.
    c. The issuer must fill the role with an individual who has experience in the issuer's industry.
    d. The audit committee financial expert must be the issuer's audit committee chairperson to enhance internal control.

37. According to COSO, which of the following components of enterprise risk management addresses an entity's integrity and ethical values?
    a. Information and communication.
    b. Internal environment.
    c. Risk assessment.
    d. Control activities.

ANSWER EXPLANATIONS FOR NEW BUSINESS ENVIRONMENT AND CONCEPTS MATERIAL

1. **(a)** The requirement is to identify the reason that effective corporate governance is important. Answer (a) is correct because the separation of ownership and management creates an agency problem in that management may not act in the best interest of the shareholders. Answer (b) is incorrect because profit maximization is an appropriate goal of management. Answer (c) is incorrect because while corporate governance is designed to prevent excess management compensation, that is not the only reason it is important. Answer (d) is incorrect because oversight by boards of directors is a part of corporate governance.

2. **(c)** The requirement is identify the form of compensation that would most likely align management's behavior with the interests of the shareholders. Answer (c) is correct because stock options that cannot be exercised for 10 years provide an incentive to manage the firm to maximize long-term stock value. Answer (a) is incorrect because a fixed salary does not provide

an incentive to maximize shareholder value. Answers (b) and (d) are incorrect because they provide an incentive to maximize short-term profit of the firm. This may not be consistent with long-term profitability.

3. **(b)** The requirement is to identify the form of compensation that would encourage management to take on excess risk. Answer (b) is correct because with a bonus based on current period net income, management has an incentive to take on excessive risk to maximize its bonuses. Answer (a) is incorrect because a fixed salary encourages management to take on little risk. Answers (c) and (d) are incorrect because stock options that cannot be exercised for 10 years and restricted stock encourage management to be concerned about the long-term viability of the firm.

4. **(c)** The requirement is to identify the item that is not a requirement of the NYSE regarding corporate governance of listed companies.

Answer (c) is correct because the rules do not prohibit the CFO from serving on the board of directors. Answers (a), (b), and (d) are all requirements of the NYSE.

5. **(d)** The requirement is to identify the organization or group that does not act as an external corporate governance mechanism. Answer (d) is correct because directors are internal corporate governance mechanisms, regardless of whether they are independent. Answers (a), (b), and (c) are incorrect because they all act as external corporate governance mechanisms.

6. **(c)** The requirement is to identify the characteristic that must apply to at least one member of the audit committee. Answer (c) is correct because Sarbanes-Oxley requires that at least one member of the audit committee be a financial expert. Answer (a) is incorrect because all audit committee members should be independent. Answer (b) is incorrect because the chief financial officer is not independent and should not be on the audit committee. Answer (d) is incorrect because while a CPA generally would qualify as a financial expert, it is not required that the financial expert be a CPA.

7. **(b)** The requirement is to identify the most effective external monitoring device. Answer (b) is correct because external auditors audit the financial statements and internal controls of a publicly held corporation. Answer (a) is incorrect because internal auditors are an internal monitoring device. Answer (c) is incorrect because the SEC relies on external auditors to audit the corporation's financial statements and internal controls. Answer (d) is incorrect because attorneys only advise management on legal issues. They cannot take action if management does not take their advice.

8. **(b)** The requirement is to identify to whom the chief audit executive should report. Answer (b) is correct because ideally the CAE should report to the CEO. Answers (a) and (c) are incorrect because reporting to financial personnel may compromise the internal auditor's effectiveness in assessing financial reporting and controls. Answer (d) is incorrect because external auditors are not part of the organization.

9. **(a)** The requirement is to identify the limitation that often is attributed to securities analysts regarding their value as an external monitoring device. Answer (a) is correct because occasionally the analyst's firm has a vested interest in the welfare of the company. Answer (b) is incorrect because while some analysts may lack competence, it is not a common limitation. Answer (c) is incorrect because analysts use all types of information to make evaluations. Answer (d) is incorrect because analysts are not employees of the company.

10. **(d)** The requirement is to identify the division of the SEC that reviews corporate filings. Answer (d) is correct because the Division of Corporate Finance reviews filings. Answer (a) is incorrect because the Office of the Chief Accountant advises the SEC on accounting and auditing matters and approves the rules of the PCAOB. Answer (b) is incorrect because the Division of Enforcement assists the SEC in executing its law enforcement function. Answer (c) is incorrect because the Division of Corporate Disclosure is not a division of the SEC.

11. **(c)** The requirement is to identify the component that is considered the foundation of a company's internal control. Answer (c) is correct because the control environment is considered the foundation of all of the other components of internal control. Answers (a) and (b) are incorrect. While they are both components of internal control, neither is considered the foundation. Answer (d) is incorrect because the audit committee is one aspect of the control environment.

12. **(d)** The requirement is to identify the item that is not a control environment factor. Answer (d) is correct because control monitoring is a separate component of internal control. Answers (a), (b), and (c) are all incorrect because they are all aspects of the control environment.

13. **(c)** The requirement is to identify the component of internal control that encompasses the routine controls over processes and transaction cycles. Answer (c) is correct because control activities policies and procedures are designed to ensure that management's directives are followed. Answer (a) is incorrect because the control environment is a high-level control. Answer (b) is incorrect because information and communication encompass the controls to ensure that management and employees have the information to perform their functions. Answer (d) is incorrect because risk assessment encompasses the organization's processes to identify, assess, and control risks.

14. **(b)** The requirement is to identify the item that is not a component of the COSO framework for internal controls. Answer (b) is correct because segregation of duties is an aspect of control activities, which is the component. Answers (a), (c), and (d) are all incorrect because they are components of internal control.

15. **(a)** The requirement is to identify the statement that best describes how technology can improve the monitoring component of internal control. Answer (a) is correct because monitoring involves collecting information to determine that controls are working. Answers (b), (c), and (d) are incorrect because while they represent control advantages to the use of technology, they do not relate as directly to the monitoring component.

16. **(d)** The requirement is to identify the item that is not a benefit of enterprise risk management. Answer (d) is correct because sharing risk is only one way of responding, and this technique cannot be used for all risks, nor should it be. Answer (a) is incorrect because ERM involves identifying events with positive effects (i.e., opportunities). Answer (b) is incorrect because ERM involves designing appropriate responses to risks. Answer (c) is incorrect because with ERM, capital is deployed to opportunities that are consistent with the organization's risk appetite.

17. **(b)** The requirement is to identify the item that defines the term "risk tolerance." Answer (b) is correct because the COSO ERM framework defines risk tolerance as the acceptable variation with respect to a particular organizational objective. Answer (a) is incorrect because it defines risk appetite. Answer (c) is incorrect because it defines residual risk. Answer (d) is incorrect because it defines risks that are accepted.

18. **(d)** The requirement is to decide what type of response is illustrated by hedging a risk. Answer (d) is correct because hedging involves sharing the risk with another party. Answer (a) is incorrect because avoidance involves exiting the activity that gives rise to the risk. Answer (b) is incorrect because acceptance involves no response to the risk. Answer (c) is incorrect because reduction involves managing the risk to reduce its likelihood or impact.

19. **(c)** The requirement is to identify the item that is not a technique for identifying risks. Answer (c)

is correct because probabilistic models are used for risk assessment. Answers (a), (b), and (d) are incorrect because they are all methods used for event identification.

20. **(c)** The requirement is to identify the next step in the ERM process. Answer (c) is correct because the next step in the process is to determine the risk response to the assessed risks. Answers (a) and (b) are incorrect because they are subsequent steps in the process. Answer (d) is incorrect because it is part of the event identification process.

21. **(c)** The requirement is to identify the response that does not represent an advantage of enterprise risk management. Answer (c) is correct because an enterprise risk management system does not seek to eliminate all risks. Risks are avoided, reduced, shifted, or accepted based on the risk appetite of the organization. Answers (a), (b), and (d) are incorrect because they all represent advantages of ERM.

22. **(a)** The requirement is to identify the item that is not a limitation of an enterprise risk management system. Answer (a) is correct because an ERM system assumes that objectives have been set as a part of the strategic planning process. Answers (b), (c), and (d) are incorrect because they all represent limitations of ERM systems.

23. **(d)** The requirement is to identify the aspect of business process improvement that is not generally a focus. Answer (d) is correct because examination of strategic goals is part of strategic planning, not part of business process management. Answers (a), (b), and (c) are incorrect because they all represent ways to improve business processes.

24. **(c)** The requirement is to identify how business process managers view business processes. Answer (c) is correct because business process managers view processes as strategic assets that can create value and competitive advantage. Answers (a), (b), and (d) are incorrect because they all describe very limited views of business processes.

25. **(b)** The requirement is to identify the phase that involves simulation of performance of the process in a test environment. Answer (b) is correct because this describes the modeling phase. Answer (a) is incorrect because the design phase involves design of the new process.

Answer (c) is incorrect because the execution phase involves implementing the process. Answer (d) is incorrect because optimization involves identifying additional improvements in the process after it is implemented.

26. **(b)** The requirement is to identify the risk that is not enhanced by a decision to off-shore business processes. Answer (b) is correct because technology risk generally is not affected by the decision to off-shore processes. Answers (a), (c), and (d) are incorrect because these risks may be enhanced as a result of a decision to off-shore processes to a developing country.

27. **(a)** The requirement is to identify the phase that a needs assessment is most likely to be performed. Answer (a) is correct because in the analysis phase, the team attempts to get an understanding of the requirements of the system. Answers (b), (c), and (d) are incorrect because these phases occur after the requirements have been determined.

28. **(a)** The requirement is to identify the implementation model that has the advantage of a full operational test of the system before it is implemented. Answer (a) is correct because with parallel implementation, both systems are operated until it is determined that the new system is operating properly. Answer (b) is incorrect because with the plunge model, the new system is put into operation without a full operational test. Answer (c) is incorrect because with pilot implementation, the system is tested only with a pilot group. Answer (d) is incorrect with the phased implementation, the system is phased in over time.

29. **(c)** The requirement is to identify the stage that involves comparing measures of actual progress to planned progress. Answer (c) is correct because this describes an aspect of project control. Answers (a), (b), and (d) are incorrect because they represent other stages of the project management life cycle.

30. **(c)** The requirement is to identify which of the items is a detailed listing of the man-hour, equipment, and materials requirements for a project. Answer (c) is correct because this is a description of the project specifications. Answer (a) is incorrect because the statement of work is a narrative description of the work to be performed. Answer (b) is incorrect because the work breakdown structure breaks the project into manageable, independent, and measurable elements that can be budgeted and assigned. Answer (d) is incorrect because the milestone schedule sets forth the start date, the end date, and other major milestones involved in completing the project.

31. **(b)** The requirement is to identify the term used to describe the practice of adding resources to shorten selected activity time on the critical path of a project. Answer (b) is correct because this describes project crashing. Answers (a), (c), and (d) are incorrect because they are not terms used to describe this process.

32. **(d)** The requirement is to identify the scheduling and control technique that would be most appropriate when a project can be completed in a number of completely different ways. Answer (d) is correct because the Graphical Evaluation and Review Technique is appropriate for these types of projects. Answers (a), (b), and (c) are incorrect because these scheduling and control techniques do not perform as well under these circumstances.

33. **(a)** The requirement is to identify the technique used to identify critical tasks. Answer (a) is correct because ABC analysis involves categorizing tasks into groups that are urgent and important to those that are neither urgent nor important. Answers (b), (c), and (d) are incorrect because they are not terms used to describe a technique to identify critical tasks.

34. **(b)** The requirement is to identify the most reliable valuation method. Answer (b) is correct because the most reliable valuation comes from market values obtained from active markets. Answers (a), (c), and (d) are incorrect because these are all less reliable methods of determining fair value.

35. **(d)** The requirement is to identify the item that is not a way in which companies in developed countries generally can compete with companies in developing countries. Answer (d) is correct because developing countries typically have low-cost resources. Answers (a), (b), and (c) are incorrect because they all represent ways that a company in a developed country may compete with companies from developing countries.

36. **(b)** The requirement is to identify the correct statement regarding a financial expert. Answer (b) is correct because an issuer is required to disclose the names of the financial experts or the

reason that the issuer does not have a financial expert on the audit committee.

37. **(b)** The requirement is to identify the component that addresses an entity's integrity and ethical values. Answer (b) is correct because integrity and ethical values are part of the internal environment. Answer (a) is incorrect because information and communication are the way information is identified, captured, and communicated to enable people to carry out their responsibilities. Answer (c) is incorrect because risk assessment is the process of analyzing risks. Answer (d) is incorrect because control activities are policies and procedures to help ensure the risk responses are carried out.

EXAMPLE TASK-BASED SIMULATIONS—BUSINESS ECONOMICS AND CONCEPTS

Task-Based Simulation 1

Assume that you are a consultant providing services for Webster Corp. Webster is performing a significant project-based implementation of a new enterprise resource system. The company is concerned about the difficulties in performing the project. Compose a memorandum to management describing the risks involved in executing a project that is cross-functional in nature.

REMINDER: Your response will be graded for both technical content and writing skills. Technical content will be evaluated for information that is helpful to the intended user and clearly relevant to the issue. Writing skills will be evaluated for development, organization, and the appropriate expression of ideas in professional correspondence. Use a standard business memorandum or letter format with a clear beginning, middle, and end. Do not convey the information in the form of table, bullet point list, or other abbreviated presentation.

To: Webster Corp. President
Re: ERP project management

Task-Based Simulation 2

Skyview, Inc., a small start-up company, has hired you as a consultant to assess its financial systems and related processes. During your review, you learned that the company accountant is responsible for providing general ledger access to others in the company, processing transactions in the general ledger, and printing checks. The president of the company must authorize write-offs in the system, but the accountant has access to the president's user name and password.

Prepare a memorandum to Skyview's president assessing these responsibilities in the context of segregation of duties. Also assess the possibility of the accountant committing fraud.

REMINDER: Your response will be graded for both technical content and writing skills. Technical content will be evaluated for information that is helpful to the intended user and clearly relevant to the issue. Writing skills will be evaluated for development, organization, and the appropriate expression of ideas in professional correspondence. Use a standard business memorandum or letter format with a clear beginning, middle, and end. Do not convey the information in the form of table, bullet point list, or other abbreviated presentation.

To: Skyview President
Re: Segregation of duties and potential for fraud

Task-Based Simulation 3

Assume that you are acting as a consultant for Winston Co. The president of the company is considering implementing an enterprise risk management system. To evaluate whether to go forward with the project, the president has asked you to describe the limitations of an ERM system.

Prepare a memorandum to Winston's president describing the purpose and limitations of an ERM system.

REMINDER: Your response will be graded for both technical content and writing skills. Technical content will be evaluated for information that is helpful to the intended user and clearly relevant to the issue. Writing skills will be evaluated for development, organization, and the appropriate expression of ideas in professional correspondence. Use a standard business memorandum or letter format with a clear beginning, middle, and end. Do not convey the information in the form of table, bullet point list, or other abbreviated presentation.

To: Winston Co. President
Re: Limitations of an enterprise risk management system

SOLUTIONS

Solution to Task-Based Simulation 1

To: Webster Corp. President
Re: ERP project management

You have requested that we provide information about the issues in executing a project to implement an enterprise resource management system. You should understand that the cross-functional nature of this project creates additional risk of failure that must be controlled. The most important requirement for success of a cross-functional project is full support by top management. The team must have this support to get adequate cooperation from the various function managers of the organization. This also means that the relationships between the project manager and various functional managers must be clearly defined to avoid conflict. Finally, senior management must support the project manager's decisions, recognizing that these decisions must be made quickly and with limited information to ensure that the project remains on schedule. If senior management recognizes and resolves these issues, the risk of failure will be significantly reduced.

If you have any additional questions about the issues regarding completing of the project, please contact me.

Solution to Task-Based Simulation 2

To: Skyview President
Re: Segregation of duties and potential for fraud

You have requested that I perform an independent assessment of Skyview's financial systems and related processes. In a properly controlled financial system, the duties of authorization of transactions, approval of transactions, custody of assets, and record keeping should all be segregated. In other words, these functions should all be performed by different individuals. Your current financial system and processes do not include this proper segregation of duties. Skyview's accountant has incompatible duties that would allow him to make an error or perpetrate a fraud and prevent its detection. He processes transactions and has access to assets (printed checks). As an example, he could process fictitious purchase transactions to his own shell companies and cause payments to be made for goods or services that were not received by Skyview.

In addition, the fact that the accountant has access to your user name and password allows him to circumvent the control provided by your being the only individual authorized to write off accounts. This would allow the accountant to process an unauthorized sales transaction to his own shell company and use your user name and password to write off the account.

I would recommend that we develop a new financial system that would include appropriate segregation of duties to ensure that no individual in the organization has the ability to perpetrate errors or fraud without it being detected in the normal course of operations. In addition, we will establish polices regarding the maintenance and confidentiality of user names and passwords to ensure that the controls cannot be circumvented.

If you have any questions, please contact me.

Solution to Task-Based Simulation 3

To: Winston Co. President
Re: Limitations of an enterprise risk management system

You have requested that I provide you with information about an enterprise risk management system. You are particularly concerned with the limitations of such a system. The primary purpose of an enterprise risk management system is to provide processes to identify potential risks to achieving a company's objectives and to manage those risks to be within the company's risk appetite.

In considering implementation of an enterprise risk management system, it is important to recognize that these systems have limitations. All enterprise risk management systems rely on judgments about future events that may or may not occur. Also, while an enterprise risk management system provides information about risks to achieving the company's objectives, it does not even provide reasonable assurance that the objectives will be achieved. The company may have a well-established enterprise risk

(continued)

management system and still fail. Finally, as with all control systems, an enterprise risk management system can break down for a number of reasons, including bad judgments about risks and their impact, collusion among two or more individuals, or override by management. Also, due to cost-benefit constraints, no enterprise risk management system can be perfect.

If you have any additional questions about enterprise risk management systems, please contact me.

RESHUFFLED MATERIAL—BUSINESS ENVIRONMENT AND CONCEPTS

This represents material that was previously tested on the Uniform CPA Exam but was covered in areas other than BEC:

This section came from Wiley Module 21, Professional Responsibilities, which was previously tested in the Regulation Section.

NEW RESPONSIBILITIES AND PROVISIONS UNDER SARBANES-OXLEY ACT

1. This act is predicted to generate not only provisions summarized here but also new laws and regulations for at least the next few years. New information for this module and selected changes in other modules will be available when relevant for your preparation for CPA exam
   a. The Sarbanes-Oxley Act, also known as the Public Company Accounting Reform and Investor Protection Act, is receiving much attention in accounting profession, Congress, and the business community at large.
   b. This act already has and will continue to have further important impacts.
   c. The act is the most extensive change to federal securities laws since 1930s; it formulates a new design for federal regulation of corporate governance of public companies and reporting obligations.
   d. The act changes some accountability standards for auditors, legal counsel, securities analysts, and officers and directors.
2. New federal crimes involving willful nonretention of audit and review workpapers:
   a. Retention required for five years (in some cases seven years).
   b. Destroying or falsifying records to impede investigations.
   c. Provides for fines or imprisonment up to 20 years or both.
   d. Applies to accountant who audits issuer of securities.
      (1) Now also applies to others such as attorneys, consultants, and company employees
   e. The act requires the SEC to issue new rules and then periodically update its rules on details of retaining workpapers and other relevant records connected with audits or reviews.
3. Creates new Public Company Accounting Oversight Board.
   a. The board is a nonprofit corporation, not a federal agency.
      (1) Violation of rules of this board are treated as violation of Securities Exchange Act of 1934 with its penalties.
   b. Consists of five members:
      (1) Two members must be or have been CPAs.
      (2) Three members cannot be or cannot have been CPAs.
      (3) None of the board members may receive pay or profits from CPA firms.
   c. The board regulates firms that audit SEC registrants, not accounting firms of private companies.
   d. The main functions of the board are to:
      (1) Register and conduct inspections of public accounting firms.
         (a) This replaces peer reviews.
      (2) Set standards on auditing, quality control, independence, or preparation of audit reports.
         (a) May adopt standards of existing professional groups or new groups.
         (b) Accounting firm must have second partner review and approve each audit report.
         (c) Accounting firm must report on examination of internal control structure along with description of material weaknesses.
      (3) May regulate nonaudit services that CPA firms perform for clients.
      (4) Enforce compliance with professional standards, securities laws relating to accountants and audits.
      (5) Perform investigations and disciplinary proceedings on registered public accounting firms.

      (6)   May perform any other duties needed to promote high professional standards and to improve auditing quality.

      (7)   Material services must receive preapproval by audit committee, and fees for those services must be disclosed to investors.

4. Additional new responsibilities and provisions recently added:

   a. The company must disclose whether it has adopted a code of ethics for its principal executive officer, principal accounting officer, principal financial officer, or controller.

      (1)   The company may have separate codes of ethics for different officers or may have a broad code of ethics covering all officers and directors.

      (2)   The company is not required to adopt a code of ethics, but, if it has not, it must disclose the reasons why.

   b. Company officials found liable for fraud cannot use bankruptcy law to discharge that liability.

   c. Attorneys practicing before the SEC representing public companies must report evidence of material violations by the company or its officers, directors, or agents of securities laws or breach of fiduciary duties.

      (1)   The report must be made to the chief legal officer or chief executive officer.

         (a)   If this officer does not respond appropriately, then the report of evidence must be made "up the ladder" to the audit committee of board of directors, another committee of independent directors, or finally to the board of directors.

   d. SEC adopted new rules requiring more events to be reported on Form 8-K and shortening filing deadlines for most reportable events to four business days after the events.

      (1)   If a company becomes directly or contingently liable for material obligation arising from an off-balance-sheet arrangement, it must describe this, including its material terms and nature of the arrangement.

   e. A company must disclose several items if a director has resigned or refused to stand for reelection because of disagreement with the company's practices, operations, or policies, or if a director has been removed for cause.

      (1)   The company must disclose such items as circumstances regarding disagreement with company.

   f. If a new executive officer is appointed, the company must disclose information such as his or her name, the position, and description of any material terms of employment agreement between the company and the officer.

5. The act lists several specific service categories that an issuer's public accounting firm cannot legally do, even if approved by audit committee, such as:

   a. Bookkeeping or other services relating to financial statements or accounting records.

   b. Financial information systems design and/or implementation.

   c. Appraisal services.

   d. Internal audit outsourcing services.

   e. Management functions.

   f. Actuarial services.

   g. Investment or broker-dealer services.

   h. Certain tax services, such as tax planning for potentially abusive tax shelters.

   i. The board is permitted to exempt (on a case-by-case basis) services of an audit firm for an audit client.

        Note that the act does **not** restrict an auditor from performing these services to nonaudit clients or to private companies. Also, the act permits an auditor as a registered public accounting firm to perform nonaudit services not specifically prohibited (e.g., tax services) when approved by issuer's audit committee

6. The act requires that both the assigned audit partner having primary responsibility for a certain audit and audit partner who reviews audit can do the audit services for that issuer for only five consecutive years.

   a. If a public company has hired an employee of an audit firm to be its CEO, CFO, or CAO within previous year, that audit firm may not audit that public company

7. The act requires increased disclosure of off-balance-sheet transactions.

8. The act mandates that pro forma financial disclosures be reconciled with figures done under generally accepted accounting principles (GAAP).

9. The act creates new federal laws against destruction or tampering with audit workpapers or documents that are to be used in official proceedings.
10. The act increases protection of whistle-blowers by better protections from retaliation because of participation in proceedings against securities fraud.
    a. Also, the act provides that employees may report securities fraud directly to the audit committee to provide information anonymously and confidentially.
11. With a few exceptions, public companies may not make or modify personal loans to officers or directors.
12. Annual reports filed with the SEC that contain financial statements need to incorporate all material corrections noted by CPA firms.
13. Each company must disclose on a current basis information on its financial condition that the SEC determines is useful to the public.
14. The SEC is authorized to discipline professionals practicing before it.
    a. The SEC may censure, temporarily bar, or permanently bar a professional for:
        (1) Lack of qualifications needed.
        (2) Improper professional conduct.
        (3) Willful violation of helping another violate securities laws or regulations.
15. The Public Company Accounting Oversight Board was set up to register CPAs providing auditing services to public entities.
16. The auditor reports to the audit committee.
17. Auditors are to retain workpapers for five years.
    a. Failure to do so is punishable by prison term of up to 10 years.
18. The Sarbanes-Oxley Act directed the SEC to perform various tasks, including several studies to formulate regulations. Some of these studies have deadlines in the future and are expected to be used to promulgate new important regulations; others have been completed, resulted in regulations by the SEC, and have force of law, including:
    a. Require disclosure of differences between pro forma financial results and GAAP.
    b. Require that "critical" accounting policies be reported from auditors to the audit committee.
    c. The SEC will tell NYSE and Nasdaq to prohibit any public company from being listed whose audit committee does not meet specified requirements on auditor appointment, oversight, and compensation.
        (1) Only independent directors can serve on the audit committee.
    d. Companies are required to disclose if they have adopted a code of ethics.
    e. Names of "financial experts" required who serve on companies' audit committees.
    f. Actions prohibited that fraudulently manipulate or mislead auditors.
    g. New conflict of interest rules for analysts.
    h. The SEC may petition courts to freeze payments by companies that are extraordinary.
19. CEOs and CFOs of most large companies listed on public stock exchanges are now required to certify financial statements filed with the SEC.
    a. This generally means that they certify that information "fairly represents in all material respects the financial conditions and results of operations" of those companies and that the:
        (1) Signing officer reviewed the report.
        (2) Company's report does not contain any untrue statements of material facts or does not omit any statements of material facts to the best of his/her knowledge.
        (3) Officers have internal control system in place to allow honest certification of financial statements.
            (a) Or if any deficiencies in internal control exist, they must be disclosed to auditors.
20. Blackout periods are established for issuers of certain security transaction types that limit companies' purchase, sale, or transfer of funds in individual accounts
21. Stiffer penalties for other white-collar crimes including federal law covering mail fraud and wire fraud.

INDEX